A Hunger to Kill

A Hunger to Kill

**A Serial Killer, a Determined Detective,
and the Quest for a Confession
That Changed a Small Town Forever**

Kim Mager WITH Lisa Pulitzer

ST. MARTIN'S PRESS
NEW YORK

First published in the United States by St. Martin's Press,
an imprint of St. Martin's Publishing Group

A HUNGER TO KILL. Copyright © 2024 by Kim Mager.
All rights reserved. Printed in the United States of America.
For information, address St. Martin's Publishing Group,
120 Broadway, New York, NY 10271.

www.stmartins.com

The Library of Congress Cataloging-in-Publication Data is available
upon request.

ISBN 978-1-250-27488-5 (hardcover)
ISBN 978-1-250-27489-2 (ebook)

Our books may be purchased in bulk for promotional, educational,
or business use. Please contact your local bookseller or the Macmillan
Corporate and Premium Sales Department at 1-800-221-7945, extension
5442, or by email at MacmillanSpecialMarkets@macmillan.com.

First Edition: 2024

10 9 8 7 6 5 4 3 2 1

I dedicate this book
to my dad and mom, Alva and Carol Lee,
who taught me the true meaning of perseverance
and always challenged me to defend those
who are most vulnerable

Contents

Note to Reader

What follows is my telling of the Shawn Grate case. Dozens of law enforcement officials from multiple jurisdictions worked on the case. I am but one of many officers, detectives, BCI and FBI agents, prosecutors, and countless others who worked innumerable hours to bring Grate to justice and bring closure to the victims' families.

When I was interrogating Grate, I was approached multiple times to tell my story. I had no intention of ever putting pen to paper; I didn't want to give any more attention to this man than he had garnered himself. But I began to realize that only by processing what occurred can we improve as agencies and also assist the public in identifying indicators of danger that are more nuanced than people realize.

I began seeing a torrent of articles, podcasts, documentaries, and other accounts of the Grate case, and in so many instances, the facts were incomplete and incorrect. What motivated me was when one victim's mother approached me in tears, asking me to tell the *real* story. She wept as she told me that she believed her daughter was being marginalized. It was only then that I decided to write my own account of what had happened; the victims' families deserve that.

What follows is a progression of my interactions with Grate. In some interviews, he would talk about one victim; in others, he would talk about all of them. It is impossible to include all the details from my thirty-three hours with Grate. This book will highlight a portion of our exchanges.

My children, husband, parents, sister, as well as other family members and friends have all sacrificed throughout my law enforcement career. I don't talk to them much about my job or the evil that I see on an almost daily basis. Still, I want my children to know someday that their mom got something right.

Also important to me is that a portion of the proceeds from this book will go toward the benefit of crime victims.

Prologue

Temperatures were in the high teens, and a light snow was falling on the morning of March 16, 2015, as an employee for Columbia Gas Transmission drove along County Road 1908, a narrow lane that ran through cornfields and wooded areas of Ashland County, Ohio. The driver was proceeding slowly because low fog hung over the area and visibility was hampered by both the haze and snow.

Veering right, he turned onto the unpaved right-of-way, where he planned to check on gas wells for the company. As he neared the well's location, something caught his attention by the trunk of a majestic oak tree. Climbing out of the cab, he walked over to get a better look. Horrified by the sight before him, he ran back to his truck to call 911.

That tree had stood witness to the region's rich history, including the area in Mifflin the Native Americans had once heavily inhabited. It had seen progress as the region developed over time and eventually became a center for industry. Perhaps it had also stood guard over the woman whose remains were propped against the gnarled, old trunk. She was strangely well preserved, her features still recognizable, even though her body had been left there more than two months earlier.

Four days after the chilling discovery, the Ashland County

Coroner's Office confirmed her identity as that of thirty-one-year-old Rebekah Leicy of Mansfield, whose family had reported her missing the previous month.

Coroner Dale Thomae ruled her death an overdose and associated dumping by unknown individuals in the narcotics realm. Rebekah Leicy was known to consort with drug users and dealers, and her family believed she had died as a result of her addiction.

At the time, the Ashland County Sheriff's Office saw no reason to suspect foul play. But the following August, Rebekah's death would be linked to one of the most prolific murder investigations to ever hit the state of Ohio—and become one of the most haunting cases of my career.

DAY ONE

September 13, 2016

1

The Abduction

Nineteen minutes. Nineteen heart-stirring minutes. That's how long it took our officers to locate the female victim now waiting for me in the interview room. My stomach still tightens every time I hear the nail-biting 911 recording that ended in her rescue.

My name is Kim Mager, and in the fall of 2016, I was a detective with the Ashland Police Division in Ashland, Ohio. I'd been with the department for twenty-three years, and for much of my tenure, I was one of the only women on the small, thirty-member force. Being a lone female wasn't always easy. I don't care how tough you are, as a woman, you have a constant awareness of the physicality of law enforcement.

But I knew I had other skills that made me a good cop. For one, I was a good shot. I grew up in rural America, and my father taught me to shoot a gun beginning when I was four; by eight, I was regularly accompanying him hunting for small game like rabbits and squirrels.

I grew up in the country, where the farm culture and lifestyle required hard physical work, mostly outside, in good weather and bad. If you had a big piece of property or any farm animals, like we did, it was what you did. Everyone helped, whether it was tending the gardens or keeping the woodpile stocked for the wood-burning stove, with the biggest kids carrying several logs at a time and the little kids carrying one or even just the kindling sticks. But everyone participated, boys and girls. Those were the rules.

We lived in the middle of nowhere, and we had a driveway that was at least a couple of hundred feet long. When it snowed, even us kids would chip in to shovel out the truck, followed by Dad, plowing the driveway. In the spring and summer, my sister, Tamra, and I were tasked with helping water and tend to our family's vast vegetable garden. We didn't have a hose that stretched to the field, so we carried buckets of water to get that job done. We were always lifting water, hay, or feed for the animals.

We had horses, chickens, and a couple of cows, and their food came in fifty- to one-hundred-pound bags that we had to carry.

Like most country people, we'd get up early in the mornings because there was work to do. Disrespect wasn't tolerated in my household, so I always had to watch what I said and how I said it. My father was strict, so I learned to present my points respectfully. I didn't know it then, but this would be a skill that I'd rely on later.

Early on in my law enforcement career, I watched how veteran detectives at the department like Dennis Evans and Tom Lattanzi used their communication skills to deescalate tense and sometimes life-threatening situations and also to gain confessions. I was a young officer, and that made an impression on me. I'm not saying good communications skills always work. I've had a few run-ins where it didn't matter what I said or how genuine I was.

Being mindful and thinking before I open my mouth is a skill that has served me well throughout my life and in my law enforcement career. And I have worked to hone it, beginning in the early days when I was an investigator for the Ashland County Department of Job and Family Services, working with families who were often going through a rough patch or children who came from hard places.

I've never passed up on training to improve my verbal skills. Through my work with children and families, I learned that communication can often be the key to progress and breakthroughs. With practice, my interviewing skills improved over the years, too. I was often tasked with interviewing suspects in some crime or another, and I had to learn how to type a personality and establish a rapport with a person, then get them to open up. I became proficient at securing confessions.

As a female detective investigating sex crimes, I feel that danger is always there like some dark shadow following me around. I have a bad habit of getting intensely focused on my work—sometimes to the point that I fail to even consider potential risks to my safety. I'll barge into a halfway house or interview a potential offender in his or her home without thinking about waiting for backup. In hindsight, it seems I sometimes put myself in harm's way rather than risk that someone else gets hurt because I didn't get an offender off the street. I can't count the number of times I've been yelled at by other officers who've been worried about me. Sometimes I can see them trying to quietly back me up, without getting in the way of an investigation.

One time I was investigating a case, and I peered out a window only to see one of our uniformed officers hiding behind a tree a few feet away. He flashed me the thumbs-up, signaling that he was there for me if and when needed. I should be more grateful for their quiet care.

Fortunately, I am married to an incredible man with Southern roots with lots of brothers and a sister and a deep well of goodwill and love of family. Dan gets it, and he doesn't worry about things that other people worry about. He is hardworking, tough inside and out, and the most active father our children could ask for. He treats me with respect and compassion; he is my pillar. Both of us know that being in law enforcement can be brutal for both husband and wife; fortunately, with God's grace, we survived. Being a police officer was challenging. *Perhaps all of it was in preparation for what I was about to encounter?*

Never in my life could I have imagined that one day I would find myself playing the role of a real-life Clarice Starling seated across the table from Ashland, Ohio's version of *Silence of the Lambs'* villain Hannibal Lecter. My perpetrator wasn't a cannibal, but he was a prolific serial killer.

Little did I know that when I woke up that Tuesday morning to prepare for my 8:00 a.m. shift, I was about to come face-to-face with one of the most malevolent men I'd ever met.

The sun had not yet risen that mid-September morning in 2016 when the desperate call came into the Wooster-Ashland Regional Dispatch Center.

"Nine-one-one, what is the address of your emergency?" Dispatcher Sarah Miller responded.

A long silence ensued, followed by a whispered utterance. "By the Fourth Street laundromat."

"What is it?"

Again silence.

"What's the problem?"

"I've been abducted," the caller claimed.

"Who abducted you?"

After several whispered attempts, Miller was finally able to decipher a name. "Shawn Grate?" she repeated.

"Yes," came the breathy confirmation.

"Where's he at now?"

In a voice so low that Miller could barely hear her, the woman explained how her abductor was next to her in bed. He had fallen asleep, and she had somehow managed to get hold of his cell phone, which he kept on a table next to the bed.

"What's the number you are calling from?" the dispatcher asked.

"I don't know."

"What's the address?"

"I don't know."

The only information the woman could provide was that she was being held in one of the two yellow houses across from the Fourth Street laundromat, a low-slung, barn-red building marked by an old Pepsi billboard–style sign that sat on the corner of Fourth Street and Covert Court. It was a busy place, with locals doing their weekly wash, and neighborhood kids playing in nearby parking lots.

The place had a negative association for me. Several years earlier, an eight-year-old boy failed to come home from school, and we were out looking for him. I found the child near that laundromat. When he got in the back seat of my patrol car, I could see his eyes in the rearview mirror. He appeared to show evidence of trauma. It's hard to put into words, but I could see it. I stopped the vehicle, got out, opened the back door, and knelt beside him. I asked where he'd been, and he didn't want to tell me. After several minutes of building a rapport, he explained that he had been in the laundromat and that an adult man had sexually assaulted him in the restroom.

We eventually tracked down the suspect, who confessed during an interrogation. He was arrested and charged.

I don't want to, but every time I pass those houses, which are directly in front of the laundromat, I remember that little boy. Now, I don't just think about that precious child. The man my colleagues were about to encounter and arrest inside one of those houses changed all that for me.

"Does he own the house?" Dispatcher Miller asked our distraught caller.

"No, he broke in."

"Does he have a weapon?"

"He's got a Taser . . . Please hurry!"

"Okay, stay on the phone with me," Miller advised, hoping to keep the caller calm and talking until officers could reach her. Miller had been on the job long enough to know the importance of maintaining a cool demeanor and getting as much relevant information as possible.

I was not yet on station that morning when central dispatch contacted the Ashland Police Division, where three fellow officers—Officer Curt Dorsey, Lieutenant Tim Shreffler, and Sergeant Jim Cox—were in the middle of a shift briefing. Roll call was cut short when the three were dispatched to the scene.

Dorsey had joined the force eight years earlier in 2006; the two other men were seasoned veterans with more than four decades of law enforcement experience between them. So, as the "rookie" of the group, Dorsey knew he would be the one doing the grunt work once on scene.

There was no sign of life at either of the yellow, two-story colonials when our officers arrived at the location that morning. There were no cars parked in either driveway, and no lights or sounds coming from either place. At first glance, Officer Dorsey and the others wondered if perhaps the dispatcher had made a mistake. Until recently, the Ashland Police Division had used Ashland County 911 dispatching operations. But the city had just transitioned that operation over to a new regional dispatch center that serviced several law enforcement agencies in multiple jurisdictions and counties. Perhaps the dispatcher had been mistaken. Lots of places had their own Fourth Street. And this place was in the middle of town, with lots of passersby. It made little sense the suspect would be holding a woman against her will there.

Further complicating matters was the fact that the caller could not provide an exact address. It was unclear which house she might be in; the pair of wood-framed houses with the wood front porches stood side by side and looked nearly identical. The two structures dated back to the 1800s and had once been occupied by supervisors who worked at the old F. E. Myers & Bro. Company plant—a now-defunct factory complex in the center of Ashland that had once provided good, steady work for some 850 people, nearly a tenth of Ashland's population at that time.

In its heyday, Ashland, once known as Uniontown, was a prosperous manufacturing hub with nearly fifty factories producing a variety of items that were shipped all over the country. Its founder, Francis E. Myers, was a local boy who left his father's farm in the late 1800s to work as a salesperson, peddling tools and hardware to area farmers. Eventually, he and his brother Philip started their own company, F. E. Myers & Bro., which they operated from the basement of a rented building in the center of Ashland. Soon, two more brothers joined the company and constructed their own building to manufacture the pumps.

At the time, there were forty-eight factories operating in Ashland, but F. E. Myers held the title of the city's biggest manufacturer. By 1915, they expanded their facilities with a new complex of four- and five-story redbrick buildings that covered several city blocks and spanned twelve acres in the Fourth Street area. Those buildings still stand, but the operations have long ceased.

Beginning in the 1960s, companies began to shut down manufacturing operations in the States and move them overseas to take advantage of lower labor costs. The city of Ashland was one of many communities throughout America's heartland that fell on hard times as a result. Thousands of area residents lost their jobs as one plant after another closed. F. E. Myers was sold to a local competitor, and its operations were eventually moved to a new plant outside the city.

Over the years, the complex was sold a couple of times and eventually donated to a local nonprofit Christian entity, Pump House Ministries, run by local pastors Bruce Wilkinson and his wife, Marylou. Wilkinson had only wanted the building that had once housed the pump factory, but he agreed to take the other properties as part of the deal.

The ministry had already made some progress, converting one of the sturdy, old brick buildings into a small catering and events center that was used primarily for weddings. They also opened a men's shelter, an emergency food pantry for the needy, and the Revival Thrift Store, which would play a minor role in the unfolding case, in particular the donation drop box outside the establishment.

As for the two old, yellow colonials across from the laundromat, somebody had tried to upgrade them years ago by adding a layer of cheap vinyl siding to cover up the peeling paint on the original clapboard. But the structures were still in serious disrepair, and it would have cost tens of thousands to make them habitable again—money that the charity simply didn't have. Pump House Ministries had plans to renovate them someday and turn them into housing for the homeless.

Neighborhood kids liked to hang out in the crumbling factory structures. Our officers have searched them countless times for trespassing complaints. But I never saw any activity at the two yellow houses, which now stood boarded up and vacant. Or at least that's what everybody—including my fellow officers and I—had assumed.

Dispatcher Miller was in radio contact with our three officers as they circled the two structures on foot, looking for any indication that something was amiss. The entry doors on both houses were locked, and after peering in the windows, the officers determined that the one to the north was obviously empty; the walls on the first level had been gutted in preparation for a remodeling. They had no way of knowing if the upstairs had been gutted, too, and it was impossible for them to determine if anyone was up there without breaking in and physically searching the structure.

The officers had been on scene for just a few minutes when they learned from the dispatcher that the alleged perpetrator was asleep in the bed next to her and that even the slightest noise could wake him. Doing so would risk putting the victim in great danger—and perhaps lead to a hostage/barricade situation or further violence.

They tried to be as stealthy and quiet as possible, peering in windows, and hoping they might see something that could help them determine in which house the woman was being held. Minutes were ticking by, and still they hadn't found any sign of the female caller or anyone else in either of the houses.

The three were ready to head back to their cruisers when Officer Dorsey was suddenly overcome with a sense that something was off. Dorsey, like many in our small community, is a devout Christian and lives his life honorably. As a believer myself, I appreciate his deep commitment to his faith, so I understood when he later confided what he thought happened in that moment. He believed that God was sending him a message, telling him to turn back, that he was needed and should not give up the search.

Following his gut, Dorsey decided to retry a rear door he'd seen during his first pass of the home to the left. But there was a problem: there was no stoop or landing to get up to the door. The ground level was significantly below the door, meaning that there was no way to look inside or make any kind of quiet entry. The door didn't have a typical landing, so it made the option of kicking it in more difficult.

There was a flimsy storm door there, and he was able to pull it open without much noise. But the wood entry door was locked solid and wouldn't budge. He stood and listened for any sign of life inside but didn't hear a thing. He was just starting to circle back toward the house on the north when the dispatcher radioed.

"The victim says she hears you at a side door," Miller said.

Dorsey stopped dead in his tracks and immediately went back to the side door, with Lieutenant Shreffler and Sergeant Cox arriving shortly thereafter. He was just starting to reach up for the door-knob when he saw it—a woman's outstretched hand flat against the windowpane. It was quite literally like something out of a horror movie, only this time, it was all too real. His heart skipped a beat as he realized he'd found the 911 caller. He hesitated, contemplating if he should try to break the door down to get to the woman or if that would make the situation even worse.

Dorsey got on the radio with the dispatcher, asking Miller if she could convince the caller to unlock and open the door. He knew it was a lot to ask of someone who feared for her life, but it seemed like their best option. Miller agreed and asked the caller if she could help.

"Ma'am, are you still with me?" Miller asked.

Throughout the call, the dispatcher had managed to maintain a cool demeanor, aware that losing the element of surprise could greatly elevate the risk of further harm to the victim and poten-tially the responding officers, as well. She explained that a uni-formed officer was now at the side door but was unable to get inside without the potential for a good deal of noise and delay.

"Do you think you can unlock the door?" she asked.

But the woman was reluctant, terrified that her abductor would wake up and come after her. She resisted time and again, but Miller kept at it, coaxing her along, encouraging her to help free herself. Finally, the dispatcher managed to convince the woman to act, gently cajoling her as she slowly unlocked the door and looked down at Dorsey.

The young officer was taken aback at the sight before him. The slender brunette was completely nude, with part of a restraint hanging from one arm. She looked to be in her mid- to late thirties and had extensive bruises on her arms and legs. What he saw in the woman's eyes was her terror. There was no question in his mind that this was a true abduction, and that the woman—whom we will call Jane Doe to protect her identity—had been through hell. He would later tell me that her frightened stare was something he will never forget.

Dorsey wanted to get Jane out of the house and away from any danger as quickly as possible. Mindful to avoid any noise, he waved his arm and motioned for her to walk toward him.

But she was petrified with fear. She stood frozen in place, staring straight ahead, uncertain what to do next. The officer quietly asked her to come through the door, but again, she stiffened, unable or unwilling to move.

Dorsey could hear his colleagues approaching behind him as he remained focused on the woman standing in front of him. "It's okay. You're safe now. Please walk to me, and I will get you out of here."

Despite his best efforts, it still took several seconds before Jane finally took her first step toward him—and freedom.

"Where is he?" Dorsey whispered as he steered her through the door.

"The bedroom," she replied.

Once outside, Dorsey made sure the woman was safely in the hands of law enforcement personnel before joining his colleagues, Lieutenant Shreffler and Sergeant Cox, for a search of the house. Their weapons drawn, the three men moved left into a kitchen area, where they encountered a fetid odor. A swarm of gnats hovered above the sink, which was piled with dirty dishes.

Continuing down a hallway, they came to what appeared to be a bedroom door. It was partially ajar, but there was something on the ground blocking it from the inside.

Dorsey kicked the door open, then entered the room with Shreffler and Cox on his heels. To the right of the door was a bed, where a man lay face down beneath a blanket; he was awake, but groggy.

"Get up!" Dorsey instructed. Pulling the blanket back, he saw that the man was naked. "Show me your fucking hands right now!"

The man complied, throwing his hands out in front of him.

"Now put them behind your back!" Dorsey directed.

Sergeant Cox pulled his handcuffs from his belt and closed them around the suspect's wrists as Dorsey picked up a pair of blue shorts from the floor and assisted the man in putting them on. The officers noted various articles of women's clothing tied to the handles of the mattress, likely makeshift ligatures that the man had used to confine Jane; the restraint was the same type that Dorsey had seen on her arm when she came out of the house.

What at first blush appeared to be a case of kidnapping and rape would soon unfold to reveal the most heinous crime saga this small city had ever seen.

2

Fair Week

We have four seasons in Ohio, and each one is equally amazing. Fall is my favorite, with the changing leaves, the cooler, crisper air, the fresh-picked apples, stockpots of soup, pumpkin patches, hayrides, and the annual county fair.

The Ashland County Fair is among the best in Ohio. It has been in existence for over a hundred years and is held at our local fairgrounds every year in late September. It's a countywide event with exhibits, food stands, amusement rides, animal shows, demolition derby, tractor pull, livestock sales, and lots of youth engaging in 4-H projects. Just about everybody in our county shows up there at least once during the weeklong event, and many of us go several times.

As a child, I loved going to the fair with my family. My older sister, Tamra, and I showed our rabbits at the fair. We'd bring them to the fairgrounds on opening day, and they'd stay in the rabbit barn, where they were judged on different criteria—weight, balance, composition, teeth, fur, and other attributes. My rabbits never took home a prize, but Tamra's did. I also entered fair week cooking competitions and was over the moon when I won a blue ribbon with Grandma Lee's homemade noodle recipe.

Now that I was a mom, I looked forward to going with my own

family: my husband, Dan, and our three kids, Corbin, our eldest at nineteen, and Macy and Reed, eight and six, respectively. Dan and I were both regulars even before we were married, but it was even more special experiencing it with our children.

Opening day was fast approaching with the women's skillet toss on the calendar as Sunday's kickoff event. The skillet toss was a chance for women to test their strength by seeing how far they could throw a cast-iron pan, kind of like a shot put competition—only with a frying pan.

I was excited, but also a bit stressed. This year, fellow detective Brian Evans and I had volunteered to run the booth for the regional drug enforcement task force known as the METRICH Enforcement Unit, a joint task force of the Mansfield Division of Police and the Richland County Sheriff's Office. Detective Evans and I were hired on the same day and had worked together for more than two decades.

Detective Evans was head of our narcotics squad and a member of the METRICH unit. Like much of the heartland, Ashland had a drug problem. Addiction was a serious issue, with Ashland County experiencing its deadliest years of overdoses from 2014 to 2015, according to figures from the Ohio Department of Health.

I was not on the narcotics squad. My area of expertise was sexual assault, violent crime, and child/domestic abuse. But I was usually willing to volunteer. I could certainly benefit from talking with fairgoers, getting to know them, and letting them get to know me. Our department had sponsored a booth before this year and saw just how many people we could reach by being at the fairgrounds where we were approachable.

Community policing was a key component of the Ashland Police Division's prevention and law enforcement efforts. Over the years, we'd learned that participating in public events like this allowed people in the community to get to know us and trust us.

But our efforts didn't end there. As a department, we had introduced our own community-outreach initiatives. We had an annual fishing derby, where kids could come with their families to throw out a line with a cop. Several of our officers were avid anglers, so they were all involved. Fisherman or not, we all participated, dressed in civilian clothing, our families in tow, all with the goal of making ourselves more approachable to the city's most vulnerable. Even while on duty, we made a point of making ourselves accessible to the public.

During mild weather, we'd drive around keeping our windows down so we could better hear what was happening on the streets we patrolled and shout hi to friends, neighbors, and just about anyone we saw. We very deliberately parked in areas where community members could see us and strike up a conversation if they were in the mood to do so. If we saw a group of kids engaged in a game of hoops or throwing a football, we'd join in if we had the time.

During my shifts, I gravitated to the Fourth Street area near Pump House Ministries, where there was always a lot of foot traffic, especially in the summer. I'd park in the lot behind the two old houses across from the laundromat and just watch the people come and go.

People in our community love us, and we've earned their adoration. We appreciate our community, so community policing comes authentically easy, rather than doing it because we have to. Visitors from Cleveland and other nearby cities consistently remark about how polite we are.

Ashland is a small city. Not only can you cross it within fifteen minutes, but you are also going to see people all along the way that you know. During a typical shift, I traverse the city's main drags. People wave as I go by, and if by chance I fail to wave back, I hear from them. I will inevitably see them again later, and they are going to stop me and ask, "Hey, I was waving at you. Didn't you see me?"

I prided myself on being familiar with many of our residents.

God knows there was no way I could ever know everyone who lived or worked within the city limits, but I could at least try.

The relationships went both ways. We needed to hear from the community about trouble spots, and they needed to feel like they knew somebody on the force that they could approach. We made it our business to know the people in our community. If just one interaction led to a community member coming forward to seek help, it was worth the effort.

I'd taken it upon myself not only to man the METRICH booth but to help Detective Evans conceive, design, and construct it. There were a lot of moving parts, and there wasn't much time to get it all done. Between planning for fair week, juggling my kids' sporting events, and working my detective caseload, the next few days were all planned out.

But the universe had other plans for me.

I was at home and in the shower getting ready for my 8:00 a.m. shift at the department that Tuesday when I heard my cell phone ringing on the bathroom vanity just before 7:00 a.m.

I was in a hurry to get to the police station because I had a sex offense interview scheduled that morning, so I let it go to voice mail. But it rang again, followed immediately by the ping of a text. Clearly, someone was anxious to get hold of me.

I cut my shower short, stepped out, grabbed a towel, and looked at my screen. I saw a message from my superior, Captain David Lay, asking me to call him ASAP.

Captain Lay was on temporary assignment as commander of the detective bureau. Normally, we had a lieutenant in charge of the detectives, but because of a manpower shortage, the captain had been involuntarily pulled back to the detective bureau and was handling the work.

Typically, captains spend most of their time managing administrative issues. But David Lay was different. He was a working captain, kind of like in the 1930s when there were major-league baseball managers who played the game as well. Lay was as comfortable on the streets as he was behind a desk in headquarters.

The captain wasn't happy about even my five-minute delay getting back to him and made it clear right at the start of the call. "Two calls and a text?" he grumbled.

"I was in the shower getting ready for my shift," I explained.

The captain quickly detailed what he knew: uniformed officers had just rescued a woman from an abandoned house near the laundromat on Fourth Street and were bringing her to the police department. He needed me to report in immediately to interview her.

"I'm on my way," I told him.

As the only female detective, I was the one responsible for interviewing most victims of sexual assault, as well as many victims of domestic violence and child abuse. I'd assisted other jurisdictions on innumerable cases during my twenty-some years with the department and before that for three years as a child abuse investigator with the Ashland County Department of Job and Family Services, so I knew that getting a detailed account promptly from a victim could provide law enforcement with the material we would need to make a strong case.

Dan was in the kitchen preparing breakfast for our two younger kids when I hurried past him, my long hair still damp from the shower, and raced out the front door. "Going to interview a kidnapping victim!" I yelled back.

My husband was used to hearing things that would cause most people to stop dead in their tracks and ask for clarification. I'd been to all sorts of emergencies over the years, and he knew little bits and pieces about many of them. It was pointless to keep things from him. He had spent twenty-five years as a law enforcement officer. And now, as a retirement job, he was working as a probation officer and periodically heard about cases I was involved in.

Like many households, ours was a busy one, with Dan and me juggling our three kids, demanding jobs, and lots of after-school activities. Keeping our schedules straight and figuring out who was driving the kids was always a challenge.

The kids were just back at school after the long summer break, and Dan and I were still settling back into our schoolday routine. Our two youngest, Macy and Reed, attended the same elementary school, so morning drop-offs were not too complicated.

Our eldest, Corbin, was preparing to enter the police academy. I like to think he was following in the footsteps of Dan and me, as well as his three uncles Bobby, John, and Cody, when he announced that he wanted to become a police officer. He was basically self-sufficient, although he liked a good home-cooked meal every now and again. Remarkably, his instinct to pursue a career in law enforcement would quickly prove invaluable with his insightful input in the case that was about to land in my lap.

In addition to my detective work, I also served as a crisis negotiator for the Ashland PD, responsible for all of Ashland County, encompassing some 427 square miles and fifty-two thousand people. I never knew when an emergency would arise, and I'd have to drop whatever I was doing to head to a scene.

My husband, Dan, was balancing two jobs. He'd recently retired from his longtime position as regional manager of the Muskingum Watershed Conservancy District and had started a second career as a probation officer for the city's only elected municipal judge, John Leroy Good. The Ashland Municipal Court was housed in the same building as the police department and was reached through a secure door, so sometimes we'd see each other during the workday.

Dan was also the varsity football coach at my former high school, a job he loved. When he took over as coach of the Crestview Cougars in 2015, he inherited a program with low participation. Now, a year later, there were more than eighty players on the roster. Coincidentally, I had been a cheerleader at Crestview back in the day.

Still, it was routine for either Dan or me to get a call during dinner and have to head out to work, either for an emergency or, in my case, to begin investigating some new case.

I was raised with a mother who had a home-cooked meal on the table every single night when my father got home from work. I love to cook; I find it therapeutic. But I don't always get to prepare the meal I've planned, so I find myself cooking in a Crock-Pot or preparing two meals in one night. That way, I usually have something ready in case I can't get home on time.

As much as I loved my job, it was difficult juggling the demands of motherhood and a full-time career, so I'd taken to some strategic planning. Generally, I'd get all the kids' school stuff ready at night to take some of the stress out of the morning routine. It also ensured that the kids felt organized and could walk out the door in clothes that matched.

Lately, Dan and I had a pretty good schedule going. On the days I worked the early shift, Dan would drive the kids to school, and I would go into the station early to get some of my never-ending paperwork done while my office was still quiet. I always hoped that if I got in early, I could get out of work early. But that rarely happened. The detective bureau was inundated with cases, and being a small department, we were forever short-staffed and overworked, with no end in sight.

I was out of breath by the time I reached the police department that Tuesday morning. I couldn't shake the uneasy feeling that lingered from my call with Captain Lay, as though I had done something wrong because I hadn't answered his earlier call. My own anxiety grew when I entered the building to find that nobody was around. *What's happened?*

The captain was waiting for me in the hallway of the detective bureau in the back of the building, and I could tell from his posture that we were dealing with something serious. His was a commanding presence, with a shaved head that enhanced his air of authority. He had Southern roots and spoke with a hint of a Southern accent.

"What's going on?" I asked.

Captain Lay directed my attention to the woman seated in the interview room.

The door to the room was ajar; I looked through the opening and was disturbed by the bruising I saw on Jane Doe. She looked to be in her mid-thirties, and there were indications she had been beaten, with marks on her arms, legs, and face. She was dressed in only a tank top and shorts, so her injuries were clearly visible. Her hands and feet were noticeably dirty, and her long brown hair was messy and greasy to the point it appeared wet. It was clear she had not showered in days.

The captain had spoken to Jane Doe briefly before my arrival and said he recognized her name from a missing persons case our department was investigating.

Six days before we rescued Jane Doe, a case had presented itself involving a local woman named Elizabeth Griffith. Although we didn't know it then, it would turn out to be an integral part of the Jane Doe story and the story of Shawn Grate.

That past Wednesday, therapist Tina Swartz from the Appleseed Community Mental Health Center had called the police station to report that Elizabeth, who was one of her clients, had failed to show up for her last two counseling sessions. Nobody had seen her for weeks.

According to Swartz, Elizabeth suffered from paranoid schizophrenia with some mania. She would often hear voices and see things that weren't there, and she called Appleseed's helpline about every other night. But a check of the center's records showed her last call was more than three weeks earlier on August 16, when she'd told a crisis counselor she was "hoping God would get the evil out of her life."

Our youngest officer and newest hire, Kody Hying, was on duty that Wednesday morning and took the report. Officer Hying and all the officers on the force knew Elizabeth. She was a regular caller to 911—sometimes due to emotional challenges she had and other times to report criminal activity going on in her apartment building.

To the irritation of her neighbors, Elizabeth, an unreserved twenty-nine-year-old who wore her blond hair cropped short, had assumed the role of "neighborhood watchwoman" and considered no offense too small to overlook.

Over the years, I had responded to some of her calls. One time, I had barely pulled up to the curb when she emerged from the building anxious to file a report against a couple in a downstairs apartment for smoking weed, which was illegal in Ohio at the time.

When I suggested that lodging a complaint might make her a target of her neighbors' ire, she grew outraged, telling me, "It's against the law, and I am not going to breathe it in, so do your job and go arrest them!"

Sometimes I'd see Elizabeth out walking with her headphones on. If I wasn't busy, I'd offer her a ride, which she usually accepted. She'd throw her head back and laugh, then climb in. My job allowed me to be something of a protector for her and others like her, helping to ensure that they all safely made it through another day. That kind of small gesture gave me a different kind of job satisfaction, far different from the one I got from solving a sex crime or making an arrest.

We knew Elizabeth had a good heart and cared about the community and her neighbors. We also recognized that she was met with challenges, so we tried to help keep watch over her. Her regular stream of 911 calls came at all times of the day, especially when we were in the middle of a busy shift. Still, we responded when we could and tried to be polite even when her complaint was trivial at best. Elizabeth was ours. That's how it is in Ashland. It's a city, but it feels more like a small town, and that's the way we patrolled it.

After taking Swartz's report, Officer Hying did some investigating of his own. A check of police department logs revealed that Elizabeth had not been in contact with our office since August 11. This, coupled with Swartz's account and Elizabeth's mental health issues, triggered an investigation with Officer Hying entering her name and particulars—height, five foot five; hair color, blond; date of birth, September 29, 1986—into the statewide LEADS database as a "Missing and Endangered Person." This meant that agencies around the state and beyond who keyed in Elizabeth's name could access Officer Hying's entry.

My friend Sergeant Garry Alting was playing a primary role in the case. Sergeant Alting was a twenty-year veteran, and his infectious smile, sense of humor, and storytelling skills made him one of the most popular officers on the force. He had a young face and kind eyes hidden behind tortoiseshell-framed glasses. He took his job as lead detective seriously and was focused on doing everything he could to find Elizabeth.

I wasn't assigned to the Griffith case, but Sergeant Alting and Captain Lay had many of us assisting with the investigation. It was not like Elizabeth to just disappear, so I was eager to keep up with the latest developments and help with the case.

Our officers had worked through the weekend chasing down leads and opening new avenues of inquiry. One witness they interviewed was a local woman named Tamara Whelan. Whelan said she knew Elizabeth through the Eastgate Bible Church, which had a facility a couple of blocks from Elizabeth's apartment. Whelan said that both of them had been members of the congregation for many years. But Whelan had recently begun attending meetings of a new church group called the Hebrew Roots, which was actively recruiting members.

Ashland is a strong faith-based community with more than seventy churches operating within its city limits, among them Baptist, Roman Catholic, Lutheran, Methodist, Evangelical, non-denominational, and at least two dozen Brethren houses of worship. We even have a large Amish community, with members belonging to the Old Order sharing our roads in horse and buggies. But I had not heard of this new congregation.

Whelan referred to it as "house church," because it didn't have a building of its own, so meetings were held at the home of the rabbi, who lived in the Rowsburg area, an unincorporated community about two miles from downtown Ashland. Whelan said that Elizabeth was interested in the new church and that she'd given her a ride there on several occasions. One time, Elizabeth brought a friend along, a woman they both knew from church—our victim, Jane Doe.

"Ask her about Elizabeth," Captain Lay instructed before releasing me to begin my interview.

Little did he know how prescient his request would be.

3

Jane Doe

I had barely entered the room when I was hit by a pungent, musky odor. It was as if the assailant were nearby, although in truth, his scent had been carried in by his victim, a mix of male sweat and androsterone, a derivative of testosterone that sometimes produces a foul-smelling odor.

There was nothing comfortable or inviting about the interview room; it had been designed that way. So, I motioned for Jane Doe to follow me to my tiny but quiet office at the very end of the hallway. I'd decorated it with things that made me happy—plants, photographs of my family, and lots of books and toys for the young victims of sex crimes that I interviewed all too often. Basically, I had everything from battery-operated trucks to crayons to Play-Doh, and all kinds of craft projects that I could do with kids as we talked—anything to help release some of the emotional pressure they invariably felt.

There were some personal items of mine in there, too, including things that my own kids had made over the years, such as drawings and hand-painted rocks. Those were the things that I could look at to bring a little joy and mental diversion when the crimes I was investigating were weighing on me.

I also kept a small metal heart with a bell inside in a special spot on my desk. The heart was yellow, with hand-painted flowers, and was given to me by Karen Kellogg, a local attorney who would later become Ashland County Court of Common Pleas Juvenile and Probate Divisions judge. It wasn't uncommon for people in various agencies, like Sherry Bouquet of Fostering Family Ministries, to provide things like weighted lap blankets or fidget spinners, items that aid victims and help bring them to a place of comfort.

In the right situation, I hand it to a victim during an interview. It is ergonomically pleasing and assists them in revealing details of the crimes perpetrated against them.

My office is what we in law enforcement would call a *soft room*, intended to feel more like a room in a house than a sterile office where police work and criminal investigations are conducted. But the work done there was gritty in nature, and the case files were not for the faint of heart.

Like all offices, my cubbyhole had the requisite desk and a couple of chairs. But I would only sit behind the desk when I was by myself doing paperwork. Most of the time, I was sitting directly opposite the person I was interviewing. That, too, was meant to make victims feel more at ease and able to confide in me about whatever may have happened to them. And, on that Tuesday morning, that's where I motioned for my kidnapping and sex-crime victim to sit.

"I'm Detective Kim Mager," I said softly. I knew from experience that I needed to move cautiously and not push too hard given the extent of her trauma. I also knew that this woman needed medical attention, and so there was a clock ticking; I needed to get what I could in this first interview, pass her on to the medical team, and then circle back to talk more after she'd been treated. I needed to be attentive and empathetic and let her know that I was there for her.

But inwardly, I was pissed. This incident had happened in my city, on my watch. It was my job to protect people here. And I am not an anomaly. Most police officers feel that ownership for their community members.

As Jane eased into the chair, I saw she had bruises all over her face, arms, and legs. There were scratches that appeared to be fresh and some that appeared to be healed. Some of her injuries were bluish purple in color, while others were swollen and red. I fully expected that hospital personnel would find even more bruises hidden by her clothing. I suspected, too, that many of those injuries were deep and painful. She was still wearing the clothes that she'd had on when she was abducted; investigators had found the garments at the scene for her ride to the police department, and one of my officers had thoughtfully provided her with a jacket to help cover herself and stay warm.

I let Jane settle in and look around the room for a minute before saying anything, using the time to make further mental notes about her injuries. I now saw reddening on her neck and upper torso, too. Her eyes were swollen and bloodshot, and her face was streaked with tears. There were pieces of lint and debris stuck in her hair and dried matter around her lips and in the corners of her mouth. This woman had clearly been brutalized by her abductor, and she showed both the physical and emotional toll that it had taken on her. I'd been involved in innumerable rape and sex assault cases over the years; the injuries here were extensive.

I was about to explain my role as a detective when Jane suddenly burst out, "Are you going to stay with me? I don't want him to see me."

Jane's comment was yet another indicator of how deeply she'd been traumatized. Even here, safely inside the police department, she perceived her abductor as a clear and present danger. I assured her that she was safe now.

"The man who hurt you is in custody, and he can't hurt you anymore." I also informed her that we were coordinating arrangements for her medical evaluation and care.

Before entering the interview room, I had asked an associate to contact Safe Haven, a rape crisis center that always wanted to be brought in as soon as possible to help provide direct support to victims. The center would be sending a victims' advocate to the station.

Normally, we would transport a victim with injuries like Jane's directly to the hospital, but officers on the scene had wanted to get her to safety and quite likely didn't realize the extent of what had happened to her.

Based on what we could see, it was clear she required medical attention. I told her I could interview her at the hospital, or we could talk briefly now and then she could go to the hospital for treatment. It was decided we would do a short interview at the police department, and then she would be taken to the hospital.

"This is so horrible," she exclaimed tearfully. "I'm scared, and I'm hurting."

I explained the interview process and asked if she would feel comfortable talking with me.

"Yes," Jane replied in little more than a whisper. She started by describing her 911 phone call to our dispatch center and telling one of our dispatchers that she'd been abducted by Grate.

"Does Shawn know where I am?" she sobbed. Speaking his name aloud triggered her terror again. "Can he get access to me?"

I assured her once again that she was safe now and that her attacker could not hurt her anymore. I expected her to begin by explaining to me how she was abducted—but she didn't.

"Elizabeth's been missing for two weeks," she blurted.

Her remark sparked concern. *Is Jane referring to our missing woman?* "Are you talking about Elizabeth *Griffith*?" I asked as plainly as I could.

The victim nodded. She was, indeed, talking about our missing twenty-nine-year-old.

Jane explained that Elizabeth lived in an apartment across the street from hers in a subsidized housing complex off Mathews Avenue, and nobody had seen her in weeks.

"Do Grate and Elizabeth know each other?" I asked.

"No, I don't think they know each other very well."

"What do you mean by 'not very well'?" I prodded.

Jane shifted her body around in the chair, wincing with pain from her injuries as she sought to find a comfortable position. She explained that she and Grate would sometimes play badminton together on the lawn in front of her apartment building. During one of those casual games about a month earlier, Elizabeth had come out of her apartment and observed them with badminton rackets in hand.

"She came out of her building and just started talking to us," Jane recalled. "Elizabeth has mental problems, and she was telling him everything. I told her to stop telling him about all her problems, and the conversation ended shortly after that."

When I asked if she could elaborate, she explained that Elizabeth was "sweet, like a child," but sometimes she exhibited poor judgment about what to say and whom she should be talking to, that when Elizabeth met someone new, she would blurt out her entire life story right off the bat.

"I'd talked to her before about needing to first build trust, because people can use that information poorly," Jane said. "I'd tell her, 'You are gonna make yourself a victim.'"

The whole situation was becoming more complex. We had a traumatized victim, Jane Doe, and her alleged assailant, Shawn Grate. Jane seemed to be suggesting that there was a loose connection between Grate and Elizabeth, but it was unclear exactly what she was intimating. Was she suggesting that there was a connection between Elizabeth's disappearance and her abductor?

Ashland is a small city, so it was certainly possible the two were acquainted. Although I didn't have a true suspicion that Grate was involved in Elizabeth's disappearance, the fact that she was miss-ing did raise concern. I knew from experience that the first twenty-four to forty-eight hours are the most critical and that with each passing hour, the likelihood that a person will be found declines.

Elizabeth had been missing for nearly a month. Still, if Grate was somehow complicit, there was a remote chance we might still find her. He had held on to Jane for three days and hadn't killed her. Perhaps he was still holding on to Elizabeth, as well. The of-ficers who had responded to Jane's 911 call had done a sweep of the residence and hadn't found any live victims. Perhaps he was holding Elizabeth somewhere else? Suddenly, my interview had taken on a new urgency. But before I could explore that possibility, I needed to understand what had happened to Jane.

Jane spoke in a soft voice and had a gentle demeanor. Her long brown hair had a slight wave; she was not the type to dress up or wear makeup. She didn't have a full-time job or any sort of steady income. Instead, she relied mostly on unemployment and made some pocket money for herself by babysitting. She was well-read and knew the Bible in great detail. She spent a good portion of her time at home painting, re-creating religious stories on canvas. I would get to view them in the coming weeks and found them moving and emotional. Some of them were vibrant, like the biblical stories they depicted; others were more subdued.

I also discovered that Jane loved to sing and had recently learned to play the guitar. She performed at church and in small groups with friends. Much of her life revolved around her faith. Her paint-ing, writing, and the music she listened to centered around her religious beliefs.

She was a devout Christian who chose to live by the teachings in the Bible. She did not prefer one version over another; she'd read them all. In fact, she'd recently committed to learning Hebrew, so that she could study the Bible in its original language.

Jane did not have any family in Ashland. But she'd made some good friends over the years as a congregant of the Eastgate Church, as well as other local Christian organizations, where she sometimes volunteered. She'd only recently become affiliated with the Salvation Army's Kroc Center, the local community center run by the Salvation Army, where she often ate her midday meal.

The Kroc Center was an integral part of the Ashland community. It had its own chapel, classrooms for after-school activities, Bible study, and lots of summer programming; there was even a spray park for the kids. And its Summer Food Service Program provided free lunches and snacks to hundreds of area children and adults.

It was during one of those afternoon lunches at the Kroc Center that she was introduced to Shawn Grate, and they ended up in conversation. She learned that Grate, too, relied on the free food being provided. "He is a really friendly guy," she offered, missing the painful irony of her comment.

Jane explained that when she first met Grate, he was working part-time at Save A Lot, a discount supermarket on Center Street. In addition to working there, he also did various other jobs—which meant that his weekly work schedule was fluid, and he often had time in the afternoons to get together for some casual outdoor fun. She said the two liked to walk, so after lunch, they'd take a stroll together, sometimes to Brookside Park, about two miles from the Kroc Center, where they'd play tennis or walk to the store, if either of them needed something.

Jane insisted their relationship was strictly platonic. She said Grate had expressed interest in becoming romantic, but she'd told him she was not interested in being more than friends; she viewed him more like an older brother. "He's tall like my older brother and kind of goofy, but he struck me as kind."

Jane was emphatic about the boundaries she'd set for her relationship with Grate, explaining that they'd spent a fair amount of time together over the past month as friends.

Jane was presenting as a complex individual, both terrified over what had happened to her but also demonstrating an innocent demeanor. She seemed extraordinarily naive, too, for someone in her thirties.

Initially, it was unclear to me why she was so intensely focused on the social and sexual boundaries that she'd set for Grate. I suspected it might have something to do with her religious background. She told me that she was saving herself for marriage.

Jane described how Grate would walk her home after their hikes, and the two would sit on the welcome mat outside her apartment door, where they would talk. "I felt safe in that setting, because Shawn was outside the apartment, and the walls of the building were so thin that other tenants could hear if I got into trouble."

She reiterated that she would never be with him "one-on-one, alone. I am very strong in the Bible, and I know those guidelines."

As a Christian, I had some sense of the framework for her decisions. I'd regularly attend Sunday services with my Aunt Joanie and later with my husband. Over the years, my own faith has grown, and it's still growing today. I think that part of my having empathy for others comes from my sense of religion and faith, and drawing from it was a way in—a means for me to connect to Jane and gain her trust. I was curious what she meant in her reference to the Bible and its guidelines and asked if she could elaborate.

"I always take steps to do what's right based on what the Bible dictates," Jane explained. "That is why I have always taken prudent steps. I don't even have a guy's number in my phone. In fact, that's why Shawn said this has happened, 'because you don't trust guys enough.' I almost think it was a challenge to him."

Jane explained that she had strict rules when it came to members of the opposite sex; she did not exchange phone numbers with men, nor did she permit them into her apartment. Clearly, the early indications were that Grate was the aggressor and she was the victim.

"How did you end up at Grate's house?" I asked.

Jane recalled the two had walked together that past Sunday to Jamison Creek, a nature preserve with a long, creek-side trail about five miles from her apartment. He had told her about a fort he had built in the woods, and he wanted to show it to her. Normally, she attended church on Sunday mornings, but since she didn't currently belong to a "regular" church, she felt she was free to go hiking.

"We were looking for something to do that day, something new, 'cause when you walk around Ashland, it is relatively small. And I like adventure."

Grate had talked about how he'd watched the fireworks from that fort on the Fourth of July. He claimed it would take about an hour and a half to walk there. But, according to Jane, it took considerably longer.

"It was actually as he said, a cool little fort that he'd built himself," she remarked.

She said while there, Shawn dug up a box of "gems," "rocks or geodes" that he'd buried there and that once back in Ashland, he asked her to hold on to the box for him. At the time, she didn't really think anything of it. "It kind of looked cool," she said. Jane indicated she wasn't really into "worldly possessions." "I just kind of left it on the side of my couch."

After the hike, the two stopped at Dollar Tree in the Walmart plaza so Jane could buy some cleaning supplies for her bathroom. It was there that they ran into Jane's friend Tamara Whelan, who had just finished her shift at Walmart and offered them a ride back to Jane's apartment.

Whelan was the witness who had linked Elizabeth Griffith and our kidnap victim to the Hebrew Roots church group. But Jane did not recall anything of significance from the car ride; only that she was exhausted from the long hike and slumped down in the back seat to rest and recharge.

Only later, when we reinterviewed Whelan, would we learn that she and Jane had actually discussed Elizabeth's disappearance in front of Grate, who sat up front next to Whelan during the drive. Whelan told police she did not know Grate and recalled that he was silent during the conversation about Elizabeth having gone missing. At one point, Whelan said she advised Jane that police investigating the case had contacted her and that she had provided them with Jane's number, so she should expect a call.

Whelan also told police that while Grate was silent during their discussion about Griffith, he grew animated when she mentioned her plans to build a garden shed in her yard, explaining that he had carpentry skills and was eager to assist. But when she asked for his phone number, he said he didn't know it and he didn't have his phone with him to provide it.

Whelan said things got weird when they pulled up in front of Jane's apartment complex and Grate jumped out of the car without any further exchanges or pleasantries. He didn't even wait for Jane to disembark. He just started walking quickly in the opposite direction, away from Jane and her apartment building. At one point, Whelan said a cell phone tumbled from his pocket, and he stopped to pick it up; it was peculiar, since he had just claimed not to have it with him.

Jane said that once back at her apartment, she went inside to drop off her purchases and the box of "gems," while Grate waited outside on the stoop. Apparently, he had rejoined her once Whelan had driven off. Jane said she was feeling hungry and tired from the hike, so she prepared peanut butter sandwiches for them to eat.

"Shawn took his outside, and I ate mine inside the apartment," she said. "Sometimes I don't like eating in front of people."

Not long after, the two set off on foot for Covert Court.

Grate claimed that his mother and sister had put together a bag of hand-me-down clothing for Jane, and he wanted her to come to his place so he could give her the items. This would have been the second time that Grate's mother had given her clothes, and she was appreciative. I would later learn that it was a ruse just to lure her to his apartment.

As a gesture of thanks, Jane said that she put together a care package for Shawn that included some cereal, oatmeal, and raisins from her cupboard and the new Bible she had purchased for him. According to Jane, Grate had asked if she had an extra Bible, because he didn't have one, so she'd gotten him one.

Sharing her dedication to the church and God appeared to be a big part of Jane's relationship with Grate, and I wondered if he'd tried to use that as a vehicle to get closer to her and break down boundaries. She told me they would often sit together, and she would read him passages, which they would then discuss. They even talked about the Bible during their walks.

Jane recalled it was around four o'clock when the two set out for Grate's place. She admitted she had no idea that the house on Covert Court was not his legitimate residence. As far as she knew, he had a landlord to whom he was paying rent. "I was too trusting," she said with a whimper.

Once at Grate's house, Jane recalled following Shawn up the steps of the two-story colonial and into the kitchen, where he set down the bag of food she had prepared for him. The place was a mess; dirty dishes in the sink and plastic bags and assorted garbage strewn about. She had been to his place several times before. But normally, they would sit on the stoop outside, where she would read him passages from the Bible. But this time, she went inside because Grate said he wanted to give her the clothes his mother had left for her.

From the kitchen, she followed him to a small bedroom across the hall that seemed part living room, part kitchen, and part bedroom. Like the kitchen itself, this room, too, was a mess.

The bag of clothing was on the bed, just as he said it would be. Jane said she thanked him for the things, and then suggested they go back outside and sit on the front porch, where she could read him passages from the Bible. "I usually sit beside him when I read, so he can follow along," she explained.

But Grate suggested they would be more comfortable inside and grabbed a chair that he put by the bed for her to sit.

At that moment, I wished it was possible to go back in time. I wondered what was different that day that made her comfortable enough to go in. It was a question she struggled to reconcile. "I felt like I could control my ability to leave, and I knew it would be soon. I wasn't planning on staying long; I was going to leave the Bible and take the clothes."

This room served as both a living room and a bedroom, but there was no sofa, only a bed. To have Grate follow along with the reading, Jane said she ended up sitting beside him on the edge of the bed.

"I was showing him the passages, and he was looking at them as I was reading them, and that's when he turned on me. He began pacing around the room as I read the passages aloud."

At one point, she recalled, Grate walked out into the hallway, went to the kitchen, then returned to the bedroom. She could see him traversing the room, pacing back and forth. He did this several more times, before she finally asked him what he was doing. "That's when he walked towards me and grabbed the Bible from my hands. And I said, 'Don't take my Bible!'

"He . . . threw it to the side, and that's when it happened." Jane sighed heavily and closed her eyes tightly as she began reliving her time with Grate.

"Can you tell me what happened next?" I gently pressed.

We sat in silence while Jane worked to compose herself. Tears streamed down her cheeks, and her hands trembled. She then stated, "I stood to leave, and he pushed me back down on the bed and said, 'You're not going anywhere!'

"At first, I thought he was joking. I told him, 'You are over the line.'" But she quickly realized she was in trouble, with Grate growing more and more physical. "I tried to push him off, and he just showed me his strength in every way. I thought I could just kick him in the private parts, and it sounds simple, but man, I couldn't do anything to him. I was trying to scratch him and grab him, but my resistance was just setting him off. He had me pinned. I was on my back, and he was on top of me."

She choked back tears as she recounted how he forced her on the bed and began to remove her clothing against her will. He then forced her to engage in fellatio.

Jane told me that he sexually assaulted her three times that first night and at least four more times the following day, demanding she engage in sex acts that she couldn't do. "He wanted me to do all these things, and I couldn't do it.

"Most of the time, he couldn't penetrate me fully, but he would keep trying and it would be forceful. Most of the time, it was oral sex. . . . He kept telling me to enjoy it, and I told him that I didn't enjoy it and that it was wrong."

That first night, Jane recalled, he struck her in the face at least three times, cutting her lip. She was stunned by the brutality, and at some point, she realized she was bleeding from the head.

She said the room where she was being held contained an odd mix of things—a bed, two bedside tables, a television, a refrigerator, some of Grate's personal things, including clothing, and some knickknacks. The floors were wood, and the room's two windows had floor-length curtains, which he kept drawn, even in the daytime.

During her captivity, Grate was smoking marijuana from a "one-hitter," a silver pipe that looked like a cigarette. He tried to get her to smoke with him, but she declined, insisting it would make her stomach hurt.

She explained that over the three days, Grate tied her to the bed with restraints, using women's scarves and articles of clothing to bind her hands and feet to arrange her body in certain positions. She was nude, and he forced her to engage in multiple forms of intercourse. At one point, he even applied makeup to her face and body and photographed her lying there with her eyes closed and a sheet draped across her body, so that only her face and shoulders were exposed.

I would later see this photograph, and the positioning was morbid; it looked staged, as if Jane were dead. I didn't know what value to put on it, and it was a point I never got to address.

Jane cried as she described the violence she had endured. Grate, she said, would get "really violent," striking her in the head and wrapping his hands around her throat, nearly cutting off her airflow when she couldn't follow his orders during the rape offenses. Some of the blows were so forceful she thought she might pass out. "He said if I verbalized to him, if I said, 'Just don't hurt me,' he would 'go easier' on me.

"I told him, 'I can't do this anymore, just kill me, then.' I couldn't please him. I couldn't do what he wanted."

Jane recalled that at some point during her captivity, Grate left the residence. To ensure she couldn't escape, he bound her in such a way that if she moved, she would literally strangle herself to death. First, he forced her to spread her legs as wide as she could, then tied her ankles and wrists to the four corners of the bed. He next placed a thin restraint around her neck and fastened that to the bed as well. He warned her that the restraints were designed to become increasingly tighter, so she would strangle herself if she moved. To keep her from screaming, he placed two pieces of duct tape over her mouth, but not before force-feeding her a handful of muscle relaxers, which he crushed and shoved down her throat, hoping they would make her sleep.

As scared as she was, Jane said she tried to free herself the minute Grate left the house. But she could feel the ligature tightening around her neck with every movement. Minutes felt like hours as she fought to remain as still as she could, fearful even to breathe, lest she strangle herself to death.

By Monday evening, she was losing all hope. She had endured more than sixty hours of forced fellatio, vaginal and anal intercourse, beatings, and Grate's hands around her throat. She couldn't bear the pain anymore and begged him to let her die. Throughout the ordeal, he had repeatedly promised he would let her go, only to turn around and declare, "I'm not through with you yet!"

Ominously, Grate had even begun to warn her, "You'd better find yourself a way out of here, or I'm going to kill you."

Jane's body language in my office telegraphed a mix of fear, shock, and shame. For much of the conversation, she sat with her legs bent, knees together, and her arms pulled in tight to her body. Her head remained lowered, and there were long periods of silence.

It was clear the severity of her victimization had been extreme. The duration of her experience had been days, not hours, and her ability to articulate the details was so strong that from my perspective, it seemed very real and current. I could see the injuries she had suffered, smell the odor of her male attacker on her, and hear the pain in her voice. I knew I had to let her go. She needed medical attention, first and foremost, and the crisis advocate would be arriving momentarily, so I had to wrap up our interview and get whatever other information I could.

I wanted to ask her about Elizabeth and to see if perhaps Grate had mentioned her or any other women. "Did Grate ever tell you that he had done this to other women?"

Jane indicated that he hadn't said anything definitive but noted that some of his remarks had led her to believe he had done this before. She told me she had seen scars on his body that he claimed were the result of "altercations with women who were mental."

"He also has gouges on his face," she added. "He told me these women would go off on him."

"Did he have any fresh marks on him?"

"Not really that fresh."

I began to inquire about how they communicated. I asked, "Did you ever text Shawn prior to your captivity?"

"No. I don't even know his number." Jane reiterated her belief that it isn't "prudent" to have a man's number in her phone. She reiterated that Grate would walk her to her apartment door, but he had never been inside.

"During these walks, did he ever ask you on a date?"

"He asked me to marry him," Jane said without emotion or verbal inflection. She recounted that during some of their nature walks, he would talk about marriage, and she would tell him, "No way, you're not my type."

She said he'd playfully admit that he needed to "fix a few things" about himself before he would be a viable candidate—like quitting smoking.

"He knew how to play at being the perfect guy," she told me.

I began winding down the interview by introducing the need for Jane to be evaluated by a medical facility. My suggestion unleashed a tearful outburst. She expressed concern about the possibility of being pregnant because of the repeated sexual assaults. Shawn Grate had never used a condom. She revealed her religious stance that terminating a pregnancy is not proper.

"If I hadn't begun to trust him, maybe this wouldn't have happened," she whimpered. "I never saw this coming. It was so frightening."

"You've done nothing wrong," I assured her. "You are not powerless, and you are not alone."

By this point, Cindy Hudnut, the director of the Safe Haven rape crisis center, had arrived on-site and was standing just outside the door. I told Jane about her and gave her a minute to process what was about to happen before I opened the door and invited Cindy in. The two of us had worked together on several cases over the years; she exuded warmth and kindness and knew how to put victims at ease.

"We need to get you to the hospital quickly," I told Jane, assuring her she was in good hands with Cindy. "I am only going to ask you a few more questions."

I used the next several minutes to review what we had discussed and make sure I hadn't missed anything important. One of the important details I picked up was that Grate had recorded some of the sexual assaults on his cell phone.

"Tell me how you were able to get away from him," I said.

Jane said that Grate had her tied up around the arms and was next to her in bed. "He finally settled down around four in the morning and was sleeping on and off."

Around 6:30 a.m., she woke as Grate's cell phone alarm went off on the bedside table. "He'd set it to go off like every five minutes so that he wouldn't fall into a deep sleep.

"He was asleep, and for a moment, I thought that maybe I could get out of the restraints. But then I realized he is a light sleeper and worried that he might hear me. He had already showed me his force, so I thought that was going to be it, that he was going to kill me if he caught me trying to escape.

"I thought, *What can I best do?*"

Jane said she knew he had two cell phones, but she wasn't sure if either of them had any minutes left on them. "I thought, *I can at least try to call 911 on 'em*. . . . I started to reach over him to pick up the cell phone, but what I picked up was his Taser, his stun gun . . . so, I thought, what if I stun him? . . . I didn't know how to use it, so I was like . . . what if I don't do it right and he wakes up and starts to use it on me?"

Jane recalled cradling the stun gun as she slowly crept down the bed. She said at one point she accidently activated it, causing Grate to abruptly raise up. Because he hadn't slept in days, he was out of it, and dozed off again, thankfully.

"I unbound at least the one wrist and my legs," Jane continued. "I got down to the bottom of the bed, and he was still fine, and I creaked around, 'cause the floors do creak. I went slowly, and I looked around . . . every five minutes, I hear the phone going off, so I try to look for the phone, and it is still kind of dark 'cause he's got the windows all covered. So, then I realized where the cell phone ring was coming from . . . it was under a pillow by the floor."

Jane explained how she cautiously retrieved the phone. "I walked to the far end of the bedroom where the door is at." It didn't have a handle, so Grate had used a chair to barricade it shut. She realized she would have to move it to get out of the room, and even then, it was a gamble. The door made a loud, abrupt noise when opened. She didn't want to risk trying to force it open, fearful that the sound would wake Grate up and trigger another beating, or worse.

"I knew my best bet was to call 911," she continued. But first, she turned the volume on the phone down all the way so Grate wouldn't hear the dispatcher's voice. "Thank God the operator was able to hear me. She gave me courage to continue."

She said she was on the line with the dispatcher for about ten minutes when she heard the officers trying to access the back door. "That's when I became braver," she said.

She described moving the chair out of the way, forcing open the door, and running to the back door, where she placed her hand on the glass, so the officers could see it and know she was inside.

To my astonishment, she claimed that as she waited to be rescued, she "sensed" that a "Christian" would be sent to save her. Coincidentally, Officer Curt Dorsey was one of the most devout Christians on the force.

Even for a veteran cop, Jane's story was chilling. At that point, I knew virtually nothing about this woman or her background. But the reality was that none of that mattered then; what I did know was that I had a victim who appeared to be telling the truth. My gut told me that she was genuine. Learning more about Jane would have to wait until later.

Ultimately, with gentle coaxing, I was able to convince Jane to go with Cindy to the hospital for a Sexual Assault Forensic Exam (SAFE). I wasn't done talking with her, but she needed to be seen medically, so I had no choice but to cut the interview short. As was protocol, I knew I would be following up with her very quickly.

As far as I or anyone in the department knew, this was a sexual assault case—a bad one, to be sure, but an assault and kidnapping. None of us yet realized that Jane Doe had been the lucky one who had managed to escape with her life. What I was about to learn was that there were others who hadn't been as fortunate.

4

Alone in a Room with Evil

Having completed my interview with Jane Doe, I knew my next stop was the interrogation room where the alleged perpetrator, Shawn Grate, sat handcuffed. Captain Lay was in the hallway when I emerged from my interview, and he continued to look concerned. He had spent some time interviewing our male suspect. He had taken a firm tone with Grate. And although he had gained good information, Grate had become frustrated, bristled, and shut down.

I knew I needed to bring a different style to bear. My interview technique with suspects is very noncombative. I sought to establish a rapport and a sense of trust with the person, no matter what they'd been accused of doing. Over the years, I'd started to get positive results with my techniques.

The captain wanted me to steer the questioning in a certain direction. He told me that since I had interviewed Jane Doe, I needed to clarify the details about what had happened during her three days in captivity.

Just as I was about to enter the interview room, he added, "And see if this guy knows anything about our missing girls."

Missing girls? I knew from my interview with Jane that our suspect was loosely linked to Elizabeth Griffith. But I hadn't been able to make any real connection between the cases. I was able to establish that they had all eaten lunch at the Kroc Center, but nothing beyond that.

Now the captain was not only proposing a link between Grate and Elizabeth but also a possible link to the disappearance of a second woman, a forty-three-year-old mother and grandmother named Stacey Stanley Hicks, who had also been reported missing the previous week.

Unlike Elizabeth, Stacey was not from Ashland County. But Ashland was the last place she was seen. According to Stacey's family, she had come to our city on Thursday, September 8—the same day Elizabeth Griffith was reported missing—for a late-afternoon manicure appointment. But she never made it home that night, and two days would pass before family and friends realized that she had disappeared.

Stacey's adult son Kory reported to authorities in Huron County, where Stacey resided, that he'd received a frantic call from his mother around 8:30 p.m. that past Thursday. Her car had a flat tire, and she was at the BP gas station on East Main Street in Ashland. "She was freaking out because she didn't know what to do," Kory said. She had a spare tire, but she didn't have the tools to change it.

Kory was supposed to meet his mother at the Applebee's near his house that evening, but it was getting late, and now she had a flat tire. He worked nights, and he would have to go in for his shift soon. Concerned, he called around to family and friends to see if he could find someone in Ashland County to go to his mother's aid.

Family friend Wayne Bright, a farmer who lived in Ashland, agreed to help. When Kory called back to tell his mother that Bright was on the way, he said his mother was no longer frantic. He said she told him not to worry, she "had a helper" who was going to get the tire changed. Kory didn't like to hear that his mother was talking to some stranger, so he let Bright proceed to the BP station.

Bright told police he arrived sometime after 9:00 p.m. to find a male stranger working on Stacey's tire, and he joined in to help. The tire would not hold air, so the man, who Bright described as six feet tall, slender, clean-shaven, and dressed in a striped shirt with cut-off sleeves and baggy shorts, suggested they change it out for the "doughnut" in the trunk.

With the compact spare securely in place, Stacey told Bright she was going to go inside the BP station to buy herself a coffee, and then she was heading home. She thanked Bright for his help, and he went on his way. But the male stranger was still hanging around when he left.

Kory said he next spoke to his mother around 10:15 p.m. and was relieved when she told him the tire was fixed; she was going to get herself a coffee inside the station and be on her way.

Stacey never made it back to the small village of Greenwich that evening. But Kory, and the rest of her family and friends, would not become aware of her absence right away.

After hearing from his mother that evening, Kory went to work for his late shift. He then slept in the following day and put in another shift that night. It wasn't until he was leaving his job the following morning that he realized he hadn't spoken to his mother in nearly two days, which was out of the ordinary because they were close and spoke frequently. But repeated calls to her cell phone went unanswered.

Alarmed, Kory and several other family members went to Stacey's home that past Saturday, September 10, and when she didn't answer their knock, they broke in to find Stacey's two dogs locked in their cages and soiled with feces and urine. Her one cat was roaming the house, its litter box an untidy mess.

Worried something may have happened to her, the family reached out to the Huron County Sheriff's Office, the police agency that covers their town. We later learned that she was known to police, who, over the years, had responded to calls involving Stacey.

But Stacey's family knew something was wrong. According to Jenae Stanley, Stacey's sister, Stacey was in recovery from addiction and had been clean for nearly a year. Friends and family agreed she looked the best they'd ever seen her. She loved to cook and maintain her home. She held family functions and kept the pulse on her family at all times. Sheriff's deputies reached out to us the following day, Sunday, September 11, to request our assistance with the investigation.

While it was highly unusual to have not one but two women reported missing in the same week, the circumstances of their disappearances appeared quite different. Elizabeth had a diagnosed mental health condition and was considered an "at risk"—endangered person—while Stacey Stanley Hicks was not from Ashland and didn't have mental health issues like Elizabeth. On the surface, there didn't appear to be a connection between the two cases. Not yet, anyway.

Upset that law enforcement was not doing enough to locate Stacey, the family commenced an investigation of their own. They printed up dozens of flyers featuring two photos of Stacey, her short dark hair styled in one photo and tied back in a black-and-white bandanna in the other.

"Missing," it read in bright red lettering, "Stacey Stanley, DOB 04/21/73. Last seen 09/08/16 10:00 pm, BP/Duke & Duchess on E. Main, Ashland County. Had a flat on 2003 Mitsubishi Eclipse. Please call Huron County Sheriff's Department, 419-668-6912."

Her family are a tight-knit group, and during the search for Stacey, they basically led the charge. They were relentless in their efforts. I have never seen anything like it in all of my years in law enforcement. They even spoke to the clerk at the BP station, where Stacey had purchased her coffee.

Nathaniel Keck remembered seeing the petite woman with the short, black hair in the store just after 10:00 p.m. "She was chipper, in a good mood," he recalled. She was on the phone for about fifteen minutes, and then she came up to the counter accompanied by the man who had helped with her tire, he said. To show her appreciation, she bought him a coffee, and the two left the store together.

Certain that Stacey was in trouble, Kory, his younger brother, Kurt, and several other family members decided to search the area around the gas station to see if they could locate her gray 2003 Mitsubishi Eclipse. They'd driven just five blocks when they spotted it parked along the curb on Ninth Street. The keys were still in the ignition, and her identification was found inside the vehicle.

More troubling was the positioning of the driver's seat, which was pushed all the way back from the steering wheel; Stacey was short in stature and would not have been able to reach the gas pedal from that distance, indicating that someone else may have driven the car. That scenario became more likely when they noticed several Camel cigarette butts in the ashtray. This was not Stacey's brand.

It was an ominous discovery and only added to the family's frustration with law enforcement. Determined to find Stacey, the family launched a coordinated search effort. They went door-to-door asking questions and showing Stacey's photo, but no one remembered seeing her in the Ninth Street area.

A witness who lived on Ninth Street would later tell police that she noticed a strange car, one that didn't belong, parked across from her house one evening sometime around September 11. She also recalled seeing a man exit the vehicle and walk down the street. But we would not learn of this witness for several more days.

My radar was already up after learning that Jane Doe and Elizabeth Griffith were acquainted and that they both knew our suspect. But again, in our small city, this was not something that was alarming at this point. Still, the captain appeared to be exploring the possibility that the two cases were linked and that Grate might also be connected to our missing grandmother, Stacey Stanley Hicks, whose disappearance we had learned about just two days earlier.

Coming fresh out of my interview with Jane gave me an edge and afforded me the opportunity to formulate my questions based on information about our suspect that I had gleaned during that conversation. I felt like I knew this guy's personality already; I'd worked thousands of cases and interviewed hundreds upon hundreds of sex offenders. This was my niche.

I would be alone in the room with Grate, but that was not unusual. Officers would be watching my interview on a monitor in the adjacent room. I didn't have time to get nervous or even plan out a strategy for my interrogation. The clock was ticking, and we needed to learn more about what Shawn Grate had been up to. Was he holding Elizabeth and Stacey at some other location? What if there were others?

The one thing I did know going in was that Grate had become argumentative with Captain Lay during their conversation. We all knew that once a suspect shut down, it was tough to get them talking again. But I was confident I would find a way in.

The interview room had its own audio and video system specifically to record interviews. But there was always a small risk that the equipment might someday malfunction. So, I'd gotten into the habit of carrying a small digital backup recorder on my person. Before entering the room, I dropped the recorder down my blouse. I knew the quality of the recording wouldn't be as crisp as if it were captured on our professional equipment, but at least I would have a fallback if, heaven forbid, something went wrong with the system.

It was 10:53 a.m. when Captain Lay handed the interrogation off to me. He entered the room with me and made the perfunctory introductions. "Shawn, this is Detective Mager."

"Hi, Shawn," I said. "Nice to meet you."

I hadn't expected him to look as he did, unremarkable beyond being unshaven and unclean. His light brown hair was a tousled mess, and he was bare-chested, barefooted, and muscular. His most outstanding feature were his eyes: they were blue, and they were piercing. I did notice some healed gouges on his forehead. His sole garment was a pair of blue shorts that hung loosely from his waist.

Lots of officers like to come on hot and heavy during interrogations. But I'd learned early on to be less commanding and allow myself to exhibit a level of empathy for the suspect despite any negative feelings I might have about what they were suspected of doing. Over time, I realized that this tactic gave me an edge over other investigators, whether I was communicating with a victim or suspect.

For me, at least, interviewing a victim or alleged perpetrator is nothing like what you see on TV crime shows. Often, there is no straight path from beginning to end. My interviews appear more casual, with lots of questions and back-and-forth. I find myself trying to pick things apart and slowly extract bits and pieces of information. I may bounce from one topic to another and try different angles. Sometimes I push, and other times I might back off.

Power and personal ego have never been my friends during interviews. Standing over someone, slamming a fist on a table, and demanding answers like fictional TV detectives Danny Reagan of *Blue Bloods* and *Law & Order*'s Elliot Stabler may work for some, but it doesn't work for me. I've learned to check my ego at the door and use a far more deliberate and probative style. I look for a way to connect and establish a rapport, all the while trying to find what brings a person to a place where they will talk.

That could be different for every person. It may be that they were abused as a child or that they had received backlash for their gender identity. For others, it may be someone they love or the fear of losing something that matters to them. It's whatever causes them anxiety or worry, whether it's present or something in their past.

Every case is complicated and has multiple dimensions. I always remind myself that even the most heinous offenders are somebody's son or daughter. At the end of the day, I'm just a detective trying to find the truth so that I can get justice for the victims. Having empathy for the person I'm interviewing is important to me and comes authentically, no matter what the circumstances may be. Sometimes it's the little gestures—asking if someone's okay or offering to get somebody a cup of coffee or a soda—that can make a difference.

"We're going to get these cuffs off you," I told the suspect now seated before me, motioning for Officer Dorsey, who had transported Shawn Grate from the scene, to remove the steel handcuffs from his wrists.

I knew he had the potential to be dangerous and that I was taking a calculated chance by leaving him without his handcuffs on. But I also knew that fellow officers were always keeping an eye on the interview room and that help was literally seconds away.

"Are you doing okay?" The first words face-to-face with a suspect are critical. And although clichéd, a first impression goes a long way.

"It's hard," Grate replied as Dorsey removed the handcuffs.

I could rarely get a confession from a handcuffed suspect because 90 percent of communication is body language. Having them handcuffed inhibits my ability gain an accurate account of what transpired. Sometimes suspects act out their crimes using their hands, and that proved to be true with Shawn Grate. If I'd kept him handcuffed, I would have missed a lot of direct demonstrations and a lot of nuances. Beyond that, being handcuffed while talking about something that can get you in trouble can cause someone to shut down or never talk in the first place.

"Can we get you something to drink?" I asked Grate.

"I'd like some coffee, whenever."

I wasn't certain, but as Grate recited his order, cream and sugar, same as his earlier cup served to him during his interview with Captain Lay, I thought I saw tears welling in his eyes. "All right, bud, all right," I said in a soft voice, eager to forge a connection. "We're going through a lot, okay. A whole lot.

"So, I talked to Jane, okay, so I want to touch base about a few things . . . Boy, she's got a beautiful heart, doesn't she?"

"She does," Grate replied flatly.

"It sounds like there was a lot of reading the Bible with her, and it looks like you were trying to find your walk with Christ. Am I right?"

"Yeah."

"Okay. And wow, does she know her stuff when it comes to that, doesn't she?"

"Yeah, she's on my case all the time, which is good," he replied, flashing a quick grin.

"Yeah, it is, it is." I am specially trained as a forensic interviewer and have vast experience working with children and vulnerable adults in situations where allegations of abuse are made or a traumatic event has been witnessed.

Forensic interviewing is a means of gathering information from a victim or witness for use in a legal setting, such as a courtroom. And while there are numerous techniques I employ during my interviews, the foundation for most interviews is typing the subject's personality, finding commonalities between myself and the interviewee, assessing their value system, and identifying their trigger. I look for a connection, a way in. With Jane, it was her connection to God and the Bible. I sensed that something about Jane's deep faith had attracted Grate to her, and I decided to run with that theme for a bit.

"Here's what I know," I said. "I know that sometimes good people do stupid things and sometimes things just explode when that thing kind of turns into another bad thing. So, here's the deal, Shawn, and I'm Kim. You can just call me *Kim*, okay?

"I don't think we can really be defined by a little block of time in our life. We can make mistakes and we're going to be defined by that. Sometimes things happen, sometimes good people do stupid things, and I know that, so we try to be pretty delicate with situations like this, try to be kind of careful.

"Jane came in, and she was open and honest, and it sounds like you're trying to be open and honest as well. Now, what I do know is sometimes people will kind of perceive things differently when they're in a situation, but it sounds like you're pretty honest.

"I want to kind of go through what she said and see what we're missing, okay? So, I appreciate your candidness, I appreciate your openness that you're already trying to explain some things. It looks like you have a conscience, you feel, you have some feelings, I can see that. I saw you tear up when I came in, so . . ."

Lowering his eyes, he muttered, "Yeah, it's rough . . . I'm involved in things . . . but . . . it's no excuse for what's happened."

"If you could say something to her, what would you tell her?"

"What I've been telling her, that she's hanging in there, she's doing a really good job. Don't ever change."

"Would you tell her you're sorry?"

"Oh yeah."

"Well, I can see that you're hurting. I can see that—"

Grate interrupted, "I could be hurting more, but I'm just trying to stay strong. I think she knows that I'm sorry."

"I think with her it's a little more difficult because, the whole sexual part, it's just not something she does."

"Not until marriage," Grate added.

"Right, she doesn't believe in sex without marriage, so she's what, she's thirty?"

"Six."

"Thirty-six, she doesn't have sex at all. That's just not something she believes in. Her boundaries are pretty strong, aren't they? I mean, you weren't even allowed in her apartment, were you? And did you guys ever talk on the phone, or would she ever give you her phone number?"

"No, she doesn't do the phone thing."

"Yeah, she doesn't do phones, no exchanges of phone numbers, you can't come in her apartment, she's pretty strong on that. Let me ask you this—"

Before I could pose my question, Grate began to muse aloud. "It kind of makes me wonder what's she hiding as well, because there are Bible verses all over her walls and everything, but she can just walk into where I'm staying with no problem. It's like I can't go into her place, which is fine and dandy, but it's, still, she sees it as okay that she can come with me."

How had Grate seen the passages on the walls if he hadn't been inside of her apartment? I sensed there was more that he was holding back.

Neither of these people had been on my radar. Not Jane, and not Grate. There was no way that I could ever know everyone in Ashland—no matter how effective the force might be at community policing. Still, this was my hometown, I lived here with my family, and I expected this place to somehow be safe. I was determined to get the facts.

Grate's willingness to have a conversation with me was a good sign, but I had no idea how long his cooperation would continue. My gut told me to keep the dialogue going and see what else he would willingly divulge.

"How many times has she been in your home?" I asked. "Just the once?"

"Twice."

"Twice. When was the other time?"

"Friday," Grate said before correcting himself. "This is the third time she's been over, just this past week . . ."

"All right. Did she give you some food?"

There was no reply. Just a long, deafening silence.

"She's worried about you," I said, hoping to coax him back into the conversation.

"Yeah."

"And did you give her some clothes?"

Grate reluctantly admitted that the garments he had given to Jane were not from his mother, as he had claimed, but items he'd stolen from the donation bin of the thrift shop run by Pump House Ministries. "That's a misdemeanor compared to what I'm dealing with," he stated. His phrasing indicated he was familiar with the system.

He explained that he routinely stole bags from the donation bin. He'd bring them back to his house, go through them, and pick out items he could sell as a side hustle. Since he could see the thrift shop from his window, sometimes he'd even use his camcorder to record other people stealing from the bin.

"I appreciate your honesty," I said. It was important for me to avoid judging him or even offering an inkling of disapproval for what he'd done. I was almost certain he'd shut down if I suggested anything to the contrary. "When all is said and done, you were obviously seeking the Lord, or you wouldn't be reading the Bible with her . . . We all fall short, right?

"When she came in your house, do you think there was any part of her that thought she would have sex with you? That's an honest question. Do you think she thought she was going to have sex, or do you think she thought she was helping another human? Be honest—for her sake, be honest."

"She's torn, a little bit of both probably," Grate told me as he stared down at his feet. "I know she does, maybe not because she's already dealt with a lot the past few days with dealing with the sexual lust, and that's a lot . . . One of the reasons why she wanted to marry me, because she's, she was horny that day."

Grate claimed that while Jane had expressed a desire to marry him, she came to realize it was "just a lust thing for her."

"Is that your take on it?"

"Yeah."

"Okay, so it's not necessarily the things she says, it's how you're evaluating what you're seeing?"

"Yeah, she finds other things to push me away when she's dealing with lust with me, instead of telling me, you know, it's not good to be around me."

"Did you find her more intriguing because of that, do you think?"

"Yeah, it was very nice."

"Probably not something you're used to?"

"No, it's not, but it was good. I like it, and I wouldn't want her to change."

I kept on thinking about the heavily bruised and broken woman I'd just interviewed. It was time to ask Grate about that. "She's hurt, kind of all over, isn't she? Tell me what happened."

"I only hit her once," Grate replied.

"You only hit her once?" I repeated matter-of-factly. I had seen her, so I knew he had hit her more than once, but I also recognized he wasn't ready to tell me that, so I stored it away to circle back when I felt like he was ready to talk about it. The key is to remember it; I can't write it down, because he will know it is notable. I don't always know when that is going to occur, because an interview is dynamic, ever changing.

"Yeah, I hit her once, and she cut me right here with her tooth. Which I didn't mean, but she flipped out on me, which I understand, and she started to claw me and stuff."

"She was scared, right?"

"Yeah, so I just tapped her."

"Well, I don't know if it was a tap, because she got hurt, right, and I think sometimes when things get out of control, sometimes stuff happens like that, right?"

I didn't want to go at him too hard this early in the interrogation. There is a formula to interviewing. It's all about timing, knowing when the right time is to confront a subject on a minor point as opposed to a more significant point. I was trying to keep the conversation going to build trust, so there would be no benefit to challenging him so soon into the interrogation.

"I don't know. Normally, I don't get out of control," he retorted.

I remained silent for a moment or two, considering what he'd said. I recognized that this wasn't the first time that Grate had lost control, and I suspected that he was responsible for other sexual assault victims—or worse—out there. "Sometimes when I talk to people, you can see they don't have a conscience. When I'm looking at you, you have some feelings, and I can see them. I can see that you're torn. Tell me what you're feeling torn about. Why do you think you're feeling torn?"

"I just want my life to be better."

"You want your life to be better or you want—"

"Well, yeah, so I can bring people like Jane in it."

"Here's what I'm seeing with you. One of your strong points is you are kind of a stand-up guy, like you might make mistakes, but you don't want to hold your mistakes inside. In this situation, the whole thing's a mistake—I mean, forcing yourself on somebody for sex when they don't want to engage is a mistake, right?"

"Well, that wasn't the intention, it was like a simple tap, and then, I get like, you know, like sorry type of thing. It's like, geez, it's okay if she just sits on my lap, but I can't give her like a pat on the shoulder or anything?"

Grate had already tried to claim this same sort of teasing behavior when he'd spoken to Officer Dorsey at the crime scene. But I knew from talking to Jane that the two had never been alone together, not inside of her apartment, nor at his home. She'd also indicated that it was anything but a tap on the shoulder. In fact, he'd struck her with such force she collapsed onto the floor, on the verge of losing consciousness.

5

A Confession

If there is one thing I despise in an investigation, it's when a suspect persists in blaming their victim, even when it's not logical. It's especially disturbing when it relates to a sex crime. I expect victim-blaming early on in the process, but typically over the course of the interrogation, suspects come to terms with accountability, or at least appear to.

I get it that people want to shift blame from themselves, that's common, and I anticipate it, but when faced with a crime that is definitively their choice, it's sometimes difficult to present myself as if I can identify with that. Shifting blame onto a victim is different from explaining why you believe you committed a crime. I reminded Grate that Jane didn't want the physical contact; she'd said no.

"Yeah, she only wanted things to happen on her time," he said.

Grate claimed that at one point during the ordeal, he had even talked about letting her go, that the two had discussed walking together to the police station, so he could turn himself in. He'd even prepared a bag of items for her to take with her, the items of clothing he'd stolen for her from the Pump House Ministries thrift shop and the Bible she'd given him.

But that's not how Jane recalled things. She said she'd repeatedly asked him to let her go, and he promised that he would—but that he wasn't done with her yet.

"So, you were talking about letting her go but then wondering what's going to happen?" I replied. "Wondering, *Are they going to come for me?*"

"It's unnerving," Grate admitted. "Nobody wants to go to jail, you know. A lot of jail is being around other inmates that aren't encouraging."

There hadn't been time for me to learn if Grate had a criminal record, but based on his answer and phrasing thus far in our exchange, I was pretty certain this was not his first brush with the law.

"You know what, Shawn," I said, "what becomes bigger than this is just, once and for all, coming to terms with anything to help you make sense of it. What's in your heart is to do the right thing; we can't take back what happened . . .

"Jane's a beautiful person inside and out; she's a doll. So, you sit here and think, *How can I make things right?* Well, I'll tell you how you can make it right, Shawn: honesty, honesty."

I'd dealt with individuals a bit like Shawn Grate in the past. I knew I had to get him to admit what he had done, to convince him that now was his chance to explain himself. It was like playing some weird game of chess with this guy; it was impossible to know exactly what moves to make. I had to rely on my skills and experience and just push through. "You can let her know that 'I did what I did. It was wrong, and it's not your fault.'"

Grate surprised me with his momentary contrition. "It's not her fault," he said.

"It's not her fault," I parroted, "and that's where the man-up thing comes in. You're a manly guy, there's a good piece of you, the guy who stands up and says, 'It was wrong, she didn't deserve that, and I want her to be okay.'"

"But she needed it, though. That's the sad thing."

"Needed what?" I queried, careful not to betray the fury rising inside me.

"Both of us needed to get through our lustful desires."

"Needed to have sex?"

"In a way . . . Not so much me. She's just battling all the time; she's battling with lustful desires, and it's a roadblock."

"Did you think by doing what you did to her that it would push her past that? I mean—"

Grate stopped me midsentence. "It did get overboard," he interjected, "but you know what? She's equipped with what it takes to emotionally get through something. But there's a lot she doesn't understand because she's not sexual with anyone."

Having a suspect accused of a sex crime behave as though the situation was reciprocal is not uncommon, and Grate was proving to be no different from the many other sex offenders I'd interviewed during my tenure. He persisted in the narrative that Jane had equal culpability for what had occurred, unwilling to own up to what he had done.

It was already becoming clear that he became angry if he believed that someone had betrayed him or lied to him, and I needed to be hyperaware of that. If I said, "I don't believe you," I would erase the relationship between us and effectively shut the interview down.

At this point, Grate acknowledged that when Jane entered his residence on Saturday, she carried his stuff inside and had intended to read the Bible to him. He further acknowledged that while she was reading, the situation got out of control. "At some point, she decides she wants to leave, and that's where the switch happened."

I commented about Jane's body hurting, to which Grate stated, "I wore her out." He admitted that he tied her up when he left the residence, but claimed he untied her when he returned home.

What he didn't admit, and what we would learn later during our investigation, was that while Jane lay bound and gagged on a putrid mattress, Grate went through her purse, stole her house key, went to her apartment, and let himself in. While there, he stole thirty-four dollars from the green wallet Jane kept on a bookshelf in the living room for emergencies. It was likely during this visit that he observed the Bible verses that Jane hung on her apartment walls. He then paid a visit to the Circle K convenience store to buy cigarettes and soda with the stolen money.

Video surveillance we later obtained from the Circle K captured footage of Grate at the register.

Grate claimed that it had always been his intention to let Jane go. But had it really? I pressed him about his plans. Had he secured another place to hide out? Perhaps a fort in the woods? Another abandoned building?

Grate hesitated. "I . . . I don't know what I would have done," he finally blurted out. "I lied to her. I told her I'd hide out and stuff like that."

I also pressed him about a threat he had made to burn the place down once he freed Jane. "What would be the purpose of that?" I asked.

"Just angry."

"Angry because of what you did?"

"Yeah."

Grate's half-hearted response was unconvincing. Surely, he intended to set the place alight to cover his tracks—and his crimes. But did he really intend on letting Jane go? Or was he going to burn the house down with her still inside?

I wanted to keep him talking, so I didn't challenge him at that point. "Did you have anything you could use to set it on fire? Gasoline? What would you use?"

"I don't know . . . I was just rambling . . ."

It was time to press him harder. "I want inside, Shawn. I want inside. Who do you have that you're close to that you talk to in your life? Do you have any special friends, or do you have a church? Who do you have?"

"Jane."

"Just Jane?" Had he just named his victim, the woman he had abducted and sexually violated, as his sole friend and confidante?

"Pretty much . . ."

At this point in our exchange, I told Grate I wanted to go through what Jane had told me, to confirm her version of things. "What I'm trying to do is figure out if you're being honest or not. What I know about you so far is you want to be honest."

Grate agreed.

I already knew from my interview with Jane that Grate had known her through the Kroc Center for about two months. I wondered if he would tell me the truth.

Grate confirmed the time line that I already had from Jane. He said he'd gone to the Kroc Center to speak to a counselor about finding housing. "There are no places to live around here," he railed. "The homeless shelter is shut down, so really, it's Ashland's fault for everything that I've done."

Grate's remark was laughable. To be sure, Ashland, like every community, could do better at providing for the homeless. But that was a national problem that literally stretched from coast to coast. And his homelessness had absolutely nothing to do with what he'd done to Jane.

I pondered whether he actually believed that or if he had tossed the comment out there waiting to see how I'd respond. He looked directly at me, and I could tell he was waiting for my reaction. But I offered him nothing in return.

"I'm just joking." He grinned.

Grate claimed he'd been running from the law since that past June, and that's how he'd ended up in Ashland.

Cops in the neighboring county were looking for him on a child support warrant, so he came to Ashland to hide out. His criminal record would show a number of offenses, both misdemeanors and felonies, dating back to his high school years. His first arrest came when he was seventeen.

Grate admitted that he had fathered three children with three different women, one of whom he married and then quickly divorced, but that he was not involved with any of them and had been negligent when it came to child support, necessitating he find a new place to hide.

Grate explained that for the past several months, he'd squatted in abandoned houses and buildings around Ashland County. He'd also camped for extended periods in wooded areas around Richland and Ashland Counties. He would set up what he called "forts," makeshift refuges where he would hide when he had no other place to go.

It was all very MacGyver-like. He put a lot of time and effort into constructing these hideaways of branches and pieces of stolen wood. Some were hidden in the woods around Mansfield; others were in abandoned buildings or defunct businesses, including a former cigarette store in Ashland.

The place had gone out of business; the doors were locked, but there was still inventory inside, including candy and cigarettes. It was a very small building on Claremont Avenue. The place had been closed for a long time, but Grate said the candy was still good, that the "preservatives" had kept it "fresh." He admitted that he ate the candy and smoked the cigarettes; he also sold the items for quick cash.

I paraphrased some of what he said: "You're here in Ashland, you don't have a place to go, you end up in an abandoned house, you're always looking over your shoulder, wondering if someone's going to show up here, and you're in some place you're not supposed to be.

"Then, you meet somebody. She's pretty . . . you got somebody who's almost angelic. Her boundaries, they make her almost angelic, too, which might be the thrill of the chase, because I am certain you can get all the women you want. I'm sure you don't have a problem with that.

"But then you have one who will not be intimate. It's not happening, so it becomes kind of a quest. So, add to the stress of not having a place to go and maybe the stress of some other things that have happened, that puts you in this position at this time, and it is the perfect storm. And there you are.

"So, when you say it's Ashland's fault, well, you know what, we can't blame that, but sometimes we are where we are because of all those little things that are going on around us, and anybody who thinks otherwise is wrong, because you have to look at it and think, *You know what, why was I in this position?*"

"Things might have been different if I'd been in a homeless shelter instead," he offered.

"Yeah, you're right," I said, being careful not to show judgment. Grate's statement didn't surprise me at all. I knew there was no point debating the matter with Grate, and in fact, it would have been detrimental to the interview if I'd engaged him.

"It's not hard for us to figure out what happened," I said. "What we can't figure out is why is this happening, so when I'm talking to you, I think I've got to dig into your heart. I've got to figure out what's in your head and what's in your heart. We don't just take anything at face value, no matter how bad it is. We try to figure it out. How did this happen? Why is this guy who, when you're talking, you're articulate, you communicate well, why is this guy who seems like he should have everything going okay, not okay? What happened?"

I suggested there may have been some other issues at play that might have triggered his action—some stressor or perhaps something that happened to him years ago.

Grate claimed his troubles started when his mother, Theresa McFarland, abandoned him and his older brother. Shawn was just eleven at the time, and his brother Ronald, who went by his middle name, Jason, was thirteen. "I come home from school, and she's gone," he said. "But I don't blame her, I don't. I used to, but . . ."

"Why did she leave?" I asked.

"Ah, she had to go find herself."

"I'm sorry," I said. I contemplated whether it was time to do a deep dive into his childhood. I could already tell it was a trigger point for him. And the timing for introducing sensitive topics is crucial.

There was no doubt that Grate harbored some intense feelings for his mother, and it needed to be addressed. It was my in with him, but I had to be careful with the topic, as to not cause him to shut down.

"Do you ever get to see your mother?" I asked.

"No, not no more. She left when I was eleven, and she tried to come back in my life when I was seventeen." At this point in the interview, Grate launched into a story about "this lady." Grate explained that many years ago, while visiting his mother's house, a young woman knocked at the front door. "She said, 'You wanna buy some magazines?'"

He recalled that his mother ordered magazines from the woman and paid her forty dollars for the subscriptions. "But she never got them," he said.

I had no idea why he was telling me about this woman and the failed magazine exchange, but it would soon become clear. I listened intently and let him elaborate, which quickly morphed into a rant against his mother. "She is supposed to be a Christian woman, but she'll get hers. Something will catch up with her someday."

His anger was palpable, especially when he said that he was "wishing her dead."

"I haven't been out to my mom's place for a while," he continued. "There was a time I needed some help, you know. I was in between jobs, and she didn't help. She just bugged me. I mean, this is the time that I could, if you're going to help me, you should help me, because I'm going to forget you.

"I did, I forgot her. It's about five to eight years now I haven't had a Christmas."

"Wow, that explains some things, Shawn." I suggested that this was a perfect example of how the people who mattered in his life had let him down and what that had created in him. "I'm not a counselor, but I talk to people who are hurting, on both ends of situations."

I projected empathy as he told me more about his dysfunctional childhood, his abandonment by his mother, and later by his father.

"My dad moved across the street when I was fourteen and my brother was sixteen."

"He just left you boys there?"

"Yeah." According to Grate, at some point, his father became romantically involved with the woman who lived across the street, and one day, he just packed up and moved in with her, leaving Grate and his brother to fend for themselves. Grate explained that absent a parent, the place became a "party house," with kids from all the surrounding schools coming by at all hours of the day and night to drink and get high.

Grate said he would leave the house and drive around just to get "peace of mind." He would take his books with him and do his homework. His relationship with his brother was good when they were in high school. "He was my older brother. . . . I listened to him." But at some point, Jason told him he didn't want him around.

Despite it all, Grate boasted at his ability to finish high school and graduate, something of which he appeared proud.

"I at least had to make Ds," he remarked.

When describing his childhood, Grate spoke as if the events had just occurred, and the wounds were fresh. Like many of the suspects I'd interviewed, he appeared vulnerable, even though he had committed horrific acts. Our interview was dynamic. Still, it was an arduous process to get him to a place of comfort and trust, which is imperative in gaining a confession.

"That's hard," I acknowledged.

"It don't really matter. I'm used to it."

"Well, I don't know that you are. I mean, I think all those little pieces play a part in where we are, why we do the things that we do. No matter what goes wrong or what has been wrong, when it comes down to it, sometimes your whole life hinges on a moment. Like today."

Time and again, I suggested to Grate that being truthful with me would be akin to giving Jane a gift of sorts. I knew that it was difficult for someone to heal from a trauma unless the perpetrator actually acknowledged what had happened—and validated what took place. In Grate's case, I knew that he cared about the truth, and at some level, he also struggled with how he felt about Jane. I tried to convince him that being honest about what he had done to her was like a first step in bringing her peace.

"You're doing the right thing," I said, hoping that he'd continue to be honest. But for the time being, it was not to be.

Grate started to cry. "It doesn't matter. Life sucks anyways, so my wish is to just be put away in a cell."

Grate's apparent regret for what he'd done to Jane proved to be momentary. Despite the emotional outburst, he failed to exhibit any remorse. In fact, he seemed to be coming to grips with the fact that he was in serious trouble. He was more concerned about himself than his victim. In that aspect, he was no different from my other suspects. This form of self-preservation is common among many of the people I've interviewed.

We were forty-five minutes into the interrogation when I started to question him about how he'd restrained Jane and kept her quiet during her captivity. She had told me that at one point he'd tied her to the bed and put duct tape over her mouth.

"That's when I had to step out [of the house]," he replied flatly. "I asked her permission first."

"To put duct tape over her?"

"To tie her up. I wasn't going to. I had to punish her and tire her out. I wasn't ready to take her home yet."

"Do you think this will impact her for a long time?"

Grate's response struck me as brutally cynical. "It'll clear her lustful thoughts," he claimed. "She'll be able to move on and stay focused now."

"Do you think it will cause her some trust issues?"

"She's always had trust issues, anyway."

"Do you think they will be worse?"

"They can't get no worse. She's still single, hasn't been married, she's thirty-six—she has really bad trust issues."

"So, you think she needed to have sex with somebody, but do you think she needed to be forced into sex? Be honest."

"She needed it, because she wasn't going to do it herself, because it's so wrong, she needed to be free of that."

"But tying her up and forcing her?"

Grate claimed he didn't tie her up to have sex, only to prevent her from fleeing. This was inconsistent with what Jane had alleged, that he had tied her up in various positions allowing him to access her for sex. "But you're five times as strong as her . . . She tried to fight you off. I mean, looking at this whole thing, you forced her to have sex. She didn't want to—"

"I abducted her," he interjected, "and I raped her."

And there it was—Grate's confession to Jane's abduction and rape, not only in a layered narrative but in a direct exclamation. But I still needed detail and context to access Grate's veracity. Although it was a critical moment in my interview, and one that would almost certainly be used against him in court, there was more information to gain.

"So, looking at it, you still think that's what she needed, or do you think it should happen in a different way? Be honest."

"If we would have gotten married, I probably would have been disappointed, and I wouldn't know how to act. I would have flipped out, just like I did, I don't know if I would have flipped out, but I would have been, 'All right, let's step up and get her on the ball.' Do you know what I mean?"

"Meaning sexually, do what you want her to do?"

"No, no, not so much, just like, maybe there would be more effort, though, do you know what I mean? . . . But then again, we might not even have had sex on the honeymoon, you know, like one of them things . . . But then again, maybe she would have rocked my world, it's one of them things we probably should have just waited until we marry."

I found Grate's insight into a possible future with Jane to be crass and blatantly disrespectful. Not that everything he'd said to this point wasn't, but I was particularly taken aback by these remarks.

At this point in the interview, I decided to revisit our earlier discussion about Grate's promises to let Jane go. He explained that throughout her captivity, she would repeatedly ask to leave, and then she wouldn't ask for a while to get him to believe that she was okay with being there. "I told her to relax . . . I need some time. Time was just going too fast."

Grate claimed that he'd been planning to let her go on Monday evening, but it was already dark by the time he was ready to release her, and she was tired, "so I told her to go to bed.

"I don't regret it," he added. "Let's get this shit on the road. It don't matter to me. I died a long time ago on the cross."

His comment warranted clarification. "You say you died a long time ago, meaning emotionally, you feel like you're dead?"

"Yeah," he affirmed. "I died on the Cross with Jesus."

During my thirty-three hours interviewing Shawn Grate, he would make numerous remarks like this referencing Jesus, the Bible, and crucifixion. We were still early in the interview, so I didn't know what value to put on all of it. What did he mean, and what relevance did it all have to what he had done?

From our conversation thus far, I knew that he was raised in the church, had some familiarity with the Bible, and seemed concerned about the impact of his alleged crimes on his salvation. But what wasn't clear to me—at least not yet—was if Grate's interest in Christianity was genuine or if he was just using it as a vehicle to get closer to Jane—and other women he may have preyed upon.

6

Father Knows Best

Being a girl should never stop you from reaching your goals.
—Alva Lee

I was seven years old and in the second grade when I first became aware that there were cruel people in the world. People who like to prey on those they perceive as weak.

I was on the playground at recess when I saw one of the boys in my class trying to pull down a little girl's pants. She was my friend, and she was tiny. I remember looking around at all the kids standing idly by while she screamed. *What is wrong with you guys?* I recall thinking. *Why aren't you doing anything?*

I managed to talk a couple of my classmates into joining me in intervening, and that's what we did. It felt good to do the right thing and help protect someone else. I yearned for the opportunity to experience that blend of happiness and quiet pride again.

When I was a little girl, my parents talked to me about my strengths, and they convinced me that my options were limitless. Throughout my childhood, they gave me small life lessons around everyday situations. Most involved standing up or speaking out for those who were vulnerable. They were staunchly protective of my sister and me. Still, I was aware that I really didn't have people outside my family sticking up for me when I needed them most.

I was born in a rough area of Mansfield, a small city of just under fifty thousand residents in the western foothills of Ohio's Allegheny Plateau. Our home wasn't anything great, but it didn't look all that different from others nearby. I guess we didn't have a lot of money, but the truth was, I didn't notice it much, because my parents always made sure we had what we needed.

As a child, I thought the guy from the meat market was just being friendly when he gave us free hot dogs and that my neighbor was being thoughtful when she made my sister and me peanut butter sandwiches. To this day, I honestly don't know if it was friendliness or people helping a family.

My dad, Alva Lee, was a lifelong resident of Ashland County who worked as a mason. He was handsome, intelligent, and incredibly tough. In my eyes, he was an amazing man who was bigger than life. Alva Lee loved to joke around, and his wholehearted laugh was contagious. He believed in doing your best, standing up for what you believed in, and persevering through difficult times.

My dad didn't have full-time work during the winter, when it was too cold to pour concrete, so he made money plowing snow, trapping foxes, and picking up money here and there at poker games.

My mother, Carolyn, was raised in Kentucky, one of eight siblings, all of whom are still alive. For the first twelve years of my life, she was at home with my sister, Tamra, and me. She was nurturing and openly loving. She raised huge gardens that we helped work, canned a lot of our food, and was an outstanding cook and seamstress.

When I was four, we moved to the "country," what we in Ohio call the rural area, mostly rolling hills and farms, on the outskirts of the city. My parents bought a thirteen-acre plot and built us a home. Right after the move, our former house in Mansfield was condemned and razed, which seemed weird to me at the time. Looking back, I realize that it was in very poor shape and probably needed to be torn down.

My dad had an incredible work ethic and was eventually promoted to supervisor. Still, he continued to work long hours and supplement his salary with part-time work when he could.

My mom would always have dinner ready when he got home, and we would all eat together at the kitchen table. It was, by some standards, a typical American household. I was incredibly close to my mom, but I was also a daddy's girl. I couldn't sleep until he came home from work. He would take off his T-shirt after a double shift, and I would wear it to bed as my nightshirt. He was my everything, and it made me feel secure.

Mom would brush my hair every night. She helped me with my homework and had a particular skill with English. She hadn't gone to college, but she read a lot. She was ladylike and was never attached to or controlled by material things.

Growing up, my sister, Tamra, and I were close. She was two years older than I and incredibly intelligent and beautiful. We bickered as siblings, but we were protective of each other. She actually fought an older girl who was picking on me when I was in the fourth grade.

My sister and I attended the local public school. Tamra was a straight-A student without even having to work at it. I was not. She helped me with my homework, and we played together all the time.

When he wasn't out making money, my dad was an outdoorsman. And, since he didn't have any sons, my sister and I became well rounded, to say the least. My dad had several boats that he docked on Lake Erie. We'd spend summer weekends fishing at the lake, and both Tamra and I became accustomed to running the family boats from an early age. Taking the wheel and handling the throttle on one of the boats was no big deal for either of us. I started running a big boat when I was just eight. When we weren't out on the lake, we'd be out hunting and shooting with Dad and Mom.

I was four the first time I held a gun. I started out with a Daisy BB gun, and Dad and I would go out squirrel and rabbit hunting. At the age of nine, I moved up to a 20-gauge shotgun that I used to hunt rabbits and squirrels. I bagged my first deer in my early teens and continued to hunt with my dad throughout my teenage years and beyond.

I would also go to turkey shoots with my father; he was an amazingly accurate shot. His Browning 12-gauge shotgun, which dated to the 1950s, was one of his proudest possessions, and he always told me that it would be mine someday.

At one turkey shoot competition, a man accused my dad of cheating because he kept winning. But my father remained calm and offered to swap guns with the man. My dad knew full well that it was his skill that allowed him to win, not that he had a trick shotgun. I watched him hand the guy his gun and accept the man's weapon in return. My father's opponent was cocky as they began the next round of shooting, thinking that he was sure to come out on top. But he was wrong.

My dad outshot the guy in the next round, even while using a shotgun that he'd never touched before. It was his skill that brought home the prizes, which included hams, slabs of bacon, and various butchered meats—and not the Browning that he treasured. I remember thinking he was the coolest and toughest man on the planet.

The year I turned nine, we got horses. My mother would pack a lunch for my sister and me, and we would ride off on adventures on the neighboring farmer's property. Over the years, we also had dogs, chickens, and a couple of cows. Throughout my childhood, my parents were flirtatious with each other, making their love obvious.

They were playful and outwardly affectionate, so it came as a surprise when I arrived home from junior high one afternoon to learn that they were separating for a few months.

I didn't know it then, but my father had come home drunk and laid a hand on my mother. It only happened once, but my mother rightly judged that even one time was unacceptable, and we temporarily moved out. At twelve, I went from living in our family home in the country and attending the local public school where I was comfortable and familiar to living in a tumbledown rental property with my mother and sister in another county where I didn't know a soul and just didn't know how to fit in.

It was in that rental that I saw cockroaches for the first time. I walked into the kitchen one night, flicked on the light, and spied the bugs crawling all over the countertops.

I was devastated that my parents were apart and that I didn't get to see my dad. It was tough for my sister and me—and my mother, too. She had been a stay-at-home mom, but now she had to go out and find a job. She found work and made do. Remarkably, she went from being a housewife to later becoming a barber to quickly owning her own shop.

I watched her trying to make it on her own; I knew she had to be struggling, even if she tried not to show it, so I was hesitant to approach her with anything that might upset her.

Our move happened the summer before I was to enter the seventh grade, so I started junior high school in a new, and much bigger, district. On the first day of class, a boy talked to me, and a jealous girl who looked like she was fifteen walked up to me in the middle of the lunchroom and knocked my lunch tray out of my hands, sending my plateful of *Marzetti*—what we in Ohio call pasta with sauce and hamburger meat—onto the floor in front of the entire grade. That silenced the room, and everyone was staring at me.

At first, I was mortified and humiliated, but within seconds, I was pissed. Although the girl was bigger than I and clearly had been in those situations before, she didn't realize that I was dealing with my parents' separation and that my dad had taught me how to defend myself. I took her to the floor and had to be pulled off her. Looking back, I realize she was likely dealing with a lot in her own life.

I remember being grabbed by a male teacher/coach who took me into a classroom. I was resisting him, struggling to get away when he pushed me down in a chair and abruptly pulled out some paper and a pencil from the desk. Intrigued, I stopped fighting and watched as he proceeded to draw a giant *Y* with a little stick figure standing right where the letter split. That figure was supposed to be me.

He told me I was sitting right there on the edge of going one of two directions; it was up to me to decide which way I would choose. He asked me where I wanted to go with life and encouraged me to come up with some short-term goals and some long-term goals for myself and offered me some advice—to stop worrying about the things you can't control and focus on the things you can.

Looking back, I realize he had a profound impact on my life. During my short time at that school, he periodically checked on me and kept encouraging me to do the right thing. He helped me to recognize that Henry Adams, the father of teaching, was correct when he said, "A teacher affects eternity." That year, I learned that there are some things I can control in my life, and if I set short- and long-term goals, I don't have to freeze in a situation I have no control over.

Happily, I didn't get in trouble for punching my classmate. The school counselor told me that the girl had been picking on kids for the last three years and that, because I had challenged her, he believed I would never have a problem with her or anyone there again.

I was only in that school for another six weeks; after that, my parents got back together, and we returned home to our old life. But the impact of their separation, as well as another traumatic experience I prefer not to share that occurred during my six weeks there, probably shaped my life. We all have events in our lives that shape how we live and what career paths we choose.

I had reenrolled at my old junior high school, and life resumed as it once was. Once in high school, I got involved in more activities, including cheerleading. I had an incredible group of friends, but my best friend was my big sister, Tamra.

My family was very close, and we continued to do lots of things together—especially around the holidays when we'd always carve out some time to go look at Christmas lights and have big dinners.

I was invested in hunting and trapping and would set my own traps. In the early mornings, I would take my dad's truck out before school to check on my trapline in hopes of catching a fox.

My grades in high school were okay, except for one class. In the first weeks of class, my teacher called me up to his desk. He motioned me around to his side, and he ran his hand up my leg. I was so shocked that momentarily I thought I was going to pass out. After that, he would ask me to stay after class. I avoided him. I couldn't tell my dad, because he would have killed that man, so I kept it to myself.

From that moment, I was rendered useless in that class. I couldn't focus at all. Just like the mean girl in the school cafeteria, this man was a bully. But I did not yet have the wherewithal to deal with him, and it nearly cost me my opportunity to go to college.

Looking back, I praise God it went no further than that. It was also a learning moment that helps me recognize why so many of my victims freeze when something traumatic happens to them. Events like that impacted my path. And, if there is any positive in my life events, it gives me a strong frame of reference during my countless investigations.

When it came time to apply to colleges, the school counselor advised me that I wasn't someone who seemed likely to succeed in collegiate studies, because of my terrible grades in that subject, and suggested I look for a different path for my life. He refused to give me an application to fill out, claiming he reserved those application forms for kids who were "college material." Back in the day, it wasn't an option to jump online to access an application; we had to get one from our guidance counselor.

I had no idea what that meant, but I took offense. This person who was supposed to be advocating for our futures had taken it upon himself to decide who was worthy and who wasn't.

With my mom's encouragement, I applied to Ashland University on my own and was accepted.

To help pay for my college tuition, the summer after my freshman year, I took a job as a gate guard at Charles Mill Lake Park, a two-thousand-acre park and campground located on the Black Fork of the Mohican River in Ashland and Richland Counties.

Little did I know that I would meet my future husband, Dan, an operations assistant there, during that summer at Charles Mills Lake Park. We forged a relationship during an afternoon boat trip on the lake, when it became apparent that we had so much more in common. Dan came from a big family; he had four brothers and a sister and grew up in a classic 1800s farmhouse just outside the city. His parents, Bruce and Sue Mager, were both from West Virginia but had made Ashland their home.

I dated Dan through college. I graduated with a bachelor of science degree in criminal justice and a minor in sociology. That December,

Dan and I were married in a big church wedding. My sister, Tamra, was my maid of honor. To our delight, Santa Claus—a wedding guest who dressed up in a red suit and white beard to surprise us—turned up for the celebration!

After college, I moved to join Dan in southeast Ohio, where he had been transferred by the Parks Department. We lived in an historic farmhouse in an area rich with history.

My first job was in the crime prevention office of a local sheriff's department. Not long after securing the position, I enrolled at the police academy in Akron to begin my law enforcement training. I was one of thirty cadets and one of only a few women. Back then, law enforcement wasn't on the top of the list for most women when they were searching out a career.

At the end of our training, we competed against each other in the Top Gun competition for the individual in the class with the best shooting skills. The competition was held at a large range house where active-duty officers were always streaming in and out.

As all the candidates were shooting the course, I wasn't really focused on how well everyone else was doing. About halfway through, I knew I hadn't missed any shots—but didn't really know where I stood in the event.

As the competition progressed, the field of people who had shot without missing narrowed, and ultimately, I was informed that I was one of two individuals who had gone through the entire course without missing a single shot.

Everyone began to hover around, and I could hear the academy commander telling the range instructor that there was going to be a shoot-off between the other guy and me. I then heard the academy commander inform the range instructor that no woman had ever won Top Gun in the academy class, and "it's not going to happen today either!" To ensure I didn't succeed, he wanted the shoot-off to include *moving* targets.

"That's unprecedented," the range instructor shot back. "You are trying to make the course impossible for her to win."

The two men continued their verbal sparring, and it wasn't long before the academy commander suggested that I might not do well with moving targets compared to the other guy. The arguing continued as I stood by with the other contestant. Neither one of us knew quite what to do, and we both opted to let the higher-ranking officers battle this one out.

At the time, I was embarrassed and just wanted the situation to go away. Then something happened inside me. Instead of shrinking back, I became determined. The arguing went on for several minutes with other people chiming in that it wasn't fair that the commander was trying to keep me from being the Top Gun. There was cursing, and more people started coming around. I initially felt humiliated. Then the academy commander repeated that no woman was going to be Top Gun of his academy, causing some in the crowd to get behind me in a show of support. Even officers from the city where the range was located started encouraging me, telling me that I could do it.

Maybe I saw the commander as an egotistical ass. Or perhaps it was my instilled sense of determination driving me forward. But something gave me the will to push ahead. I stepped forward and told both the range instructor and my academy commander that I was fine with a contest involving moving targets. So, they set them up. I remember feeling a sense of calm and resolution.

Of course, no one there that day knew that I had been firing shotguns since I was a child. By this point, shooting at a moving target was second nature to me. The only thing that made this different was that these moving targets were a good deal more predictable in their movements than an animal in a field or forest. It wasn't fear of the moving targets that had prompted me to hesitate at the range. It was the thought of being the cause of conflict and, worse, being the center of attention.

I took a moment to contemplate the consequences of winning, both good and bad. Although my father wasn't there with me, I could almost hear him telling me to focus and "show those sons of bitches how to do this!"

When the academy commander asked who wanted to go first, I stepped forward. I volunteered because I didn't want it to be said that I was afraid or that I wanted to see what the other guy might do before I had my turn. As I began to shoot, I was taken aback by the noise of the moving targets; that was a distraction that I hadn't anticipated. I could hear people encouraging me, too. I had never shot at an indoor range, nor had I ever shot at cabled moving targets. What I could hear even though he wasn't there was my dad in my ear, telling me how to aim and how to use controlled breathing to calm my nerves and focus.

"Take a breath, breathe in through your nose, slowly breathe out through your mouth, and focus," he used to whisper.

When it emerged that I was performing well on the course, the academy commander intruded again—this time directing personnel to speed up the targets and make the course even harder for me. For a moment, the guy running the cable operation refused the commander's order. But I told him to go ahead, that I was fine with it.

I was so hyperaware of what was going on that it felt as if I were on the outside looking in. I knew I was a good shot, but I also think God smiled on me that day. Despite the higher speed, I continued to hit one target after another. My male competitor was going to have a very tough job, indeed, to meet or exceed my score.

Lo and behold, I emerged Top Gun.

After the results were announced, I turned and realized for

the first time that the range was packed with observers—most of whom I did not know. All but one of them was congratulatory. Not surprisingly, the commander angrily threw his arms up in the air and stormed out without a word. I only wish my father could have been at the shooting range that day to see me put his words into action: "Being a girl should never stop you from reaching your goals."

After graduation, there was a banquet to mark our achievement, and I got to stand up in front of everyone to receive my award, the coveted Top Gun honor and a plaque to memorialize my victory. Dan was with me, and when they called my name, he smacked me on the back and said, "Get up there, girl!"

Dan and I were in southeast Ohio for only a short time when he received a transfer back to Ashland, and we happily returned to our hometown.

I was hired as an investigator for the Department of Job and Family Services. The office was in the Fourth Street area, with its parking lot just behind the old yellow colonial where Shawn Grate had been squatting. It was a demanding but rewarding position. I worked sex offenses and child abuse cases. The department was short-staffed, so I was constantly being called out at all hours of the night.

By then, Dan and I had our first son, Corbin, and I wanted to spend more time at home with my infant. Much of my work with the agency had me interacting with officers from the Ashland Police Division, and over the three years, many of the guys of the force had become my friends. They knew I'd been putting in long hours with the agency and suggested I consider joining them at the police department.

At the time, it was an all-male force, and the department was eager to have a woman join the team. Police admin assured me that if I could score in the top ten on the police exam process, I could have a position, even if they were hiring only a few people. But that's not how I wanted to join the police force. I recall telling the interview team, "I am not going to have anything handed to me just because I am a woman.

"If you are hiring three officers, and I don't score in the top three, I don't want to be hired."

I remember looking up and seeing them look at each other and nod.

I went through the process and scored in the top four. The department was hiring four officers, so I earned my place. I was one of two female officers hired that year, making us the only women on the all-male force.

From day one, I felt accepted by the majority, but there were a couple of old-timers who were not accepting at all. They couldn't come to terms with the concept of a female in law enforcement. They were of the mindset that if a woman performed this job, then it marginalized how manly you had to be to do it. I learned quickly that my ability to communicate was my greatest asset.

I'd worked for three years with the Department of Job and Family Services as an investigator with Children's Services. When you are alone in a house, and you don't have backup and are not afforded the luxury of having a gun or pepper spray, and you are talking about whether someone can keep their children or not, your survival is your ability to communicate. Those peripheral things are what a Children's Services worker must deal with, so you must focus on your surroundings, because you don't have a partner. Performing the job made me confident in myself and later in my abilities as a police officer.

At the start of each shift, I would hear the guys banging around in the adjacent men's locker room, but I was usually by myself. Yet, oddly, I didn't feel isolated or alone. I was like the den mother half the time, but at the same time, they were protective of me.

Over the course of my career, I have always worked cases

involving sex offenses and child abuse, whether I was on patrol or as a detective. I've interviewed hundreds upon hundreds of suspects, including sex offenders, during my tenure, and I've gotten confessions from most of them. One of my main goals in my interview is creating an environment, both physical and emotional, where a suspect feels comfortable disclosing the most heinous act they've ever committed.

And it was no different when Shawn Grate surfaced.

7

A Ticking Clock

As my interrogation of Shawn Grate moved into its second hour, I knew that I had his bare-bones confession to the abduction and subsequent rape of our victim, Jane. But there was a ton more digging I needed to do. The admonition from the captain to find out more about our two missing women, Elizabeth Griffith and Stacey Stanley Hicks, was top of mind for me. And I had an ominous feeling that there were likely others.

We knew that time was of the essence if Grate had been involved in other abductions and was perhaps holding somebody at another location. Jane was in bad shape when we rescued her; we could only speculate what condition these other victims might be in—if we were lucky enough to find them still alive.

Grate had bound Jane in a way that she could harm herself if she tried to escape. The possibility of some other woman out there bound and gagged in that manner haunted my thoughts. "I want to talk a little bit about some other stuff," I said, my way of setting the stage for a change of topic.

Grate responded affirmatively.

"I told you that we always figure it out. We do. And for you, Shawn, you want to be a stand-up guy. You try to be one. So, right now, I want to talk about some other things we are digging into.

"We can't find Elizabeth," I said. "We will find her. But we can't right now." My mere mention of Elizabeth's name provoked an immediate response of Grate refusing to look at me.

"Hey, look at me," I appealed. "I need your help. I'm not here to judge you. I'm going to ask for your help here."

My solicitation was met with silence. "Are you hearing me okay? Are you understanding me when I talk?"

"Yes."

"Can you help me?" My plea seemed to reach him. The way he looked at me told me I had him. At that moment, he locked eyes with me, and although I didn't know what he had done, I knew he had bought into me. I had established a connection with the suspect, and my gut told me that he would eventually confess.

Looking back, it was the profoundest moment of our interview. There was just something about the way he looked at me and allowed me to look into him. He trusted me; he believed me. His eyes telegraphed that, at some level, he wanted to help me. And it wasn't just some desire to please me. I knew he wanted to say what he'd done. I knew he wanted to talk. I didn't get a confession or even a partial confession right then, but I knew the truth would come if I could find a way in.

It was clear that Grate had come to a moment of resolve. I knew that he would waver back and forth for some time to come, like some imaginary pendulum he would swing back and forth before finally spilling what he'd done. He'd debate the merits of what his next step was going to be, and we'd talk, and then talk some more. I'd ask questions, and he would be responsive for a bit—but then retreat. The two of us would verbally spar with each other.

Grate would try to find some way out from under the trouble he'd created, but ultimately, he'd relent. At some point, he'd try to deny that anything happened, and there would be a moment when he would backtrack, too. Ultimately, though, I would get a confession. I just had to wait it out and keep him talking.

His gaze fixed on mine, Grate replied, "I don't know if I can help you."

"Why? This might be one of those moments," I said. "This might be your moment to do the right thing, Shawn."

"What's the right thing?"

"The right thing is to tell us where she is . . ."

"You're asking me?"

"I'm asking you."

"I don't know."

"I'm asking you to tell me where she is. Do I think she's okay? No, I don't. But I know you have a conscience. I know you have a heart. I need your help, that's what I'm asking for. You came in and said, 'I don't care about me anymore. I died a long time ago.' . . . Let's just put it in perspective, with what you've described with Jane, as far as doing things going wrong . . . Really anything that's happened with Elizabeth is the same exact thing. Am I right, or am I wrong?"

"I'd say it's a whole lot different."

"Tell me how. Because you cared about Jane?" I pressed.

Grate reiterated his previous statement. "No, it's just different . . . a whole different situation."

"I agree . . . two different scenarios. Two whole different scenarios. I don't think Elizabeth's okay," I said, raising the possibility she may no longer be alive. "We're past that, I think."

"How do you know she's not okay?"

"That's what I believe."

"Maybe she's better off, though."

Grate's comment was telling. Perhaps he knew her better than he was letting on.

"I only hope she's in a better place. I don't know for sure," he stated.

"I think you already know that. I think we both do. I believe she's gone, and if she is, she is walking with God," I stated.

"She's gone?"

"Yeah, that's what I believe," I responded.

"Yeah, she's probably more like a child of God who automatically goes to heaven," he remarked, growing agitated and deflecting my gaze. "She was so abused by so many people that still have their freedom and do whatever they want."

I did not know to what Grate was referring, and I didn't want to spend a lot of time probing him. I just wanted to get to Elizabeth if she was still alive. "I just want to find her," I told him. "Will you help me?"

I saw Grate look at me. I'd appealed to him by saying that I wanted him to help me. And I could see it was impacting him, so I repeated it. Then I took it a step further. "She has a mom," I said. "She has a mom."

I noted that Grate seemed to have a lot of emotion in relation to his mother and her perceived betrayal. How would he react to my comments about another mom, a mom who, perhaps, was more invested than the one he had?

"What's her mom like?" he asked.

"She feels like a failure. She's devastated," I said.

"Feels like a failure?"

"Yeah, she wants to bury her daughter. That's what she wants."

"I know you're just giving me a chance. You already know," Grate said.

I shot him a puzzled look. "I am?" I didn't know what value to put on his response. Clearly, he was assuming that I knew something about what had happened to Elizabeth—and it would soon become clear why he was making this assumption. But at that moment, I had no idea what he was referring to. I could only proceed with the interview and pay special attention to his reactions.

"Yeah, you're giving me a chance," he added. "You already found her."

"I haven't found her," I told him.

"No? Because you act like something happened to her already," Grate said. "I don't know, like you're trying to find somebody that did something to her."

I was not at all surprised by his comments. This was all part of the continued discussion that I expected to take place. Here, again, I tried to telegraph two things to Grate: the severity of his situation, and the opportunity for him to do something that was morally right and just. I continued to project that he had a conscience, whether or not he did.

At that point, I still did not know if Elizabeth was dead or not. But I wanted to probe the issue with Grate and see what I could learn. I didn't dare push too hard, for fear of shutting him down. Instead, I needed to push past awkward moments and continue with my line of questioning—poking and prodding and trying to gain small insights. I didn't know if he was responsible for killing anyone, but I was interviewing him as if he had done so. It's almost as if you are playacting and treating someone as if they'd done something without knowing the truth, like a blind interview, where you don't know what you have but progression momentum is a guide.

Sometimes, people who aren't trained police officers ask me what happens if I wrongly accuse someone of a crime they did not commit. In return, I ask them what happens if I don't go after that person, and they *did* do something.

"More important than finding what happened to Elizabeth is finding her body," I told Grate. "Can you do that much for me, Shawn?"

"I think you already have," was his response.

"I don't have it."

"You don't?" he asked, playing what felt like a verbal game of tennis. Back and forth we went.

"No," I replied. "Remember when I told you I'd be honest with you? I'm not going to tell you something different, because I may need your help with something, and if you don't trust me, you're not going to tell me."

"Right."

"Can you take me to where she is?" I asked.

"I can't."

"Why, Shawn? It's the right thing to do. Shawn, look at me," I pleaded. "It's the right thing, I know it is. Can you do it? If I take you in my little detective truck, can you take me out and we can go find her, and go get her where she is?" My heartbeat suddenly quickened. I sensed that he was ready to open up, to let me in. "Hey, are you willing to do that?" I pressed.

"I don't know what you're talking about right now."

"I'm looking for Elizabeth's body. Can you take me to it?"

"She . . . she's dead?" he asked.

"I believe she is."

"Maybe it's another guy. Just because I did this one, you know, doesn't mean I did all this other stuff."

"Listen to me. This is your moment."

"Is it my moment?"

"I believe it is," I said.

"My moment when I die," he said glumly. "Once I'm put in a cell and the key locks, that's my moment."

"Listen, things are never the way they look at face value. Even the thing with Jane is not exactly the way you think it is right off the bat. Do you know what I mean?"

"I might not be able to take you to her. Maybe someone else . . ."

At that moment, I understood that Grate's crimes might be more prolific than we first suspected. His reference to "someone else" made me realize that he was most likely speaking about another victim. My mind raced to determine whom he was referencing. Was it someone we already knew about, or was it someone else? I was aware he wasn't from Ashland, so I began to theorize that the situation was more widespread than we knew and could even include crimes in other counties.

I sensed that he was ready to divulge more about his transgression, but I also knew I needed to be strategic. Grate had a particular aversion to being viewed as a liar, and an even stronger aversion to someone lying to him. Worse, it could potentially destroy any rapport that I had established with him thus far.

Just as I had my goal—to get to the truth—Grate had his, though I had no idea what path he would take. Clearly, he sensed that he was in trouble. Having admitted to what he'd done to Jane, he was facing a criminal prosecution and, if found guilty, a lengthy prison sentence. There would be no benefit to him admitting to any further crimes.

I had no idea what crimes he had committed or how many other victims were still out there. If there were multiple victims, was there some hierarchy of importance he placed on them? Some order in which he wanted to revisit his crimes? My priority was on obtaining a confession. But how did Grate want to proceed?

Oftentimes, a suspect will confess because he feels some sort of guilt or remorse for what he has done and can't live with it any longer. But I had not witnessed any guilt or remorse from Grate.

I needed to focus. "How many are there?" I asked.

Grate shot a look at me. "I don't know. It depends on what you say is many."

Many? Was he ready to purge, or was he toying with me?

Elizabeth Griffith had been missing for several weeks before anyone noticed. Grate could have abducted several more women during that time. I was feeling the pressure of the moment and my responsibility as a detective. I knew I was just one question away from shutting him down, and that it would be on my shoulders if I screwed up here. I didn't want to be the cause of this case not being solved. The bigger pressure I have in all of my interviews is letting the victims or their families down. Grate had already said a few things that were concerning to me, but I needed to be strategic in my line of inquiry. "How many are there?" I asked for a second time.

"I don't know. There might be none," Grate shot back. "You say Elizabeth's dead?"

"What?" I replied, refocusing my attention on the conversation.

"You think that she is dead?" Grate repeated.

"I believe she is. I don't know one hundred percent," I said. "I'm being honest with you. I think she is."

"Why don't you know one hundred percent?"

"Because we haven't found her," I replied.

Grate shot me an incredulous look.

"Hey," I said, hoping to find a way in, "you know how bad your parents hurt you? Elizabeth's mom is decent. You know what she's doing right now? She's begging. She's begging to have her daughter; she doesn't think she's okay either."

I had not had any contact with Elizabeth's mother, nor was I aware of any interactions between her and our officers. But I decided to revisit the parallel between how *he* was impacted compared to how this current situation was impacting a mother who was kind. I recognized the risk of it triggering him into silence, but there are no easy victories.

"I think you're broken inside, and I think everybody you've cared about has let you down," I continued. "I'm asking you to stand up right now, to stand up and do the right thing, to take the things that have happened, the things that are wrong and right now, right now, do the right thing.

"Do you know where Elizabeth is right now? I don't care what you told anybody else. I care what you tell me."

Grate lowered his head and closed his eyes. I could tell that he was taking deeper breaths, the way he was exhaling, he was having an internal struggle over whether he should tell me the truth. And all the while, whatever he'd done, he hadn't told anybody about it, so I needed him to buy into me.

I don't like to see anyone in front of me hurting. I am not saying I support a rapist, but I am human, and I feel empathy. Having empathy doesn't impact my goal in a case, but again, empathy guides my life. I can't turn it on or off.

At that moment, I could almost feel it in the air in the room, that I had established a connection with Grate. I didn't have to be manipulative or fake; I could be myself and get him to trust me enough to confess.

I recognized he had trust issues, because instrumental people in his life had let him down and betrayed his trust, or at least that is how he perceived it. I couldn't just say, "Hey, trust me." It's like going to a pastor that gives one-liners—"Praise the Lord." Why should I trust him? Some people need the why, not just the phrase.

"Look at me," I said. "I do not know where Elizabeth is. I'm not lying. Why would I lie about that? What do I have to gain?"

A heavy silence sank down on us. Grate shut his eyes, leaned back in his chair, and drew a long breath. "You already know I can't answer your question right now," he said, "because if I knew where she was, then I'm just guilty."

"Hey," I replied, "look at me. I'm not going to leave your side. Okay? Believe that."

At that moment, our eyes locked.

"You would be a good person to let inside," he said as he stared at me.

I wasn't sure what he meant by that. Was he implying I would be a good person to let into his house so he could harm me or that I would be a good person to let into his heart? "We can shed some light on why things happened, right? We can dissect her personality. We can figure out a few things about her, okay?" I stated.

"Elizabeth?"

"Yeah, we can put some value to what happened. Will you take me to her?" I said. "You and me. . . . That's what I'm asking. Will you do that for me?"

"I'm confused, you know. I don't understand all this," Grate said.

Grate's sudden naivety was not new to me. Over the years, I'd sat across the table from countless suspects guilty of heinous crimes feigning innocence, playing the victim card. We were way past that, and I'm sure he knew it, too. What I later realized was that he may have been genuine in his statement about being confused, and the reason he would be confused is that some part of him thought I already knew what he had done.

"I want you to take me to where Elizabeth is or tell me where she is. You've already tried to make one situation right," I said.

Grate sat stone-faced. I could see he was at an impasse.

"Can we go to her?" I pressed.

"It's out of my hands."

"What do you mean?" I asked.

"I don't know where she is or what she's doing," he replied. "I just know she's been missing for a while now. I've heard about it three times from people . . ."

"Here's the deal. You can show me where she is. It doesn't make you have to tell me anything; it's just trying to make something right.

"Either you have a conscience, or you don't, and I believe you do. It says a lot about you; it says that you may have been dealt a hand of hell for life, but then when it comes down to it, even when you're wrong, you try to do the right thing. Am I right?"

To my surprise, Grate's expression was now one of lofty disdain. Out of nowhere, he launched into a tirade, vilifying Elizabeth Griffith. He claimed that everybody acted as though something were wrong with her and that people should be sad for her.

"That's what she wants everybody to do, to feel sorry for her," he stated. "She needs to grow up."

After a little more dialogue, Grate paused, and for the next few seconds neither of us spoke. *Where was this going?* I wondered. He was marginalizing Elizabeth, and I believed it was because he was about to face some consequences because of her, although it was his own fault. He needed to devalue her as a human as an excuse for his actions.

"Did Elizabeth ask you to assist her with anything?" From what I could decipher, it appeared that Grate was implying that Elizabeth was suicidal or perhaps contemplating suicide.

He claimed that during their evening together, she had mentioned that she didn't want to be alive anymore. But he denied any involvement in her death. "It's a good thing I'm going to jail 'cause I'm probably about ready to take . . ."

Grate paused without completing his thought, then rambled some more about his intolerance for those who needed public assistance. "Waste of lives," he grumbled. "I hate to say it. Their lives are all hunky-dory. They get their free monthly, you know, their rent, everything taken care of, and the State is damaging them more and more, and it's just accepting it."

His anger toward this segment of the population raised a red flag. I knew little about his upbringing and when and why this animosity had originated. But the picture was becoming clearer. I tried to steer the conversation back to Elizabeth when Grate suddenly asked me, "Kim, do you smoke?"

"I don't," I said, "but I can get you a cigarette, if you need one."

Grate declined, so I pressed him again, asking if he would take me to Elizabeth.

"I could take you to a place in Mansfield," he offered.

Mansfield? Mansfield is a city about fifteen miles south of Ashland in neighboring Richland County. *Why is he mentioning Mansfield?* "Is that where Elizabeth is?" I asked.

"I don't know about Elizabeth, but I could take you to another girl," Grate replied. He stared at me with his icy-blue eyes. I could tell he was struggling to decide what and how much he should reveal to me. I'd seen this look of inner turmoil many times over the years. It is the moment where I can sense that the person wants to unburden himself, that he is feeling compelled to unload, but is hesitant, unsure if he should do it and also fearing the consequences.

My thoughts went to Stacey. *Is he going to confess to something related to her disappearance?*

Grate pointed to several scars from what appeared to be numerous gouges to his temple. "She's a nut," he declared. "She put these right here on my forehead."

Some of the injuries looked completely healed. While I appeared to be listening to him, I was actually thinking, *What in the hell is happening here?* The mere fact that he had healed injuries made it abundantly clear that he wasn't referring to Jane Doe or Stacey Stanley Hicks, who had only been missing for a short time.

I didn't want to lose momentum; I needed to appear as though I were present in the conversation and that I was following him, but in my head, I was working to make sense of the time line related to our missing women, as well as our rescued victim, Jane Doe, in relation to the various stages of healing of the injuries.

"What happened to this woman?" I asked.

Grate looked anguished but said nothing.

"Is she gone?"

"She's been gone. . . . no hope," he stated, growing visibly upset.

"Did you bury her, or did you just leave her somewhere?"

There was no response.

"Is she missing?" I pressed.

"I don't know . . . I know I loved her. I couldn't stand her. She would lie all the time. She was so lost for this world. She was abused since she was eight by her stepdad. She was always threatening to kill herself."

"Is she in a house? Where is she?"

Grate was now crying.

"The woods," he uttered.

"How long has she been there?"

"I forget."

"How long has she been there?" I repeated calmly.

"June?"

"What's her name?"

"Candice," he said softly.

"Candice?" I repeated. I began to go over in my head the options for why he mentioned Candice. I wondered if he was starting at the beginning of everything he'd done, where everything first went wrong for him? Or was he telling me about the most traumatic event first? Or perhaps his victim? Maybe Candice was his only victim—besides Jane—and he had chosen me to confess this to? It was possible he didn't have anything to do with Elizabeth and he'd thrown out a name I had not heard before. I didn't have a missing "Candice." If I did, I would know, as I am in small-town America, where everyone knows everyone—and everyone's business.

Now, I was left wondering, *Why is he saying her name? Is he about to purge a litany of crimes and Candice is his first victim, and he's decided to trust me enough to confess to me?* I'd experienced this in past interviews, where someone was accused of something and they gave up other incidents they'd been involved in. Grate's remarks about Candice were so ambiguous, I wasn't sure if she was dead or alive, or if she was even missing.

"Candice?" I softly said her name again.

"Candice Cunningham."

My colleagues in the next room were already running the name *Candice Cunningham* through databases, and I knew if I took a break at some point, they would have intel. But I also knew I didn't want to break the continuity of the interview. This woman hadn't been on our radar, and we would find no missing persons report filed on her. It appeared no one in her circle had any inkling that something bad may have happened to her.

What had Grate done?

8

A Body in the Woods

Often, when a suspect mentions a crime that has occurred in another jurisdiction during an interrogation, detectives stop the interview and contact investigators from that jurisdiction to follow up. But every jurisdiction handles that scenario differently. Even detectives within the same police department make different judgment calls, depending on the circumstances.

In my department, if someone is talking, we don't shut them down. The risk you run when you do that is that the person will simply stop cooperating and go silent, inhibiting our ability to gain valuable information and precluding any chance to obtain a confession.

I believe in seizing the opportunity when someone is being remotely open, candid, or ready to purge. If you think about it, that person has sometimes harbored their secret for decades, and at that very moment, an environment has been created where they feel comfortable to reveal the truth.

I had now been sitting with Grate for nearly two hours and believed I had forged a connection. His demeanor and overall personality were not far off from some of the other violent offenders I had interviewed over the years—the ways in which they try to place blame or rationalize their actions, and the power differential between the predator and prey.

Sometimes predators will choose victims over whom they have significant power or a strength differential. Perhaps one is older and the other young, or one is in a position of control over the other or is physically stronger. There are also those who will act when they identify someone who's vulnerable—perhaps someone who is walking alone by the side of the road. These are one type of opportunistic predators because they don't necessarily always follow a defined modus operandi; they don't always have a particular type of victim that they target.

These types of opportunistic predators are frightening to me because their victims are often different ages, genders, and so on. This makes investigations difficult. Those cases are also among the more difficult to solve because there's often less planning prior to the crime. It's important to note, those examples aren't all-inclusive. And the only reason to profile suspects is to save current victims and protect future ones.

Another commonality with predators is their insatiable appetite for power and control, and sometimes sex. Grate told me that he frequented prostitutes—motivated in part by his own desire for dominance. In some cases, he would transport the women around for a ten-dollar fee. He appeared to seek situations that afforded him ascendancy over others.

Instead of expanding on what he had done to Candice, he began acknowledging having raped one of the prostitutes he had frequented, describing how he had picked her up, had sex with her, become violent, and then beat her up. Although he did not try to kill that woman, it was clear from his description that the incident was very violent. Afterward, as she was crying, he walked her back to the spot where he had initially picked her up.

"Maybe it was a wake-up call for both of us," Grate claimed he told her. Suggesting that she shouldn't be prostituting herself and he needed to get hold of his rage.

Normally, a man walks a woman home to ensure her safety. In this instance, he perverted the concept for dominance. I know she is giving her body, but it should be on her own terms, rather than Grate's savagery.

At this point in our exchange, Grate was divulging information, and my intent was to find out everything I could about his crimes, including past crimes, starting with Candice Cunningham, then going backward or forward in time, depending how the organic nature of the interrogation led me. So, I offered him a fresh cup of coffee and pressed on—hoping to strengthen the connection between us and keep the conversation going.

I reintroduced the topic of Candice by stating, "Tell me about your relationship with Candice."

Grate explained that he and twenty-nine-year-old Cunningham had been together about seven months. They had even talked about getting married, the same claim he made about Jane Doe. He said they met when he was doing some work on an eight-bedroom "sleeping house" on Second Street in Mansfield. While there, Candice came to the home seeking a place to stay.

We would later learn from Candice's mother, Dianna Gardener, that her daughter had been telling family and friends that she'd finally met "the right one, the perfect guy." Gardener said that both she and Candice's sister were ecstatic to hear Candice so happy.

Candice, a wisp of a brunette weighing just 110 pounds with a gap-toothed smile, had grown up in the city of Canton, about an hour west of Ashland in Stark County. Standing just four foot nine, she spoke in a booming voice and liked to make people laugh.

According to her mother, she was headstrong and a bit competitive, and being the middle child, she sought to do everything better than her brother and sister.

While attending Timken High School, Candice announced plans to pursue a career as a massage therapist. But she fell in with a bad crowd and got into drugs, her mother said. In 2005, while still in high school, Candice gave birth to a son, and three years later, a daughter.

Gardener insisted that Candice loved her children, but her struggles with addiction had her in and out of rehab, trying to get clean. In 2009, both of Candice's children were removed from her custody. Gardener believes the two were adopted by new families.

Despairing, Candice turned to "whatever made the pain stop," her mother said.

I believe Gardner was right. Police officers sadly watch so many people give up everything important in their lives for drugs. Addiction is that strong.

Sometime around 2013, Candice announced that she was moving to Mansfield, and her mother didn't question it. Gardener said she was happy that her daughter was getting away from her friends "that like to pop pills" and hoped the move would help her daughter stay clean.

That past May, she said she received a call from her daughter, who excitedly told her she was moving to South Carolina and promised to call once she settled in. By August, nobody had heard from her, and family members were growing increasingly concerned. But they opted not to file a missing persons report out of respect for Candice's independence, holding out hope that she would be in touch soon.

During my interview with Grate, he claimed he was living in a small rented room on West Second Street in downtown Mansfield when he met Cunningham. He'd been there a little over a year, and during that time, he had become friendly with his landlord, Jim Crisman. Much like the house on Covert Court, this place also had no heat, electricity, or running water. At one time, the small space, measuring just eight by fifteen feet, had served as a sitting room for the occupants of the old Victorian house. There was no kitchen and no bathroom, so Grate used a bucket for a toilet. An extension cord running from the second-floor apartment, where his landlord lived, provided electricity. Grate used a space heater in winter to warm the place.

Grate explained that Jim Crisman was not just his landlord, he was also "kind of a supervisor." He would have Grate do jobs like taking care of his dog. He even bought Grate some woodworking equipment to help him launch his new business venture, making handcrafted wood signs. It was a comfortable arrangement, Grate claimed, until he and Candice fell behind on the rent and Jim evicted them that past May, rendering them homeless.

Grate said he "prayed for a place to stay" and "was guided" to an abandoned house just off the Lincoln Highway Historic Byway in Madison Township. "There's a MotoMart near there, and it's down the street from the sheriff's station," he explained.

"Are you referring to Route 430?"

Route 430, also known as Park Avenue East in some sections, is a state highway that runs through portions of Ashland and Richland Counties; the area of highway Grate was describing is rural, with long stretches of open space and cornfields in summer. The Richland County Sheriff's Office is also there.

"Yup, Route 430," he confirmed.

I handed him a piece of paper and a pencil and asked him to sketch me a map of the location. As he drew, he narrated, stating, "If you're going this way, there's a street, a light, a gas station, and a little landscaping place. The landscaping place is closing down."

I watched as he roughed out a simple sketch showing the house and a nearby creek. "Burned house, big creek, right there," he said, pointing to the area behind the house. "Right up about twenty feet."

"And you put her there in June?"

"Yeah."

"Tell me what happened."

Grate explained that when he found the abandoned house, he brought Candice by to see it. It seemed like a viable place to squat, and he was excited to show it to her. But during their time there, things went sideways. They had a volatile relationship, and something she said upset him, causing him to fly into a rage.

"She kept attacking me," he recalled. "I told her, 'You keep hitting me and I'm going to just choke you out.' . . . So, I did."

Grate claimed that at some point, he released his grip on her throat, hoping to see that she had calmed down. "She didn't. She still attacked me, so then I just choked her, and she went limp. She woke up, though, and she went crazy again, so then, I'd had enough."

"How did you end it?"

Grate hesitated for several seconds, then stated, "Twenty-five to life, right there." I watched as he realized the momentum of our conversation. He then blurted out, "This whole situation's killing me."

"I can see that," I said. "How does it feel telling me what you did to Candice?"

"Now, it's the law," he replied. "I feel much freer. And now I know I'm definitely going to be in the custody of the law for a long time.

"That's why there's people who raped kids to keep me occupied, you know what I mean?" Grate disclosed that he had a four-year-old daughter—the youngest of the three children he'd fathered with three different women. "If someone molested my little girl, I would take care of them. We'll get a group going, don't worry, we'll narrow the prisons of all the child molesters. Something to do, 'cause I always have to stay busy."

It was no secret there was a social hierarchy among prisoners based solely on their offenses and that child molesters occupied the lowest rung. Still, I found it striking that Grate, now an admitted rapist *and* murderer, viewed himself, and his crimes, as somehow less egregious.

Grate's initial telling of Candice's murder made it appear as if he had killed her during their first visit to the residence, but he now indicated that they had been staying there at least a few days when the altercation that ended her life occurred.

"It was three o'clock in the morning," he recounted. "I got hit in the face with a bag of tobacco, I just snapped. I did. When she did that to me, I freaked out."

Grate said he asked Candice why she had done that, and she told him, "Roll me a cigarette."

He said her flippant response made him angry, and he retorted, "'You woke me up to roll you a cigarette?' . . . I just snapped."

"How did you get the body from the house to the woods?" I asked.

"I wrapped her up in a blanket, and I carried her over there. She weighs only one hundred pounds." Grate claimed that once he got her to the location, he pulled the blanket off her. "She's probably naked," he stated. "When it happened, she was naked."

As he provided the details of the woman's murder, at times, he appeared upset, then would casually munch on the bag of snacks I gave him and offer me some as well.

"Will you take me to the place where you put her body after we've finished our interview?"

"It will be easy to find," he said. "You could follow the flies probably."

It was a macabre vision, made worse by Grate's dismissive revelation about killing a harmless woman.

"Who else are we going to go find?" I asked, growing convinced that Candice was not his only victim. I suspected there were others out there and some may still be alive. Jane Doe had been found alive. And he had kept her alive for days, so the possibility was there. But I needed to get him to tell me where they were, if in fact there were others out there waiting to be rescued.

Grate hesitated for what felt like an eternity, then quietly stated, "I don't know. . . . I guess I'm ready to go ahead and get my lethal injection. But I'll tell you everything first."

It would have been easier if he'd simply told me everything in one running narrative, rather than toying with me by throwing out little hints that I had to pick up on and circle back to. Looking back, I wonder how many clues he threw out that I missed, crimes that could have been solved if I had recognized the bread crumb.

I was still digesting his statement about Candice when he asked, "How many before lethal injection?"

His comment intrigued me. "Can you repeat that?" I asked.

"How many people before I get lethally injected?"

"Let's not worry about any of that," I remarked, eager to keep the conversation moving forward. "Who else is there?"

I continued to press, and eventually, he stated, "Well, I already mentioned Candice."

I wondered if he was going to shut down, so I kept at it.

"Who else are you thinking of?" I asked. Perhaps Elizabeth Griffith? Or Stacey Stanley Hicks?

After a long silence, Grate finally responded. "The house . . . the house where I came from." He was talking about the yellow colonial across from the laundromat on Covert Court, where he had held Jane hostage.

"Is there somebody in there?" I asked.

"Yeah."

"Who is it? Is it Elizabeth?"

"Yeah."

"Where is she?"

"In the closet . . ."

"In the closet? Which closet?"

"Upstairs."

I imagined that his admission about the dead body in the house would be throwing my colleagues in the adjoining room into overdrive and that they were now relaying the information to the guys on scene waiting for the signed warrant to enter the Covert Court home.

To now, we'd been operating on the belief that we had a kidnapping and rape. If Grate was to be believed, we were looking at something far more serious—at least two people had been murdered, and one of them was in the house we were about to search.

9

Jesus Loves Me

As disturbing as it was having Grate confirm my suspicion that Elizabeth was dead, I knew I had to keep the conversation going. I needed to find out how Grate had killed Elizabeth. "Can you tell me what happened?" I asked.

Grate began to weep. "I care, I do. I hate seeing people suffer."

"Okay," I replied, pushing down revulsion.

"That's it."

"Okay, all right, Shawn." I needed to press him delicately. "That's it?" I said, parroting his last statement.

"Nothing sexual or anything. I didn't hurt her."

"Okay, how did you do it, Shawn?"

"Well, she wanted more. Not at first . . ."

Grate claimed the two had met a few days earlier and that he had given Elizabeth his cell phone number. On the day of the murder, the two had been hanging out together at her apartment. They'd spent the evening playing the dice game Yahtzee. But at some point, Grate announced that he was going home to eat some barbecue chicken.

"Oh, that sounds good," Elizabeth told him.

Grate invited her to join him at his place. After the meal, Elizabeth returned to her apartment, but she was having trouble sleeping and called him at around 11:00 p.m., asking if he was up for a card game and some conversation.

"All right, that's fine," Grate told her, inviting her to come back to his house that evening.

At one point, Grate said, Elizabeth started to bad-mouth Jane. "Jane and her, they have their moments," he said. "It's like a girl thing."

He laughed when I asked if it bothered him that Elizabeth was speaking badly about Jane. "No, not really."

But, according to Grate, the conversation devolved from there, and at one point, Elizabeth started sobbing. "It made me want to smack her in the mouth," he said. "It was like seeing a big girl cry."

He claimed it was then that Elizabeth told him of her desire to end her life, proclaiming that she wished that "she wasn't around no more."

"I'm not going to marry her, and I don't see no one else marrying her," Grate continued. "She's just going to be miserable all her life. I'll free her. I'll sacrifice my life for her."

Grate claimed that Elizabeth began singing the Christian hymn "Jesus Loves Me" as he tightened his grip around her throat. Although some crazy things had happened in the case thus far, this sounded so far-fetched that as Grate related the story, I thought, *How can that be?* As he recounted the scene, I could hear the verses in my head:

> *Jesus loves me! This I know,*
> *For the Bible tells me so;*
> *Little ones to Him belong;*
> *They are weak, but He is strong.*
> *Yes, Jesus loves me. . . .*

"All I wanted to do was show her that she wanted to live. I'd say, 'Give me a hug. We're all in this together.' I'd choke her until she said she wanted to live . . . and she just didn't."

Grate's next remark caught my attention—he claimed to know that Elizabeth was a true Christian.

"How do you know that?" I asked.

Grate explained that while he was strangling Elizabeth, there was a moment when she broke free, and just as he grabbed her for the final time, she forgave him.

"She forgave you?"

"Yes," he replied. "She said, 'Lord forgive him, for he knows not what he does,'" paraphrasing Luke 23:34.

I recall wondering if he was just being sensational, or if Elizabeth had actually said that. It remained an open question in my mind, but an answer was forthcoming.

Grate's recollection of the details of Elizabeth's murder sounded like a scene that most people would only see in a horror flick. What he was saying was every woman's worst fear. There is always a risk when you go home with someone you don't know. This could have been any woman, which made it all the more unsettling.

My heart sank as I pictured Elizabeth forgiving this man as she took her last breath, with Grate's next statement adding to my momentary despair.

"She's set free," he announced. "No more problems. She don't have to cry no more."

The microphone hidden in my bra was capturing every word of Grate's confession for posterity—and thankfully so because, as it turns out, the recording equipment in the interview room had stopped working partway through the interview and my tiny digital recorder would be nearly the only audio record we had of Grate's confession.

In a later interview, Grate admitted that his motive for killing Elizabeth wasn't simply because their exchange had gone bad; that inviting her on a tour of his house was a ruse to get her to the second-floor bedroom, where he ultimately took her life. He claimed that at that moment, he wasn't "too far into the act that I couldn't have stopped," but as he continued to tighten his hands around her throat, Elizabeth stated, "Lord, save me!"

Grate recalled at that moment, he stopped strangling her and said, "He already has," referring to her soul.

"She kept repeating it and repeating it, and I was like, 'Now you gotta believe it,' like the Bible. We sang 'Jesus Loves Me' together," he stated. "Elizabeth was saying, 'Jesus,' and I told her, 'Jesus loves you.' And then she started saying, 'This I know.'"

According to Grate, this occurred after he strangled her and let her go, and he was trying to hug her. She was "resisting" him, so he told her, "You do want to live."

He appeared to be growing upset recalling how she kept accusing him of trying to kill her and shouting, "Jesus, save me!"

That's when he confronted her, telling her, "I thought you already asked Jesus into your heart." He claimed that they had talked about this very topic three times previously.

Grate next claimed that because of all the things he had gone through in his life, he thought he and Elizabeth would have clicked. "I didn't even put no pressure on her," he continued. "I just scared her a little bit, enough. I just wanted to show her that 'you want to live.'"

At one point, he even suggested that he didn't want to "do it," to strangle Elizabeth, he wanted to "find a reason not to do it."

"My compassion just wanted to free her from this world."

He explained that when he first met Elizabeth, he thought about the years of torment she was going to go through in her life. And he thought about how sad it was that her life was going to be horrible.

He had no idea that I knew Elizabeth. She had a kind heart, a huge laugh, and people loved her.

He acknowledged that when he was still downstairs with her, he was thinking that how things went with her would determine if he killed her. He said at one point he was giving Elizabeth a tour of the house, and as they were climbing the stairs to the second floor, he knew that the situation was going to go "one way or the other," depending on what Elizabeth did.

He acknowledged that he could feel the situation "coming," meaning that he was going to strangle her. "I could feel it like it's coming, my heart is pumping, and I hope she just doesn't say nothing else about . . . nothing that's gonna make me feel sorry for her, in a way. It depends on what she says . . . I was just going along, showing her upstairs."

Grate recalled that once upstairs, Elizabeth sat down in a rocking chair in the bedroom. His heart was already pounding in anticipation of what was about to occur. He said he sat down on the bed and showed her some stuffed animals. There was a long pause, and he opened a window. He claimed they were upstairs for about fifteen minutes before he attacked her.

"What were your thoughts at that time?" I asked.

"A lot of things flashing before me . . . like if I did this, what would I have to do next . . . then I'd have to leave, but there's really no way to get away with this. Too many people know I live here."

I asked him if strangling someone felt good to him.

"Maybe. I feel like I give up my life for this person. That is kind of how I've felt."

He recalled that as they climbed the stairs, his heart beat faster thinking about what he might do to her. No matter what Elizabeth said or did, Grate was going to kill her.

At this point in our exchange, I asked Grate if he wanted something to drink. "Can I get you some water?"

"Well, I guess I should try to drink my last cup of coffee, because it's probably going to be a while."

"Are you hungry?"

"Yeah, I am."

"Yeah, let me grab you a coffee and a granola bar, okay?"

There was another reason for me to leave the room, too. I wanted to check in with my fellow officers at the Covert Court crime scene and find out where things stood with the search. Maybe the team had found evidence that would be helpful in my interrogation. Or would at least confirm that Grate was truthful about Elizabeth being in the closet of the home.

Grate indicated that he'd like to take a cigarette break. That meant we had to walk out of the detective bureau and toward the back of the building to reach the outside.

It was 1:35 p.m. when I exited the interrogation room and switched off the digital recorder hidden in my blouse. We had been at it for nearly three hours, so a break was in order. With Grate on my heels, I stepped out into the hallway, where I noticed that there were no detectives in the entire detective pod observing my interview. I had assumed that at least one of my fellow officers was watching from the adjacent room or was stationed outside the interview room door because that is protocol and I had never known it to be broken. But the hallway was empty.

I turned around and looked at Grate and realized that he was processing the idea that the two of us were alone—and he was not even in handcuffs. I tried to remain cool and not project any concern.

Stepping out of the pod, I looked all the way down the long hallway, and that's when I spotted Special Agent Ed Staley from Ohio's Bureau of Criminal Investigation (BCI). BCI is a state resource, and any law enforcement agency in Ohio can request their help. We had called BCI to assist with the execution of the search warrant related to the kidnapping and sexual assault of Jane Doe. They would later assist with various other aspects of the case.

SA Staley was the BCI agent assigned to a multicounty area but happened to reside in Ashland County. I knew him even before I started working for APD. He and I grew up in the same area; he was older than I was, so we didn't run with the same crowd. He'd been a wrestler in high school and had retained his physical power and toughness.

I called out to him. "Eddy, can you come down here?" I was relieved when he acknowledged me and started in my direction. When he was close enough, I asked if he could go outside with Grate and me so that Grate could smoke a cigarette. The surprised look on his face told me he was beginning to understand my predicament.

"Where are the guys?" he asked quietly, referring to the other officers.

"I don't know," I replied, relieved that I now had some backup.

Before accompanying us to the rear of the building, SA Staley went from office to office, confirming that there were no detectives with me. I could see that his jaw was set in anger as he shook his head in disbelief. He was a seasoned investigator and intimidating in stature, and he indicated he would have more to say about this later.

Needless to say, SA Staley saw to it that I wasn't alone for the remainder of the investigation.

This would not be the first time I felt somewhat vulnerable as this case unfolded.

After our cigarette break, I provided Grate with a snack and confirmed that he was okay to continue. I was still absorbing the fact that no one had been watching my back during an unknown portion of my interrogation. But I was confident based on SA Staley's assurances that the problem wouldn't be repeated.

When questioned, no one in the department acknowledged they were the one who was supposed to be watching me, but they were all apologetic. The investigation was dynamic; everyone was working various parts of the case, and as a result, my fellow officers had inadvertently left me alone.

Once I got over my anger, I actually made a joke to my lieutenant. "I appreciate your confidence leaving me alone in a room with an unhandcuffed serial killer," I said.

"We try to do so much right. You could have been hurt. And what happened to you makes us look like dumbasses," he replied. "Thank God you're okay," he added. "Tell your husband he doesn't need to beat anyone's ass, 'cause it won't happen again."

Once back in the interview room, Grate and I returned to our respective chairs, and I resumed the interrogation. I don't ever interview across a table; a table is really a tangible divide. I sit face-to-face with an interviewee with no obstruction to the door and no obstruction between us, and I will move my chair closer as the interview progresses. I am aware that this configuration heightens the safety risk, but the more serious risk is not getting that confession because of a tangible barrier that equates to a mental and emotional barrier.

"I want to circle back to the details of Elizabeth's murder," I told Grate. I wanted to find out exactly where in the house he had put Elizabeth's body, aware that someone was in the adjacent room monitoring the interview and would relay the information to the agents on the scene. "About when did this happen?" I inquired.

I suggested we look at a calendar, so I accessed one for reference. I had already assessed Grate as a *visual*, meaning he processed things better visually, so having a visual like a calendar would help him to engage in the process more freely. Everybody is different. Some might be an *audible*, and do better hearing it all. Some are visual, while others are *tangible* or *kinesthetic* and need to feel or move. I can see it by what they do with their hands. They seem to touch things—the table, their hair, anything they can access, or they like to have something in their hand, like a notebook or tissue.

I knew Grate was an artist based on his woodwork and sign-making. He also told me he liked to draw. Later, when he was in jail awaiting trial, he drew a few things and put them online for people to buy. I have one of his renderings, a hand with the names of his victims on it. The curves of the fingers and the fingernails are shaped like a church window, and there's a door. I often wonder where he envisioned it led.

"So, we haven't seen Elizabeth since the sixteenth of August," I said.

Grate watched as I pointed to the dates, providing a visual, then counted out the subsequent weeks to determine the approximate day the murder occurred. "Now, it's been, one, two, three, four, about five weeks since we've seen her. So, about a month ago this happened?"

"That sounds about right," Grate replied.

I asked if Elizabeth had lost her life the same way Candice had lost hers, and he confirmed it.

"With Elizabeth, is she nude, or is she in clothes?" I asked.

Grate hesitated for several seconds before responding. "Well, she took off her shirt, right? I was just showing her around, then, she wanted, she insisted on looking around.

"So, I showed her the upstairs, and she kind of like, you know, tried to put the moves on me, which was weird, because when I was talking to her, I didn't feel that."

Grate claimed he wasn't sexually attracted to Elizabeth and that nothing sexual had occurred between them. "I didn't really feel that. Do you know what I mean?"

"Did you end up having sex with her?"

Grate grew suddenly indignant. "No, I did not. I didn't do nothing

with her at all. So, when it came to the point that . . . I was struggling, you know, her shirt did end up coming off."

"Okay, how did it come off?"

"I was moving it, like, when I was choking her."

"You were choking her?"

"Yeah."

"Did you choke her from the front or choke her from behind?" I
asked. Particular methods of strangulation can cause specific injuries. His description was important for the investigation.

"Well, it just happened. I just reached up and just choked her."
Grate motioned with his hands to demonstrate how he'd strangled
Elizabeth. "And I asked her, 'Are you sure this is what you want?'
I mean, she talked about killing herself. So, I mean, I do that as a
joke a lot of times, like even with friends, like guy friends . . . I joke
around."

Grate veered off track on an odd tangent to talk about how he
reacted when people threatened to kill themselves. Rather than
deescalating a person who is suicidal, he said that he actually encouraged them to act. He described how he'd tell them, "Well, what
are you waiting on?"

He said that he would sometimes even grab them by the neck
and start strangling them—all in some bizarre scenario to gauge
how serious they were about actually killing themselves.

"Do you know what I mean? So, I put a little fear in 'em, right?"

I asked Grate how he had Elizabeth listed in his phone.

He claimed he didn't have her entered as a contact, he had simply
given her his phone number and didn't get hers until she contacted
him. Analysis of phone data would certainly be conducted, and any
context I could gain would be advantageous.

"Everything happened so fast . . . I met her like a few days before, and then you know, like, she called me."

At this point in our exchange, I reminded him about something he had told me earlier in our conversation regarding Elizabeth talking poorly about Jane. "Did that anger you?"

"No, not really, I kind of laughed about it."

Grate suddenly turned the conversation back to Jane, which was consistent with the organic nature of interrogation. Having admitted to killing Elizabeth, he now wanted to explain his thought process for going after Jane the way he had. "I just wanted to enjoy her before all this caught up to me," he said, adding, "I'm not worthy of being her husband."

Realizing the futility in challenging his rationale, I chose to keep the focus on Elizabeth. I needed further detail. It was clear that something more had happened in the room with Elizabeth before or after her death. The indicators were nuanced, but they were there. I had no doubt the narrative he was peddling about Jane was a false one. He had already admitted to one murder. In that instance, according to Grate, Candice had been the one to provoke the violent attack. In Elizabeth's case, however, Grate was trying to sell me on the idea that he had killed Elizabeth because she had asked him to.

"So, with Elizabeth, you wanted to free her," I stated. "How did you do that?" I wanted to hear him say it. To tell me that he had strangled Elizabeth to death, just as he had done to 110-pound Candice Cunningham. "The same way as with Candice or another way?"

"Probably the same way," he said hesitantly. The purge was occurring, but he was fighting the momentum to confess. This was clear to me because he was not so forthcoming in his response.

It was an admission, but he offered no further details, and because he was so hesitant, I decided it was best to preserve the interview for now and gain further detail at a more opportune time.

10

House of Horrors

A large crowd of onlookers had gathered just beyond the yellow police tape now encircling the house and parking lot at 363 Covert Court. Ashland is a small city, and word of Shawn Grate's arrest was spreading quickly. Locals were hearing news of Grate's arrest over their scanners and others were posting on Facebook that a search warrant was being executed in the Fourth Street area. News helicopters and media outlets from larger cities were converging on Ashland.

By now, most everyone in town knew two women had been reported missing. Elizabeth was a hometown girl, an Ashland native, so talk of her disappearance had been circulating for days. People had also heard about our other missing woman, Stacey Stanley Hicks.

At some point during the morning, Stacey's family learned of the police presence in Ashland's Fourth Street area and had made their way to the location, hoping to learn something about Stacey.

By midmorning, our officers had expanded the crime scene out to North Center Street, effectively cutting off all access to Covert Court. And we'd brought in investigators from Ohio's Bureau of Criminal Investigation (BCI) to process the crime scene once a search warrant had been secured, with our officers handling support functions, such as maintaining a perimeter.

BCI special agent Ed Staley was the only member of the bureau who lived locally, which is why he was already at headquarters when I emerged from my interview with Grate earlier that day. He was now at the crime scene waiting to debrief the BCI units responding from other counties. Agents lived all over the state and traveled to wherever they were needed.

We are a small department, and a crime of this magnitude requires all hands on deck for our detective bureau. After taking Grate into custody, Sergeant Cox had remained on the scene to secure the residence and create a perimeter to keep people away and ensure its integrity.

Detective Evans, my partner for the booth at the upcoming Ashland County Fair, had been at the station for much of the morning writing the search warrant for the premises at 363 Covert Court. Much of it was based on information I had gleaned from my interview with Jane Doe. Detective Evans was now on scene, positioned at the home's perimeter entrance, where he was keeping the entry log used to record the comings and goings of everyone who entered the premises. But it would be several more hours before we would obtain a judge's signature to green-light the search of the Covert Court residence.

With Grate's arrest, most of the officers of the Ashland PD were busy working elements of the case. For a good chunk of the day, Officer Hying, our newest hire and the officer who had taken the initial missing persons report about Elizabeth Griffith, was the city's sole patrol officer. At one point, he found himself responding to a domestic dispute call on his own. This was typically a two-man call because of the potential for violence, but with the demands of the Grate case, our agency was spread thin. The captain had even called in some of the guys who were off that day.

APD officers James Coey and Lee Eggeman were summoned from home to search the abandoned factory tower where Grate had briefly stayed, as well as other vacant buildings in the Fourth Street area. Cadaver dogs were also brought in to comb through the abandoned structures, looking for possible victims. Thankfully, the county law enforcement agencies around us jumped in when they could to assist us with some of our calls for service.

The three APD officers who had responded to the initial 911 call were responding to allegations of abduction and rape. They had conducted only a protective sweep of the residence before securing it pending a warrant for a more extensive search. While I was still in the early stages of my interview, BCI agents had begun their forensic work. They had gone into the house to systematically photograph every room. Their methods were meticulous.

SA Staley and his team had not begun the formal search of the premises when Officer Dorsey phoned from the detective bureau. Throughout the morning, Dorsey had been monitoring my interview with Shawn Grate—save for those few moments when I was alone—and had been serving as a go-between, jotting down key statements and relaying them by cell phone to our officers at the Covert Court location. He had already passed on bits and pieces of information, but his latest update elevated the circumstances of the case: Shawn Grate had just admitted to murdering Elizabeth Griffith. He claimed her body was in a closet in an upstairs bedroom.

"There is no closet in the upstairs bedroom," one of the agents remarked after receiving the information. The team had photographed the home's interior, but no one had observed a closet in that room.

SA Staley and his team entered the residence through the rear side door where hours earlier Officer Dorsey had rescued Jane Doe. The air inside the house was stale; it was dimly lit and felt ominous.

All the windows on the first floor were shut tight and shielded by bed linens and miscellaneous pieces of fabric.

Just off the kitchen was a small bathroom with a toilet, sink, and stall shower that was yellow and dingy. The stairwell to the second floor was at the front of the house, close to the door that faced out onto Covert Court. It could only be accessed through an inside door at the base of the stairs that was locked and required entry tools to breach it.

The staircase was steep and narrow; one wall was covered in cheap wood paneling. It looked like somebody had been trying to do some repairs on the adjacent wall. There were extensive patches of white spackle leading up to the second floor.

At the top of the landing was a small bathroom with a toilet, sink, and antique claw-foot tub. The upstairs was laid out like an accessory apartment with a living room area, bedroom, bathroom, and small kitchen. But the officers' focus was on the bedroom, where Grate had said he'd hidden Elizabeth's body in a closet.

The bedroom was small. At its center was an upholstered green fabric sofa bed that had been opened. The mattress was bare, with no sheets, blankets, or pillows. Pieces of cloth and articles of clothing were tied to the metal bedframe to serve as what appeared to be makeshift restraints. A putrid, rotten odor hung in the air.

Against the far wall, agents observed an odd-looking wooden pole with several condoms attached to its tip. It was slender and long, measuring several feet in length. Agents would find several of these strange apparatuses in other rooms of the house. And later, as our investigation widened, more would turn up in trailers and campsites around the area. At first glance, its role was unclear. It looked to be some sort of sexual device. But we didn't know for sure.

Initially, no one knew what to call them. Later, when we learned from Grate that he'd been using them on himself, someone dubbed them "Grate rods."

Unlike the rooms downstairs, there weren't a lot of wall hangings in this upstairs space, so the odd display of clothing that stretched from floor to ceiling in the far corner immediately caught SA Staley's attention. It appeared Grate had constructed a makeshift clothes rack. He'd hammered a series of nails into the wall just below the ceiling, from which he'd hung numerous articles of men's and women's clothing—a bright pink blouse, an orange-and-green plaid tunic, a black sweatshirt, a gray-and-white flannel shirt. On the floor beneath the mosaic of clothing was a pile with more garments and innumerable stuffed animals that Grate claimed he had taken from a donation bin outside the thrift shop.

SA Staley suspected there was a closet hidden behind all the clothes and bedding and directed his colleagues' attention to that corner of the room. He was correct; it was a closet. The agents worked methodically, beginning with the heap of stuffed toys at the base of the wall.

Near the pile, they discovered a can of air freshener, an ominous find. Had Grate been using it to mask the odor of decomposition? Their suspicions were confirmed when they spotted fly pupae on several of the stuffed toys and on the wide, wood floorboards, suggesting there may be human remains nearby.

Their next task was removing the clothes and bedding obscuring the wall. They stripped away several layers before finally exposing a dark, wooden door. It was sealed shut with numerous pieces of thick, black tape. Even the old-fashioned keyhole was taped over. On the floor in front of the door was a pool of liquid that appeared to have seeped out from the locked closet. Bodily fluids, the team suspected.

Agents were dilligent, carefully removing the tape to preserve it as evidence; they then prepared to reveal what was so carefully hidden inside. One member of the team was able to pull the door open. He noticed flies in all four stages of life—egg, larva, pupa, adult—and the fetid smell of rotting flesh, an odor BCI agents experience often in their profession.

On the floor of the closet was a pile of clothing, bedding, and stuffed animals almost three feet deep. Curiously, there was no clothing rod or shelf. The dated, floral wallpaper decorating the closet's interior was covered in fly larvae and pupae.

SA Staley, who was working along the left side of the closet, removed an article of clothing to reveal a human foot. For a moment, the team paused to take in the magnitude of what the agent had just unearthed.

They had found Elizabeth Griffith.

Her body was in a prone position, covered in maggots, and badly decomposed. The top of her head was pressed against the back wall of the closet, strands of her blond hair still visible. Her legs were bent slightly upward, and her hands were positioned behind her back, as if they had been tied there.

Upon closer inspection, the agents observed black rope encircling her ankles and articles of red and white clothing tied around her wrists and hands. They appeared to be makeshift restraints and looked as though they had all been connected at some point, suggesting Elizabeth had been hog-tied before she was placed in the closet.

One of the agents got word to someone at the police station that they had found Elizabeth. I would learn of the discovery during a break.

My gut sank hearing that Griffith's body had been found. I felt helpless. There was nothing I could do to save her. My purpose would now be giving her justice.

11

Discarded Like Trash

"There's one down in the basement," Grate disclosed. I had been pressing him to be more forthcoming when the revelation finally emerged.

"Down in the basement?" I repeated. Could it be Stacey?

Nodding, Grate uttered, "Mm-hmm . . . yeah."

"Tell me about it," I said.

As the BCI agents continued to search the Covert Court house, I was at the police department and still doing my one-on-one interrogation of Shawn Grate. Detective David Rohn of the Ashland County Sheriff's Office was now monitoring from the adjacent room.

In addition to BCI and the Ashland and Richland County Sheriff's Offices, several other law enforcement agencies had joined the investigation. The FBI had been contacted, and Special Agent John Minichello of the Cleveland field office was assigned to the case.

Over the years, I had worked with SA Minichello on human trafficking and sex offenses. He and his colleagues would become invaluable assets throughout the Grate investigation and beyond.

The Ashland County Prosecutor's Office, led by Prosecutor Chris Tunnell, was also involved. He'd been looped in early in the investigation, and we kept him informed as the day unfolded.

Chris is a big guy with a long, full auburn beard and a commanding presence. He is an outstanding prosecutor and is aggressive in charging cases, but he has a warm heart. He is accessible day or night to any law enforcement officer in the county. We have called him at two and three in the morning with a question on a case, and he answers every single time.

A graduate of Case Western Reserve University School of Law in Cleveland, he spent his early years in private practice in Bedford Heights, and later Medina. His focus was on domestic relations and criminal law. From 2001 to 2005, he was an assistant prosecuting attorney in the Ashland County Prosecutor's Office. In 2005, he joined the Richland County Prosecutor's Office where he served in a supervisory position within the criminal division until 2014, when he was elected the Ashland County prosecuting attorney. Both Chris and his wife, Sandra, were active in the community, with Sandra having served two terms on the Ashland City Council, and currently serving as the executive director of Ashland Main Street.

During this investigation, we remained in contact every day. He had two special prosecutors on his team, Michael McNamara of the office of Medina County prosecuting attorney Forrest Thomas, and Mark Weaver of the Columbus law firm Isaac Wiles, who were also closely involved in the case and provided us with 24-7 support.

Grate's admission to a second deceased victim in the Covert Court house needed to be explored. I wanted to know exactly where in the basement he had placed the body, so that the BCI agents who were already in the house could be cognizant.

But Grate was circumspect. When I asked him again to elaborate, he simply repeated his earlier proclamation, "She's just down in the basement."

Determined to confirm my suspicion that it was Stacey Stanley Hicks, I pressed him. "What's her name?" I repeated.

"Stacey."

My heart sank. "What's her last name?" I asked.

Grate said he couldn't remember. "She has short hair," he remarked.

It disturbed me that he didn't know the last name of this precious woman that he'd killed. I was almost certain that this victim was none other than Stacey Stanley Hicks, but I didn't divulge that to Grate. I stepped out of the room momentarily.

Once in the hallway, I went to the adjacent room to speak to Detective Rohn. To my surprise, I found my husband, Dan, was there, too. Unbeknownst to me, someone had retrieved him from his office on the court side of our building and brought him into the observation room. Of all my suspect interviews over the years, this was the first one he had ever witnessed.

Dan told me he'd been watching when Grate confessed to murdering Candice Cunningham at the abandoned house on State Route 430. He knew the location and said that there had been a fire some months back that had burned the place to the ground. The incident had been ruled as arson, but a suspect had not been identified. The timing of the fire coincided with Grate's account of when he was there with Candice. Dan related that it was likely that Grate had set the fire intentionally, presumably to cover up Cunningham's murder.

"Now, go back in there and get him to admit it," Dan said.

Looking back, my exchange with my husband that afternoon was surreal on many levels. There I was interviewing a serial killer, and Dan was providing me with relevant information that I could actually use in my interrogation.

I returned to the interview room with a list of questions that needed answers. Switching on the digital recorder, I launched back into the interrogation. "I am going to give you a couple of names, and you tell me if you recognize any of them," I began.

I listed four names, two of them related to our victim, "Stanley" and "Hicks," and two random names.

"Hicks," Grate stated.

"Is that it?"

Grate nodded. "Hicks."

"Okay . . . does she have any tattoos or anything on her?"

"Yeah, on her hand."

"Okay. What is the tattoo of?"

"Uh, like Indian stuff."

"Any pierced ears?"

"Yeah, they were pierced, I think."

"Where's she from?" I asked.

"I'm not sure. . . . I'm trying to remember."

"Okay, how did you meet her?"

"Walking to the gas station."

At that moment, I knew we had the right woman. The last time anyone had seen Stacey was at the BP station in Ashland. My heart hurt for her family. I had prayed that she was somehow alive and I could deliver her home. But it was over. She was gone. Now, I felt the weight of getting his full confession.

"Okay. When did that happen?" I reminded Grate that today was Tuesday, September 13, and that he had been holding Jane at the home where he squatted since Sunday the eleventh.

"I'm not sure. Thursday?"

"Thursday. Well, let's look at our calendar again."

Grate straightened in his seat. It struck me that he sat casually munching on his snacks while we talked while Stacey lay lifeless under a pile of trash on a basement floor.

"All right, today's the thirteenth, so you've had Jane since Sunday the eleventh."

"Okay."

"What day do you think this happened with Stacey?"

"Let's see, it's still—it's kind of hard for me to say. Thursday. Maybe it was Thursday."

"Is that the day you met her, when you were walking by the—"

Grate interrupted me midsentence. "I met her Thursday. Yeah, it happened Friday night, I mean Thursday night."

"Okay, how did the conversation go that she ends up coming back to your place? Did you just walk up to her and start talking?"

"Well, it was raining," Grate began. "I had an umbrella. I was going to give her my umbrella and keep walking, because she was standing outside and then she had a flat tire on her car." Grate said he asked her if she wanted a hand, and she told him that someone was coming to help her. "It's only a one-man job, so I went ahead and walked down to the Circle K and then back, and she was still there waiting. Then I went back up there in about ten minutes; someone showed up.

"And yeah, I asked her if she wanted to hang out sometime, and she said sure, and she was—asked me what I was doing that evening, I tell her I wasn't doing nothing.

"She said we can hang out, so we started hanging out. She came in, and everything was fine. I mean, we ended up kissing . . . Just kind of like, it happened, and then, I don't know, it just went all bad. She's a sweet lady, though."

"Sweet lady?" I repeated.

"Yeah."

"What color hair does she have?"

"Black."

"About how old is she?" I asked.

"Young. Forty-two?" he guessed.

"Okay, does she have a car?"

"Mm-hmm."

Grate admitted he had taken Stacey's car keys.

"Have you been in that car?" I asked. "I mean, have you driven it since this happened?"

Grate fell silent. Eventually, he admitted that since her death, he had been driving the vehicle. "I got into it a few different times . . . took a drive to Mansfield and back."

I asked him where the car was now, but he couldn't immediately identify where he had left it. "I don't know what street it's on."

No doubt it was Grate that the witness had seen parking Stacey's car across from her house on Ninth Street, the same man she saw leaving the area on foot. It was clear that everything that Stacey's family said about her car, the nuances, were true.

Again, I asked if she had died the same way as Candice had, and his response was stunning.

"Tongue out of her mouth," he said.

Wanting him to elaborate, I asked him to repeat what he had just said.

"When you choke a woman out, when you choke someone, they die with their tongue out of their mouth."

I asked him to elaborate.

"The pressure," he replied. "It makes people's tongues stick out."

He had not mentioned that with Candice or Elizabeth, so why did he mention it with Stacey? I wondered how prolific his atrocities were.

Grate indicated that what he described had occurred in the bedroom on the first floor where he had been holding Jane. "Then I took her down to the basement."

When I asked if he had engaged sexually with her, Grate indicated that he had.

"See, at first, kind of like playing around and then she wanted to play all innocent, so then I kind of just snapped on her," he recalled. "She came home with me at eleven o'clock and didn't even know me. I mean, kind of like almost sent from God, or she could have been sent from the devil. I don't know. Someone gave up on her."

I remember thinking that no one gave up one her. She had a tight-knit, loving family.

Once again, Grate was blaming Stacey for what happened that night. He somehow had nothing to do with it—she was the one who may have been sent by the devil. Grate, somehow, was just there. It was almost like he was an innocent bystander that night, when nothing could have been further from the truth. Perhaps he created the alternate scenarios in his mind to avoid confronting the horror of what he'd done? Or better yet, he was attempting to justify or rationalize his own demonic actions.

"Did you have sex with her before she died or after?" I asked.

Grate displayed an expression of unease. "No one ever after," he snapped. "Nothing has ever happened afterwards."

I didn't necessarily believe him, especially considering Elizabeth was in a hog-tied position in the closet. But I had to store that suspicion for later. I have to determine in a multi-victim case whether I should go for all I can on one victim and run the risk of the person shutting down before I get all the information, or get some information related to each victim, then circle back and get additional detail per victim, in layers.

"Okay. So, what did you put her in in the basement?"

"I just put her on the floor."

"Where, on the floor in the basement?"

"Under all that stuff, garbage. Underneath the garbage," he said.

"And that's at the house on Fourth, right by the laundromat?"

Grate was answering my questions, so I kept at it in rapid succession. "Did she try to fight you when you were strangling her?"

"Yeah," he replied. "She maced me, too."

"When you had sex with her, did she want to, or did you have to make her?"

"No," he said. "I didn't have sex with her after that. I actually made her give me head, right . . . I was in that rage of like . . . with everything else that was going on, I guess I could blame it on her, but I don't know exactly why."

"Okay," I said.

"Just, she came home with me, we kind of like hit it off pretty good, and then, it didn't—it just went sour fast. I even thought, *I'm done*. It just went fast."

Like he'd done with Elizabeth, Grate attempted to deflect the blame onto his victim.

"What did she expect?" he asked at one point, suggesting that it was Stacey's fault for agreeing to come home with him after 11:00 p.m.

"We know you have videos of Jane, but do you have any pictures of other women you have been with?"

"Stacey."

"Was the video when you had her give you oral sex?"

Grate claimed that Stacey was "acting all innocent" on the video he recorded of her on his cell phone. "But she wasn't," he stated. "Once she seen the video . . . she was playing all innocent, do you know what I mean? Like once she seen that I am recording, then boy, everything changed . . . I don't know how to explain it. . . . I got her on the video, then she clicked. There was nothing on there like I forced her."

He was lying, and I decided it was time to challenge him. "Earlier, you said you forced her to give you oral sex."

"Yeah, um, I'm not exactly sure why."

"Why what?"

"Why I forced her to do that . . . What a mess. Something just triggered me. I don't know what it was."

I asked if perhaps he had been using drugs.

"No, just a little bit of beer, but not much," he stated, claiming he didn't care for drugs. I later confirmed this statement with one of Grate's long-term girlfriends, who indicated that although Grate used marijuana, he was against using other drugs.

In an attempt to determine if he ever had times where he didn't remember what he was doing, I asked, "Do you ever wake up and not know what you did the night before? I mean, wake up with blood on you and wonder if you did something to somebody else?"

"No . . . I remember everything, yeah, pretty much I remember it."

In the coming days, I would view the video Grate recorded of this forced, violent sexual attack on Stacey. The video depicts his absolute lack of regard for another human and his insatiable appetite to terrorize innocent victims. It was so profoundly disturbing, it haunts me still today.

In later interviews, it became a quest for me to get Grate to acknowledge that Stacey shared no culpability in the circumstances of what occurred that night. Still, he continued to make a number of claims in an attempt to make himself look less inhuman. At one point, he said that he had every intention of letting Stacey go that night. But as she was about to exit the house, she pulled the Mace from her purse and sprayed him in the face. "I just snapped on her."

Facets of Grate's account of what transpired weren't logical. But what I did know for sure was that Stacey was tough and feisty, and Grate had grossly offended her. It was hard to believe that he ever intended to let her leave his home that night. Instead, he again attempted to deflect blame onto his victim, stating her spraying him with Mace is what caused him to ultimately kill her, which included not only manually strangling her; because she struggled so much, he said he also resorted to using a ligature around her neck. He went on to describe that after strangling her, he dragged her body down to the basement, letting her head bang on every step because he was angry with her.

Grate grew frustrated recounting his interactions with Stacey, and I could see that he was struggling internally about whether or not to continue to talk to me. I worried that if I pushed him, he might opt to shut down, so as a way to reset his disposition, I diverted the conversation away from the murders. I knew very little about this man other than the few random details he had provided earlier in the interview. I believed that his history, including his upbringing and family dynamics, might shed light on him, so I began to dig into his past. If this was going to be law enforcement's only opportunity to talk to him, I wanted to get a comprehensive narrative, a way to better understand him, and also to secure information to create a matrix of where he had been over the course of his life.

We began by discussing his schooling. He reminded me that he had graduated from River Valley High School in Marion, reiterating how proud he was to have completed his studies despite his parents' alleged neglect. While there, he had attended building trades classes and learned some basic construction skills that he later put to use.

He said that over the years, he had done a mix of construction and remodeling work along with extensive rewiring of homes throughout the area. He claimed he had worked for a carpentry service in Mansfield for a bit. He'd also done some plumbing and heating work in Delaware, Ohio. He had even worked for a landscaper in the neighboring village of Mifflin. Grate explained that the owner of the landscaping firm saw him working on his mother's property, approached him, and offered him a job.

Grate's demeanor instantly changed when the topic of his mother arose. "Whatever I get, she should get, too," he railed, referring to any criminal charges related to his crimes. "She's the one who encourages me . . . Bad things should happen to condemned people. She's condemned. . . . The only lady higher than me. She's a nut."

He elaborated without prompting.

"My mom has been in a prison of her own all her life," he said. "She'll be like, 'Oh, I forgot to live my life.' She's probably saying that now."

I understood that to mean that Grate viewed his mother as a perpetual victim. She wasn't actually incarcerated in a brick-and-mortar prison serving time. She was a prisoner of her own making, an emotional prisoner.

Grate related that when he was eleven years old, he arrived home from school one day to find that his mother had picked up and moved to Kentucky to be with her then boyfriend. After that, he went to live with his father.

I asked if he'd ever seen a counselor.

"Yeah, a little bit when I was younger."

"Never since you were an adult?"

"No, not really."

"How do you get by financially?" I asked. "I know you've been living in abandoned houses, so you don't have rent, but how do you get the money you need for your phone? Food?"

Grate explained that he had been selling expired cigarettes. He admitted to breaking into the Eagle Gas Station on Claremont Avenue to steal the cigarettes, which he had been peddling to raise cash. A check of APD records confirmed that someone had indeed broken into the Eagle Gas Station, and the case was marked as "unsolved." I could add breaking and entering to the list of crimes that Grate could be charged with.

An awareness during every interview regarding the elements of each crime and the possibility of other crimes is imperative. That's the standard as a detective and an expectation of Prosecutor Tunnell when he is reviewing cases for charges. For example, going to a victim's apartment after you've murdered them can provide evidence for additional charging options and ultimately provide closure for the victims and their families.

Although I was interested in even the less significant crimes that Grate had committed, I was eager to redirect the interview back to our three murder victims, so I asked him if he'd worried that law enforcement might confront him if they caught him driving around in Stacey's vehicle.

"I knew eventually it was going to catch up with me," he said.

I asked Grate if he could describe Stacey's car, and he told me it was a gray Pontiac. In fact, it was a gray Mitsubishi Eclipse.

"Why, if you had a car available to you, did you keep Elizabeth's body in the house, and why did you keep Stacey's body in the house? If you knew you had Stacey's car, why did you not take them somewhere else?" I inquired.

"I didn't worry about it," Grate replied matter-of-factly. "I would still be in the same mess. Do you know what I mean? I'd still be running."

"When Jane was at your house over the past weekend, did she notice the odor, the smell in the house from the bodies? Did she say anything, like, 'What's that smell?' or anything?"

"Yeah."

"What did you tell her?"

"I told her it was something I threw away I forgot about."

"Okay, and when she was there, she said she thought she heard a thud upstairs a couple of times. What was she hearing?" During this portion of our exchange, I had thoughts independent of our conversation. I wondered if there had been yet another woman held captive in the home upstairs while Jane was being held downstairs. I knew Elizabeth had been gone for weeks. And Stacey was gone within hours of her arrival at the 363 Covert Court address. Everything Jane had said to that point was true. What did she hear?

Grate claimed he didn't know. "Sometimes I hear thuds, too."

Grate could see that I was attempting to put value on what Jane had noticed, so he claimed that he sometimes heard noises, too.

What I didn't yet know was that the BCI agents had found restraints tied to the bed in the upstairs bedroom where Elizabeth's body had been found, but there was no indication any of our victims had been tied to that bed. Still, I would never be able to get Grate to admit to having another woman in the house during Jane's captivity, although I continue to suspect that someone was in that upstairs bedroom at some point during Jane's three-day ordeal.

I later asked Grate how long he held Elizabeth before she died.

"She died right away," he stated.

"When did you tie her up?" I wanted to know if he'd hog-tied her before or after she died.

Grate claimed it was after he killed her, "just in case she came back through, but she didn't."

"You tied her up after she was dead?"

"After she let off that big scream, yeah."

"She let out a scream when she died?"

"Hmm."

I questioned Grate as to whether Stacey would also be found tied up, and he said she would not.

"How about Candice?"

He indicated that Elizabeth was the only one of the three, saying, "I tied her so if she did wake up, she wouldn't be no surprise."

I decided to challenge him, remarking that it seemed like it would be obvious if someone were dead. Little did I know, he had actual experience with women he thought were dead who weren't, something I would hear about in the days to come.

Grate half-heartedly agreed. "Yeah, I mean, kind of."

"Okay, has there ever been a girl that you kept, that you didn't kill, that you just wanted to keep for a while?"

"No. I never abducted anyone like this before," Grate claimed. "Jane's a new situation, new. I've never done nothing like Jane, other than that one Stacey a little bit."

"How long did you keep Stacey?"

"Oh, just about an hour."

"Just about an hour?"

"Short time, yeah. She flipped out, acted up, so I didn't have a choice."

"You didn't have a choice. Do you really mean that?" I pressed. "Think about it, did you really have a choice whether to kill her or not? Rationally, looking back at it, did you have a choice?"

"She knew where I was."

"And you have already made her give you oral sex, like forced that on her, so is that what you're meaning?"

"We, yeah, we already bumped heads."

"Let's jump to Elizabeth for a second. Did you say you did not have sex with Elizabeth?"

"Hmm."

"No sexual act happened?"

"Nothing happened."

"You didn't feel sexual towards her?"

"No."

Grate did finally admit that he did, in fact, remove all Elizabeth's clothes. "I wanted to get rid of them," he confessed. "Elizabeth messed her pants when she died. Her clothes were soaked, so I got rid of them because they would have that real harsh stink."

"So, when you took her pants off . . . you knew that she was dead, right?"

"I assumed that she was dead . . . but I didn't know."

There it was again, the uncertainty.

Grate said he couldn't remember exactly what happened to Elizabeth's pants, claiming he likely threw them in the trash, "just a bag down in the basement."

Returning the conversation to Grate's rage, I asked if there was a sexual component that triggered it. "When you have your thoughts, do they start out in those situations as a sexual thought, or are the thoughts something different? Like, let's say Stacey, she's in your apartment, is your thought sexual when it turns to violence? Where does it begin?"

"I think my violence starts when the lies start. I just think I've been lied to by women, and I think, *She's now a bullshitter.*"

"Okay, afterwards, do you feel bad? We talked about some regret. What do you feel?"

"I feel like, 'What have I done?'" Grate said.

"Like when you meet Stacey . . . when you decided to approach her, when she had her flat tire, did you think, *I need to do that again?*"

"No, I don't think that I have that feeling, that desire to kill again, it's always just something I have to run from, like once you snap, you don't come back. . . . I think I really snapped."

Referring to Stacey, I asked, "So, at what point while she was there did you decide you were going to kill her?"

"It wasn't planned, but . . . she just gave me these flashbacks of all these other women that's probably broken my heart to really break it down . . . flashbacks like my mom, really. I mean, I hate to blame people . . . Someone has to be blamed. I mean, I'm taking my blame," he said.

Grate's anger and resentment toward his mother were again resurfacing. It was a topic I intended to explore further in the interview process.

"So, when you told Jane that you would go find another place to stay and burn down the house or torch the house, were you thinking more about the fact that there are two bodies in your house than just covering up what you had done to Jane?"

"Yeah, it was mainly just to cover up, pretty much."

Covering the elements of abuse of a corpse, aggravated arson, and tampering with evidence. I persisted. "Did you get anything to use to start the fire?"

Grate nodded.

I would soon learn that Grate, in addition to being a serial killer, was also an arsonist and that his penchant for setting fires had begun when he was still a child. Since we had just talked about his plan to start a fire on Covert Court, I confronted him about the fire at the abandoned house on Route 430. He admitted that he was the one responsible for the blaze—and that he'd set the fire to cover up evidence of Candice's murder, just as my husband, Dan, had suspected. He admitted that when he strangled Candice, blood came out of her nose. He said they were upstairs in the "very first bedroom" to the left of the staircase and that her blood "was all over the drywall."

I asked him what he used to start the fire at the house on Route 430.

"Some type of oil . . . lamp oil," Grate said. He claimed that he'd found a container of oil in the house and used it as an accelerant. The container, too, was apparently lost in the subsequent blaze. Grate said he was not there when the fire trucks arrived but that he "came back through" on foot intending to walk toward Mifflin and eventually Ashland and "the fire trucks were still there."

He further stated that after the fire, he "stayed in the woods by Mifflin" for about three weeks, walking back and forth from Charles Mill Lake Park and Ashland.

"Did you enter the park at Charles Mill?" I asked.

Grate said he had. He then inquired if park rangers had contacted us to report any "mysteries" having occurred there.

"Is there something I need to know about the park?"

"There ain't no dead bodies," he replied flatly.

Grate admitted that during his time at Charles Mill, he broke into at least two trailers, entering through the back windows. He said he spent the next three to four weeks bouncing back and forth between the two, which were located in a cluster of trailers that remained in the park on a full-time basis. He also broke into a third trailer, where he found a "supply of food" that he divided equally to stock the two trailers where he was squatting to avoid capture by police. Posing as a camper, he regularly interacted with other campers, as well as park rangers. He was friendly with everyone, never doing anything to draw attention to himself.

"I was friends with them [park rangers]. I'd sit and talk with them sometimes," he stated.

To evade a confrontation with the trailers' owners, he rigged the front door with zip ties to make it more difficult for someone to gain entry and to give him time to escape through a rear window. On one occasion, he recalled returning to one of the trailers to find there was someone inside, so he didn't dare go in.

He claimed that while staying in the park, he befriended an older man named Freddy, and that he, Freddy, and his wife would sing gospel songs around the campfire at night. "I had a blast."

Even after the burglary of one of the trailers was reported in mid-June, Grate continued to stay in the park, simply relocating to another trailer. The owner of that trailer, a woman named Pamela, reported that her camper had been burglarized and food and electronics had been taken.

Pamela said she had last been at the trailer the weekend before and had left it fully stocked with items. At the end of June, a second burglary was reported. This time, the owner claimed his trailer appeared to have been "lived in, showing debris of beer, cigarettes and food residue." In that report, items that might "identify the culprit"—a knife, a pair of black cutoff track pants, a pair of socks, and a black T-shirt— were seized as evidence. Grate claimed he "got lucky" and saw from afar park rangers taking the report of the second burglary.

Also found in one of the trailers were several of the rodlike apparatuses layered with condoms that BCI agents had found in the Covert Court home where Grate squatted.

I asked him what they were used for, and for the first time, he stammered while attempting to provide a response. "Just to see if, like . . . I never did use 'em. It was just . . ."

I explained the necessity for his honesty. But he continued to deny that he'd done anything with the objects.

"Did you have girls in the trailers?" I pressed.

"Well, I'm not gay, but I do like to use stress relievers for me. But I'm not gay. I would never do nothing with another man."

Several weeks into the investigation, John Minichello and I would interview a man who claimed he had an intimate relationship with Shawn Grate. The gentleman we spoke to actually showed us a wood carving that Grate had given him, and he further presented pictures of Shawn Grate in a hot tub with him. Additionally, he provided text messages the two had exchanged during their monthslong relationship, which he described as "tumultuous." At one point, Grate actually sent the man a cryptic message that read something to the effect of "meet the real me," referring to his disposition when he was angry.

Did Shawn Grate also have male victims that we had not yet discovered?

Grate indicated that after the report of the second trailer burglary in late June, he left Charles Mill Lake Park and began staying in a makeshift campsite in a wooded area about seven miles west of Ashland.

He admitted to burglarizing the Island Trading Post in Mifflin, a fishing supply and convenience store near the park, to obtain provisions for his new "home." Among the items he stole was a blue-and-white cooler that the Ashland County Sheriff's Office would recover when they searched the campsite later that afternoon. He also took brass knuckles and two Tasers, which were found by BCI agents during their search of the Covert Court residence.

Regarding pornography, Grate related that he had "a little issue . . . but it could be bigger."

I asked him what type of pornography he entertained, and he stated, "Whatever I could find. It don't matter. I don't go out and buy nothing special."

He explained that he accessed pornography by purchasing DVDs. "Usually, I'll run across stuff from other people. It can be anything."

I inquired about the age bracket of female he fantasized about, and he replied, "Thirty and over."

He suddenly moved the conversation back to Jane, stating, "She's too good for me."

I remarked about the soundness of Jane's faith, then introduced a portion of her statement to me regarding a conversation that she'd said she had with Grate over a recent meal at Wendy's restaurant. Jane had claimed that they had talked about Grate repenting his sins. Before I could ask my next question, he interjected, explaining that when he was talking to Jane about needing to repent his sins, he was referring to what he had done to both Candice Cunningham and Elizabeth Griffith, although he had not disclosed either murder to Jane.

Before concluding the interview, I asked Grate to list all the places he had lived. It was clear we had a serial killer on our hands, and while Grate was emphatic that there were no other victims, I was not convinced. We had three homicide victims—Candice, Elizabeth, and Stacey—and I had no doubt that had Jane not found the courage to call 911, that number would have been four. I had gotten confessions on the three deceased women, plus the live victim, but our investigation was just getting started.

Grate stated that he'd been in Marion, Bucyrus, Mansfield, and Ashland. "Were there other, similar incidents in other places that we haven't yet talked about?"

He assured me there were no more victims, but his intonation and hesitation caused me to suspect otherwise.

It was after 3:00 p.m. when I told Grate I was going to exit the room to coordinate our transportation to Richland County, so he could show us where he had placed Candice's body.

Candice had never been reported missing. Grate's confession to me about her murder meant that coordination with law enforcement officials in Richland County needed to occur to recover her body. I was still in the interview room when my supervisor notified Richland County to advise that Grate had confessed to a murder in their jurisdiction and that, subsequent to my interview, I would be transporting Grate to Richland County, where he would be leading me to where he had disposed of her remains. Unbeknownst to me, I would soon be making a similar call to Mansfield PD in Richland County.

"I am going to go grab you a cup of coffee," I told Grate. "Then, maybe we'll head over to Route 430. Does that sound all right?"

"Yeah."

"You still okay? Do you feel better that you've talked to me?"

"Yeah, I appreciate you coming in here and not him."

I knew Grate was referring to Captain Lay.

"We weren't going to get nowhere," he remarked.

"Well, sometimes it's personalities. Or, if he already knows something, and you know, but you don't want to say it . . ."

"Well, he was lying to me, too, so . . ."

"I don't know what he said, because I wasn't in there."

Grate appeared to backpedal. "I mean, I'm not saying he's lying, but—"

"Because he's a straightforward guy," I said, defending my superior officer. Rising from my chair, I said, "Okay, let me get you some coffee."

Standing in the hallway, I was struck that Grate's arrest and subsequent confession were going to color the way Ashland was viewed.

In many ways, the city is a stereotypical midwestern town, with lots of parkland, dozens of churches, and quaint, old-fashioned storefronts along once-cobblestoned Main Street. It's a friendly place, where everyone knows everyone, and people stop to chat in the grocery line and on sidewalks.

Socializing revolves around church events, festivals, school sports, and holiday parades. It's not a place that you go to disappear, like so many of the nation's big cities are. Even Ashland's police officers, like me, make it a habit to wave to passersby.

But Shawn Grate was about to change all that for us; we'd be known henceforth as the home of one of America's serial killers.

12

State Route 430

The search of the Covert Court house was occurring simultaneously to my interview with Grate back at the police station, so information gleaned from my interrogation was being relayed in real time to agents at the crime scene. BCI SA Ed Staley and his team had just recovered Elizabeth Griffith's body when they got word that there was another deceased victim in the basement, so their crime scene went from an abduction and rape to a homicide, then a second homicide.

At the residence, SA Staley and his team were processing all the rooms in the house. The first floor included the kitchen, where the bag of food Jane had packed for Grate sat on the wood table, a small bathroom, and the bedroom / living room combo, where Grate had held Jane Doe hostage for three horrific days. The first-floor bedroom, like the one upstairs, was small and cluttered with junk. The hardwood floor was all but hidden beneath towels, assorted clothing, overturned plastic laundry baskets, and even a barbell with heavy black steel weights attached.

Blankets were hung on three of the four walls as if they were tapestries, and the room's two windows were covered by bed linens, likely to prevent pedestrians from seeing in. There was even an artificial Christmas tree by a chair in the corner.

The bed where police had found Grate asleep earlier that morning was pushed up against the far wall and unmade. The agents collected scarves and articles of women's clothing that had been tied to the mattress handles; those were the makeshift restraints that Jane had described to me during our interview.

On the nightstand was a jar of Vaseline. Jane had disclosed that Grate had used Vaseline for lubricant during the repeated sexual assaults. Agents also found the Taser Jane had mistaken for a cell phone when she first attempted to dial 911. Several more stun guns and a pair of brass knuckles were also found.

Off the hallway adjacent to the bedroom was a small bathroom with a stall shower, toilet, and wall sink. There were several bottles of cleaning fluid on the floor of the shower, but the bathroom itself was filthy—hardly a surprise since the home had no running water.

The two teams were tasked with going through every inch of the house, looking for anything that could be relevant to the case. They would open every cupboard in the kitchen and explore the house thoroughly on all three floors.

At one point during the search, one of the BCI agents opened a closet door only to have one of the "Grate rods," the homemade sexual devices Grate had used to pleasure himself, come tumbling out and strike him in the head. It was grotesque for the officer involved but provided a moment of levity.

With news that Shawn Grate had admitted to concealing Stacey's body in the home's basement, SA Staley and his forensics team moved from one recovery operation to the next.

Grate and I were already in a police vehicle and on our way to Richland County to recover Candice Cunningham's body when SA Staley led the team down a short flight of steps, where they hit a landing, then turned right to descend the rest of the way. The unmistakable odor of decomposition mixed with the toxic smell of rotting trash hit them as soon as they reached the last step.

On the floor to the right of the staircase were piles of oversize plastic leaf and garden bags, filled with weeks' worth of trash. Grate had told me we'd find Stacey beneath bags of garbage, much like he'd concealed Elizabeth's body beneath a mound of clothing.

Everyone waited while the area was photographed. It was important to document the scene exactly as they had found it. Before beginning the methodical removal of the trash bags, the agents investigated other areas of the basement that might contain a body. On the back wall, they observed a freezer chest.

Concerned the chest might contain a victim, SA Staley raised the lid and looked inside, relieved to see that it was empty. Agents also found a hole in the wall with a crawl space that led to another area beneath the house. Inside were a few discarded items, but nothing of value to the investigation.

Just as they had upstairs, the team got to work systematically removing the mounds of trash that had all been photographed. As they made their way down through the pile, they came upon a blue-and-white Circle K Polar Pop cup, a cigarette butt, and some old coffee grounds. It was likely that one of the trash bags had ripped open and the items had spilled out. Their next discovery was more ominous, a can of air freshener like the one they'd found upstairs.

The agents continued to dig through the pile, sorting through more trash—empty cigarette packs, Styrofoam cups, and rotting food. On the bottom of one of the white garbage bags, they found fly pupae and maggots. They also discovered a wood apparatus similar to the one they'd collected from the bedroom on the second floor; this one, too, was long and slender, and topped at one end by several condoms. But this one was broken into two pieces. Perhaps that's why Grate had tossed it into the basement with the trash.

Agents clearing the last of the trash bags came upon an outspread blanket. After photographing its location, one of them pulled it away to reveal a human corpse on the concrete floor; the body was in an advanced stage of decomposition. A small tattoo was visible on its left hand, and rings adorned several of its manicured fingers. The tattoo and rings would later help family members confirm that this was, indeed, their beloved Stacey.

Stacey's wallet, car keys, and debit card would also be recovered during the search. Grate had stolen and spent the forty-three dollars that Stacey had in her wallet when she arrived at his house that past Thursday evening. He also found her food card, and other plastic cards, but he decided not to use them. Items belonging to both Jane and Elizabeth were also collected during the search.

Elizabeth Griffith's house key did not turn up during the search of the Covert Court house. We would later learn that as he had with Jane, Grate stole Elizabeth's house key sometime after her murder and let himself into her apartment to rid it of any evidence that could link him to her. He was determined to retrieve the Yahtzee game pad on which Elizabeth had written both their names. He also stole some soap and shampoo, and prescription pills from bottles he found in the kitchen drawers.

BCI agents also searched the yellow colonial next door to our target location but found no evidence that Grate had utilized the house.

In the days that followed, search warrants would be executed on other properties that Grate was known to have inhabited, including the tiny apartment on Second Street in Mansfield, where he claimed to have lived with Candice Cunningham, as well as the burned-out house on State Route 430, where Grate and I were headed.

Arrangements had been made for Lieutenant Scott Smart of the Ashland County Sheriff's Office to transport us. Grate would be in handcuffs and under close watch by Smart, myself, and other officers the entire time we were outside the police station. I had been the one to escort Grate to Smart's awaiting SUV. During the short walk to the vehicle, I'd asked if he was still okay riding to Richland County with us so that he could show us the location of Candice's body.

"Yeah . . . I need to talk to you. It's gonna be hard . . . probably gonna be hard for you, too."

When I told him he would be riding with Lieutenant Smart, he asked if I could join them.

I told him that I would be in the vehicle with him and was surprised and a bit bewildered by his response.

"I'm in shackles, but you freed me," he said.

I found his remark profound. He would meet accountability, but he'd purged what he'd harbored.

During the car ride, Grate told me that he had a fort outside of Mifflin. He asked if I was familiar with the area, then provided directions to the location. "You take a left, then you go up the hill out of Mifflin. . . . There is a sharp turn on that road." He said he knew the area from when he'd stayed at his mother's home five or six years earlier and went on bike rides.

He would later admit to taking Jane to this fort. "There's a cross back there," he stated, suggesting that someone had created a makeshift memorial in the area. "Something happened with someone back there. I don't know if it was a car accident or what."

I didn't catch it right then, but Grate was providing a hint for me to follow.

At one point, he declared that he considered himself "a great deceiver." I believed he was referencing passages from the Bible that allude to Satan as the "great deceiver." He maintained that he had lied to everyone. I wondered if that declaration also pertained to me in the sense that there was more that he hadn't disclosed.

Once on Route 430, Grate began talking, and I turned on the

recorder to capture his statements. He pointed out various places where he had lived over the months—a mix of primitive, fortlike structures he had built himself, and camping trailers he'd broken into at Charles Mill Lake Park. He also admitted that he'd set fire to the house where he killed Candice a couple of days after the murder. Then he indicated that it wouldn't be difficult to find her body, as he knew exactly where he'd placed her. Having him on-site to clarify points from his confession to me was crucial and productive for the investigation.

I told him he was doing the right thing by taking us to the location.

"I felt like I did the right thing when I laid her down," he replied. "As many times as she has cried, and everything . . . I almost feel like it was the right thing . . . like I was helping her."

From the driver's seat, Lieutenant Smart asked Grate if we would be able to see the location by standing at the back of the house.

"You'd have to walk back to the creek," he said.

For a moment, Grate fell silent. Then, without solicitation, he stated, "I know I'm wrong no matter how right I felt . . . I sacrificed my life for them, 'cause all they did was talk about killing themselves.

"With Candice, mainly. I didn't know Elizabeth enough to know if anyone cared about her enough," he stated.

As we neared the location, Grate announced that we would be passing a gas station on the right-hand side. In the next breath, he admitted that after he'd strangled Candice, he'd kept her body in the home overnight and that he'd left the residence to stay in the wooded area where he'd built his fort. The following morning, he returned to the house and "took her back in the woods."

"I had to hurry up and cover her," he said. "I couldn't look at her, you know." He told us he wrapped her body in a blanket. Then, fearing that his DNA would be on the blanket, he took it back to the house and later burned the house with the blanket inside. "'Cause of DNA . . . you know . . . I wasn't trying to give up my whole life."

His remark struck me as ironic, in light of his previous comments about giving up his life for victims. In reality, I recognized that he didn't want to give up his life at all.

We approached the gas station, and Grate informed Lieutenant Smart, "It's right up the road after the light."

I asked Grate if Candice had a purse with her the night he killed her.

He said she had a copy of her social security card and a bag upstairs, but everything "got burned up" in the fire.

"I'll show you the house," he said. "It's right up after this curve."

There were multiple vehicles from the Ohio Bureau of Criminal Investigation as well as the Richland County Sheriff's Office staged along the road in front of the property. The officers and agents had been instructed to secure the perimeter, then wait in their cars until we arrived. People from the Richland County Prosecutor's Office and a coroner's investigator had also been notified and would be arriving shortly.

Grate became emotional in the back seat. "It looks like everybody's here," he said.

"Are you okay?" I asked.

He remarked that it was good that he was there doing what he was doing, but for the first time, he seemed really shaken.

I opened the rear door of the vehicle and waited as Grate climbed out. He was still handcuffed and crying. Lieutenant Smart held Grate on one side while another detective held him on the other.

"It's hard to be here," Grate said.

Being on scene with an offender gives a detective an investigative advantage. It is uncommon to get the opportunity to interview a suspect on scene, but the advantage is that they go through the scenario and almost relive it. Emotions are high, and veracity increases. I decided to inquire about details of Candice's death.

When asked, Grate launched into a diatribe about what had occurred inside the house. He said we would find Candice's body down a ravine and under a bush. "Just follow the flies," he remarked. This was the second time he'd used that phrase related to his victims. I later learned that he had a particular interest in flies as they relate to the decomposition of bodies, a fascination that began during his childhood. Still, it was a flippant comment that seemed incongruous with the tears and the anguish he had just displayed.

Grate indicated we would have to walk across the creek to get to the location. As I started toward the ravine, he directed me around because it would be easier for me to navigate the terrain. His casual remark suggested that he knew the entire area well and had probably walked it many times.

I tried to record Grate's utterances using a mini recorder as we walked, but I couldn't get close enough with the officers flanking him on both sides. I handed the device to Lieutenant Smart and asked him to ensure that he caught everything that the suspect was saying. I tried to keep the conversation going with Grate while making my way over the rough terrain.

At one point, Grate said that the dump site was roughly perpendicular to the back of the house. It would be like drawing a straight line from the back door out into the woods. He said that he had carried Candice across the creek and "straight up the hill" about ten to fifteen feet. "There's a bit of shrub, and there she is."

While standing at the rim of the ravine, Grate recalled that carrying Candice to the location "was very challenging."

I asked him if he was okay, and he replied, "Yeah."

Richland County Sheriff's Office sergeant Mike Viars asked Grate if he had fallen while trying to get Candice to the location.

"As a matter of fact, I did," he responded. Grate explained that he walked backward while dragging Candice's body, and at one point, he slipped. "She is light but seemed a lot heavier after she was dead," he said matter-of-factly.

I directed Ashland County Sheriff's Office sergeant David Rohn to photograph the area, then turned my focus back to Grate, who was now offering us advice for alternative walking routes to reach the targeted location. Grate, meanwhile, remained at the top of the embankment.

We found Candice's body in the spot Grate had described.

He was then directed to walk back to Lieutenant Smart's SUV while I remained behind with the officers to view the crime scene and provide details of Grate's confession to the Richland County detectives and the acting Richland County prosecutor. I advised that Candice was the first victim that Grate confessed to when I interviewed him earlier that morning and told them I would provide them with the recording of the interrogation. I also provided details of what Grate had revealed regarding Candice's murder.

I recall seeing Candice's nude body lying there in the ravine. There was no dignity. Her precious small frame was out in the elements, carelessly dumped. I stood for a moment recalling how Grate had so callously told us to just "follow the flies" to find her. Hearing those words was one thing, but standing over a victim's remains made the comment more visceral and disquieting. This was one of many surreal moments from the case that will always remain with me.

The location was remote and difficult to reach. We might never have found her there without Grate's confession to her murder and directions to her remains.

Candice's body was in an advanced state of decomposition when we recovered it, having been out in the elements for nearly three months. Her remains were identified through DNA by the Richland County Coroner's Office, with assistance from the Mercyhurst

University department of forensic anthropology and the Mansfield Police Department's crime lab.

A cause of death had not yet been determined.

I returned to Lieutenant Smart's SUV, where Grate had been locked in the back seat. I opened the back door and asked him about the temperature inside the car. The air conditioning was on, and I asked if it was cool. I'd made a very conscious decision not to discuss the naked body he'd just led us to in the woods. Doing so could prompt him to shut down, and I wanted to continue our dialogue for as long as I could.

"Yeah," he said, indicating that he wasn't too hot. I wondered about his emotional state and what was going through his mind at that moment.

"Are you okay?"

"Yeah," he said, then lowered his head and began to cry.

"I know this is hard," I stated.

"It's okay, though," he responded.

"You did the right thing today," I said. I asked him if there was anything else that I was missing that he needed to tell me about.

"I'm not too sure. I don't think so."

"Is there another girl to talk about?"

"No," he replied. "Just them three."

I explained to Grate that I was going to take him back to Ashland County. I told him that if he needed to talk to me, he could prepare a "kite," a written request, explaining that he needed to speak to me. He seemed anxious to maintain his communication with me, repeatedly asking when we could talk again.

* * *

Lieutenant Smart transported Grate and me back to Ashland that afternoon. It had been a long, arduous day, but it wasn't over. During the fifteen-minute-long ride to the Ashland County Sheriff's Office Corrections Division, I tried to keep the rapport momentum. I was also trying to mentally review his confession and come up with any last questions for him. I suppose that at some level, I was trying to process Candice's death; it seemed so senseless for her to be strangled and left to the elements in a ravine.

Grate appeared to be reflecting, as well. I could see him looking around and hear his forced exhale. I feared that he regretted having talked and that he might not continue to be forthcoming.

But as we neared the jail, he asked again about the possibility of speaking to me in the future. He said he wanted to talk with me "from time to time," as if to suggest that we would have a good deal more to discuss. He then asked me for a cigarette, and I told him that I would get him one. I was relieved that, from his perspective, we had forged a connection and communication could continue.

"I know I did the right thing by being honest with you," he remarked. "You didn't judge me, and you showed me compassion." He fell silent for the remainder of the ride.

When we pulled into the parking lot, we sat in the car waiting for the sally port doors to open. Grate remarked that he couldn't stand it when people didn't follow through.

"Who didn't follow through?" I asked.

"You," he said angrily. "You told me you would get me a cigarette before I went to jail."

I turned around from the front seat, and I looked at Grate, who was leaning forward. The little slide window in the prisoner partition was open, and so we were face-to-face and only a foot away from each other. He looked at me, and I told him that not everything everyone does is intentional.

He began apologizing to me over and over. "I shouldn't have

come at you like that. Just forget the cigarette. I don't need it. I'm sorry."

"We are going to wait right here until you get your cigarette," I said. And we did.

This would be the only time in the eight interviews and thirty-three hours we'd spend together that he ever got visibly angry with me.

I called Sergeant Rohn and asked that he bring a cigarette to my location, just outside the Ashland County Jail's secure and controlled sally port door. The jail was relatively new, having opened in February 2001. The facility is a state-of-the art, modular-style jail, with a capacity of 127 inmates and a staff of 34 officers.

As we waited in the patrol vehicle for Sergeant Rohn to arrive, Grate began remarking about being in jail near other inmates. He stated that he imagined people would want to kill him, but he said he wasn't intimidated by them. He talked about how "someone has to take care of" particular inmates and he had something to look forward to. He had earlier stated that he was looking forward to being in prison with "child molesters" and that it would be a "change of pace."

"If I really rededicate my life to Jesus, I really can't do that," he said, referring to killing other inmates.

I agreed with him, as did Lieutenant Smart.

"I've done some bad things," Grate continued. He then asked if he was going to be kept in a cell all by himself.

Lieutenant Smart related that he would be by himself for at least a day or so; then he would likely join the general prison population.

"I did wrong," Grate stated. "I killed people."

We watched from the cruiser as Sergeant Rohn pulled up, went into the jail, got a cigarette from one of the guards, and came back out. He gave it to me, and I passed it on to Grate. The three of us got out and stood on the sidewalk just outside the jail as Grate puffed away on the cigarette. He was still handcuffed, but he was no longer shirtless. During one of our breaks, one of the officers had located a shirt for him to wear. It was a bit ill fitting, but it served its purpose.

"Am I redeemed?" I asked, regarding the cigarette.

Grate chuckled and stated, "Yeah. You're forgiven. I'm a killer . . . but I trust you."

Sergeant Rohn and I watched Grate as he continued to smoke. "I know this is my last cigarette," he said, taking a deep drag.

He told me he would kite me to talk with me. It seemed he was coming to terms with his situation. "It has been eating me alive," he remarked. He told us he wanted to "find purpose somewhere." Then, without prompting, he turned the conversation back to Candice and the discovery of her body in the ravine.

Grate said he thought he heard someone at the crime scene say that her body was "all bones."

"I didn't think it took that fast for all her meat to be gone, right?" Grate asked. "A lot of flies, heat, I don't know, I thought bodies stayed . . . I don't know."

There he was talking about the flies again.

He suggested the idea had been planted in his head when he was a child and had watched programs on the Discovery Channel about how bodies decompose. He indicated he was enthralled by the decomposition of bodies.

He said he thought he had done Candice "a favor" by killing her. "I didn't want to play God. She just needed it . . . If I didn't do it, someone was gonna do it in the wrong situation. It's how I felt. . . . But there's no excuse for what I've done."

He admitted that after he killed Candice, he wasn't himself and hadn't been the same since.

"It would have been pretty stressful," Sergeant Rohn acknowledged.

"It's sad," Grate stated. "It's just sad how we are all designed in the first place. We're still basically perfect, but we gotta deal with a bunch of bullshit. It's just temporary anyways.

"I'll be okay," he added. "Have to be, always, even out here. Seriously, probably being locked up is probably an easier life than it is out here. I like the challenge. I'm kind of like a starving artist," he said, referencing his onetime trade as a woodworker. He said he had made about "two thousand things, personalized names in wood." He then went on to describe some of his creations.

"With the way the economy is, it is really challenging," he lamented.

At that moment, Grate noticed that there were several corrections officers waiting near the sally port doors. He asked if they were waiting for him. "Waiting for a killer," he commented and began to cry. "I'm facing the fact that I'm a killer . . . for real. It's okay, though."

It was just about 6:30 p.m. when corrections officers led Grate into the jail for processing. My interaction with him had stretched over eight hours. And in that time, he had confessed to kidnapping and raping Jane, killing Candice, Elizabeth, and Stacey, and a variety of lesser crimes, and I'd also visited the site where he had placed Candice's body. But my day wasn't over.

I now needed to return to the police station to conduct briefings and follow-up. From there, I would go to the Covert Court crime scene to meet with BCI agents and fellow officers to relate what had been described to me by Shawn Grate during his confession. I would need to do a sweep of the residence to identify any items that he mentioned during our interview that might be of relevance to our case.

13

A Narrow Escape

My last stop that Tuesday was the Covert Court crime scene, and it was already late in the day when I arrived. There were many people—most of them local residents—standing outside the crime scene tape, trying to find out what was happening and get a glimpse of investigators in evidence-collection suits and booties entering and exiting the home.

BCI agents as well as APD officers were still on scene. High-ranking superiors from BCI and APD, the coroner, Dr. Dale Thomae, and various involved agencies were also on Covert Court.

I entered the house wearing protective gear, escorted by BCI special agent Ed Staley. The odor of the decomposed bodies was beyond powerful. Wearing a hazmat suit with a mask lessened the smell, but certainly didn't remove it. It was hot inside the suit, and the combination of the heat, the stench, and what we were witnessing inside the house was overwhelming. I stopped for a second to compose myself and then proceeded to search the house.

I made my way through the rooms, pointing out items I recognized from my conversations with Grate as related to the abduction of Jane Doe. I identified the Band-Aids and medical cream Jane said she'd given him prior to her abduction. During my interview with her, she related that Grate had turned up at her apartment late one evening asking if he could borrow some first aid items. He claimed that he had a wound on his chin from helping a friend's girlfriend move. More likely, he had sustained his injuries during his struggle with Stacey Stanley Hicks.

I also identified the homemade rods Grate had described during the interrogation.

As I walked through the house, I reflected on what Grate had told me during our interview. I reviewed the upstairs bedroom where Elizabeth's naked body had been found under a pile of clothing.

When I first entered the room, I saw a bed that had restraints connected to the mattress handles. I was immediately taken aback by the fact that Grate had said nothing about tying a woman up in that bed. My next thought was about Jane telling me that she could hear a repetitive noise upstairs. Was this another indication that there were more victims? Someone he hadn't yet revealed or disclosed?

The closet doorframe still had remnants of the black duct tape he'd used in a failed attempt to contain the malodorous smell. On the door itself, there were fly larvae and maggots.

I saw the basement, which still held the mounds of trash that covered Stacey's body.

I observed the bodies of Elizabeth Griffith and Stacey Stanley Hicks after they were removed from the home. Elizabeth was nude, as Grate had indicated. Stacey was partly clothed; her tattoos and fresh manicure were visible. An autopsy would later reveal that both women likely died of cervical compression by the method of asphyxia. Grate had strangled them.

When I exited the house, I noticed several people in the assembled crowd waving their arms to get my attention. One woman, who identified herself as Tracy, was standing on the corner of Fourth and North Center Streets, just outside the taped-off perimeter, and she requested to meet with me.

Tracy was crying and told me she, too, could have been a victim of Shawn Grate. She had met Grate at the apartment of a friend several weeks earlier, and he'd given her his phone number. The two had spoken on the phone, and one day, the two went out walking. She recalled that Grate took her to a home on Orange Street, almost a mile from the house on Covert Court. He claimed to reside there, as he was "helping an elderly person" who lived there. Eventually, he invited her to his Covert Court "residence."

She explained that she went alone, and the two engaged in casual conversation. "He had a bowl of pills on a table in the main room where his stuff is," she said. "Like a living room, but there's a bed."

She was referring to the small room where Grate had held Jane captive for three days.

Tracy said she declined the pills, telling Grate she didn't use them. At first, she said, Grate was easy to talk to, because he "seemed like he cared." He asked her a variety of questions about her life but didn't reveal much about his own. She told him she was single and wasn't dating anyone.

I wondered if he had been trying to gauge whether there was anyone in this woman's life who would miss her if he killed her like he had killed the other three women.

While in the house, Tracy said she sat on the bed with him. "There was no other place to sit," she explained. Grate offered to massage her shoulders, and she allowed him to do so. After a couple of minutes, she said he began to act strangely, and she grew leery. He had beautiful eyes, she stated, but they now looked "weird" at that point in their meeting.

I asked her to elaborate.

She told me that when he was massaging her, something "seemed wrong" with him, so she turned around to face him, and that's when she noticed he was "looking at her weird."

"He looked scary, and like he was mad," she recalled.

That's when she told him she had to leave, and she ran out the door. Grate didn't follow her.

After that, she removed his phone number from her cell, and the two had no further contact. I made a mental note to follow up on the lead Tracy had just provided about the "elderly" resident and the home on Orange Street. Would we find another victim there?

It was after dark when I left the Covert Court crime scene and returned to the police station, where I sat at my desk and came up with a to-do list, a list of tasks regarding potential interviews, as well as possible items that would need to be secured as evidence.

That night, Shawn Grate's arrest was the lead story on all the local news programs across the state. My fear was becoming a reality; the city of Ashland was fast becoming known as the home of a serial killer.

With all the news coverage, my phone was blowing up with texts and calls from people checking in on me. When things go wrong and things happen, you just know it's your people reaching out to say, "Are you okay?," "Stay steady," "I'm proud of you." You feel surrounded—at least in spirit—by the ones who love and care about you. I was fortunate that I had so many family, friends, and colleagues who cared about me.

Lieutenant Geoff Thomas, who had retired just before the Grate case broke, was one of the first to reach out to me by phone. Geoff was like a dad to me. He also happened to be a real-life friend of my father's. He was a dear friend, and he told me to stay focused.

"You know what you're doing," he said. "You're fine. This is what I trained you for."

Retired Ashland Police Division sergeant Tom Lattanzi also

checked in on me, as did three women I worked with on a regular basis. Victim coordinator Ruth Rafeld of the Ashland County Prosecutor's Office called me routinely throughout the case, reminding me to practice self-care, as did my close friend Kelly Van Driest, the court advocate from the Safe Haven shelter, and Leta Plantz, a mental health professional who I had worked with many times over the years.

They understood the emotional strain that a serious case like this could put on someone; they'd all been through some tragic cases of their own.

Ashland County prosecutor Chris Tunnell gave me the same advice when I'd briefed him on the case earlier in the day. "You're doing a hell of a job," he told me. "Make sure you take care of yourself." He was supportive throughout the investigation.

Of course, there were also multiple missed calls from my sister, Tamra, and from my mom and dad. I made sure to return those right away. No matter how old your children are, you still worry about them, and it was no different in my family.

I remember calling my mom and dad on my way home. I am not sure why. Good or bad in your life, you run back to your parents. I have done that in the past after a case. That night, I wanted to hear their voices. And I got to hear both of them.

My parents had already heard some things about the case. So, when my mom picked up the phone, the first thing she said was, "I knew it was you in that room with him."

My mom put the call on speakerphone, and my dad immediately chimed in.

"Were you alone in the room with him?" he inquired. "Who else was there? Were you armed?" Both he and my mom seemed concerned about my safety.

My dad told me not to let my guard down and to be ready.

Hearing them helped to ground me. And I appreciated their

parting words. "Get some sleep," they told me. "You're going to have work to do tomorrow."

It was pretty late when I arrived home that night. The first thing I did was hug my family, which always brings me back to my center.

I was aware of the magnitude of the case, but when you are living it, you don't get to process it at your own pace. I recall being worried that my children would be impacted if they knew my proximity to someone the likes of Shawn Grate.

One of the hardest parts of being a police officer is not taking the job home with me. Parenting is difficult in itself, let alone adding a badge. Years ago, I made a promise to myself that I would try to maintain normalcy for my kids, no matter what might be happening on the job. I had had an amazing childhood and tried to replicate that as best I could. My kids have all been involved in school sports and after-school activities, and my view is always to be a mom first.

I can't say it hasn't been a struggle, and I have failed sometimes. But somehow through the grace of God and a supportive family network, we have been able to make it all work. I'm a mom who has the pulse of her children, too, which helps. I will admit to changing the day the Easter Bunny comes due to difficult shifts, but more often than not, I've had support from people at work and colleagues who are willing to make holiday schedules work so I can be with my kids. I want my children to remember me as a mom first and as a detective second. I want them to remember the smell of cookies baking in the oven and food cooking on the stove.

I don't think I ever had an epiphany that I was going to be a cop. But looking back, I know that I am right where I am supposed to be. I have my parents to thank for that because of my mother's teachings to protect those who can't protect themselves and my dad instilling in me that being a girl can't keep me from doing anything.

Being a police officer, and then a detective, required a fair amount of creativity to juggle my daily work and my homelife. I enjoyed, and indeed needed, to put a home-cooked meal on the table every night (even if it meant throwing something together in a Crock-Pot). It wasn't an easy life, but somehow Dan and I found a way to make it all work.

We were also lucky in that we had a great support system, too. My mom and dad lived about ten minutes away from us in my childhood home. My sister was also close by. Dan hailed from a big family, and someone was always around to help pitch in when we got in a bind.

Dan and I were lucky that we both worked in law enforcement; we had a shared understanding of both the demands and the challenges of the job.

What I failed to recognize is that my children catch nuances, they have that skill set, that ability, and even knowing how something impacts me can impact them. I didn't want the Grate case to be one of the things that was going to shape their lives like it was certainly shaping mine.

That night, I was not forthcoming with my children when they asked me what I'd been working on. I gave them my pat response: "I was helping people."

In the days ahead, they would confront me for not being forthcoming.

DAY TWO

September 14, 2016

14

"The Lord Is Our Rock"

My fellow officers had spent the night checking in on local women who may have been at risk or fit Grate's victim profile. These were people we interacted with on a regular basis, and we wanted to make sure they were okay. APD officers James Coey and Lee Eggeman, both military veterans, were called in to search the area around the old Hess & Clark factory buildings with cadaver dogs, as well as a dilapidated factory tower where Grate claimed to have slept in the days before squatting at the Covert Court address. Grate had made concerning remarks about his desire to harm trespassers he saw walking through the buildings while he was staying there.

Because we now had a serial murderer on our hands, multiple police departments across Ohio were busy reviewing their missing persons and cold case files, wondering if Grate may have been responsible for abductions and murders in their jurisdictions.

The Richland County Prosecutor's Office was reviewing the case regarding Grate's claim to have murdered Candice Cunningham as well as setting the fire at the house on State Route 430, as those crimes had occurred in their jurisdiction.

One of the first things I did that Wednesday morning was meet with his live victim, Jane Doe, for a follow-up conversation. In light of her situation, we had her at an undisclosed location. During our conversation, Jane provided additional details about her ordeal. She revealed that during her captivity, Grate used a razor to shave a design in her pubic region. She spoke of the pain she was still experiencing related to the repeated sexual assaults. She recounted the excruciating pain from the blows to the head and her lack of physical strength in comparison to Grate's.

She described him as being muscular and strong. She stated that when he was strangling her, she believed she was going to die. She also expressed fear of disease and her heartache for the victims who did not survive.

She also spoke at length about her faith and expressed her concern for the officers who were working the case. She again brought up her belief that "the Christian" was going to find her. "I knew he would come back around," she said.

She was referring to Officer Dorsey, who I knew was devout.

The religious threads running through this case would continue. Remarkably, Jane's faith would become even stronger after her nightmare with Shawn Grate.

During our visit, she asked me if any of Grate's other victims had been found alive. I didn't have the heart to tell her about Elizabeth, not yet. I was focused on her well-being after all she had been through.

Eager to comfort Jane, I assured her that I was there for her. "I've got you," I said. "I am going to be your rock."

Boy, did she put me in check.

She very kindly quoted scripture. Then stated, "Oh, you are not my rock. The Lord is *our* rock."

At one point in our conversation, she revisited the strange noise she'd heard coming from the upstairs of Grate's house on the first night she was there and then again the next day.

"What did the noise sound like?" I asked.

"It was like a human who wasn't able to talk, who was pounding," she recounted.

I was aware that police detectives and BCI agents had thoroughly searched the residence the day the case broke, and no other live victims were found. However, the fact that Jane recalled hearing a noise during her captivity remained unexplained.

Jane told me that on her third day in captivity, Grate drugged her with strong muscle relaxers, and for a period of time, she was "out of it." That's when Grate left the house. After he returned, she said she didn't notice the noise again.

I would visit with Jane again the following evening. People in town were speculating about the case, and there were news crews all around. I wanted to tell her that Elizabeth was gone before she learned about it some other way.

She cried upon learning the news. Then she prayed with me, telling me this was my "purpose."

As I was leaving, she handed me several Bible verses that she wanted me to read to the guys back at the police station, in particular, those officers who had been involved in the case. One she emphasized was Ephesians 6:12: "For we do not wrestle against flesh and blood, but against principalities, against powers, against the rulers of the darkness of this age, against spiritual hosts of wickedness in the heavenly places."

A few days later, I would visit Jane again, this time accompanied by Detective Evans, so that we could take her back home to her apartment to retrieve some personal effects. During the drive, I suddenly realized that Evans had taken the most direct route—meaning that we would go directly past the house on Covert Court where Grate had held her captive. Almost immediately, he recognized the mistake and shot me a look that telegraphed he knew it was too late to change direction.

I started talking to divert Jane's attention toward us, and she did not appear to notice the crime scene as we drove past. She was kind enough that even if she had noticed, she probably wouldn't have said anything.

We always try to be sensitive to our survivors, and Detective Evans and I later talked about how it could have had a negative impact on her.

My next stop that Wednesday morning was the Salvation Army's Kroc Center. I wanted to speak to people who may have interacted with Elizabeth to see if I could confirm some of the details of Grate's confession. I found a couple of lunch-goers who said they knew her. They both wept and hugged me.

I asked one of them to describe Elizabeth.

Her depiction amazed me. She explained that Elizabeth was very sound in her faith. She was also childlike, in that if she got upset or scared, she would sing the Christian hymn "Jesus Loves Me" over and over. I was astounded. Apparently, Grate had been truthful when he'd recounted his encounter with Griffith.

The other woman told me that it was profoundly important to Elizabeth that she forgive people who wronged her. She said Elizabeth forgave everyone because that was what the Lord wanted her to do. Once again, I realized Grate had painted an accurate portrayal when he'd said Elizabeth recited Luke 23:34 as he was strangling her.

I couldn't find anyone at the center who remembered Grate or had seen him with Elizabeth. But I had my answer as to Grate's honesty when it came to certain details about his crimes.

Argil Stanley, Stacey's uncle, was waiting for me in the lobby when I arrived at the police station after my visit to the Kroc Center. He was upset and expressed his grief over the news about his niece. I did my best to comfort him.

He and his family had done everything they could to try to

locate Stacey. Sadly, their efforts had not yielded the results they had hoped for. Grate had admitted to killing their beloved family member just one hour after she arrived at his house. There was nothing anyone could have done to change that outcome. By the time authorities learned that Stacey was missing, Grate had already ended her life.

The rest of my day was spent in meetings and briefings, first at the Ashland County Prosecutor's Office, where we briefed Prosecutor Tunnell's team on the facts of the case and discussed the investigation.

During the meeting, I related that Grate had admitted to breaking into the Island Trading Post in Mifflin that past summer, so I coordinated with Lieutenant Smart from the Ashland County Sheriff's Office to obtain a copy of the report related to that case.

Island Trading Post owner Curt Conner told police that someone entered the building from the roof by kicking a hole in the ceiling. He stated that the culprit stole potato chips, toilet paper, brass knuckles, two Tasers, and a blue-and-white cooler.

In the days after Grate's arrest, Sheriff E. Wayne Risner's deputies searched the woods around Mifflin, where Grate said he'd erected one of his forts. Grate had told us that this was the fort he had taken Jane to see. Deputies located the makeshift shelter in the woods about two hundred yards from County Road 1908. Inside, they found clothing, knives, trinkets, and cell phone chargers they collected as evidence.

Grate had also told us about a second fort he'd erected in the woods off Cook Road in Richland County, where he and Candice stayed after they were evicted. But he'd deconstructed that one.

In the days to come, as part of our investigation, two of our officers, Abe Neumann and patrol supervisor Jerry Bloodhart, headed to Elizabeth's apartment complex armed with metal detectors and Grate's hand-drawn map.

During our interview, Grate had admitted to tossing Elizabeth's house key into some brush on the outskirts of her apartment complex the day he returned there to retrieve the Yahtzee pad and other potential evidence that linked him to her.

The area around the complex had grass and brush. Determined to locate the key, the men began at opposite ends of the location and worked a grid pattern toward the center. They were well into the process when Officer Jeremy Jarvis showed up, got out of his patrol car, and walked to the search area, his signature toothpick in his mouth.

"What are you guys looking for?" he asked.

The officers explained that they were searching for the key to Elizabeth's apartment that Grate had ditched somewhere in the brush.

Jarvis smiled, raised his arm, and pointed to a spot in the grass. "Is that what you're looking for?" he asked.

The guys would later joke about how Jeremy had solved our missing key dilemma within seconds of arriving on scene in quintessential "Jarvis fashion."

Once back at the police station, I participated in a lengthy briefing with Captain Lay, Sergeant Alting, BCI agent Staley, Detective Evans, and our chief, David Marcelli.

At one point, someone informed me that there was a young woman in the lobby who'd requested to speak with me. I recognized her immediately from the neighborhood. I'd talk to her sometimes when I was out community policing. Her name was Brittany; she was seventeen and had a young child. She lived with her mother in one of the apartment complexes on Orange Street. She was a petite blonde with a perfect complexion and looked younger than her age.

She wanted to tell me about her interactions with Shawn Grate. Although I knew her to be somewhat feisty, she was presenting this day as extremely subdued and fearful. I took her to an interview off the lobby so that we could converse in private. She told me that she first met Grate about two weeks earlier when she was outside her apartment complex with her mother, and he'd walked past them.

Not long after, her mother went inside, leaving Brittany outside by herself. Grate must have seen that she was alone because he returned within a couple of minutes and struck up a conversation, she said. He asked her if she would like to "hang out" sometime and gave her his phone number. He told her he had an apartment nearby and tried to get her to go with him right then.

But Brittany declined. Something seemed off about him, she said, so she cut the conversation short and deleted his number as soon as he left.

A few days later, she saw him again, this time near the Fourth Street laundromat. She was carrying some laundry, and he offered to help her. He again asked if she wanted to go over to his place, and again, she turned him down. Although she was safe, she was visibly shaken and verbalized her relief at having avoided a potentially deadly encounter.

I wondered how many other Tracys and Brittanys were out there, women like Jane, who had escaped with their lives. I also worried about the ones we didn't yet know about who may not have been as lucky.

Not long after my meeting with Brittany, a detective found me in my office and let me know that he'd done an initial analysis of Grate's cell phone and had discovered thirteen videos involving Jane Doe and Stacey Stanley Hicks.

I viewed the videos. There were several of Grate's interactions with Stacey. In one, Stacey can be heard remarking that he had already forced her to engage in sex prior to the recording. There were also multiple videos of Grate sexually assaulting Jane. And there was a recording of an older woman we didn't recognize. In the video, Grate is masturbating, and the woman, a brunette, is seated on a sofa across the room. At one point in the video, they are talking about phones. According to the time stamp, the video had been shot recently. Who was this woman, and was she still alive?

The evidence strongly suggested that there were still other victims out there, perhaps discarded in some ravine or abandoned warehouse. I feared that Shawn Grate had more to tell me and that there were more places that we might visit together. That fear of finding other victims, perhaps someone who may still be bound to a bed or locked away somewhere, is what drove me forward. The fear of finding more victims, whether they were alive or dead, is what haunted me throughout the case.

And, if I'm being honest, that fear continues to weigh on me.

DAY THREE

September 15, 2016

Two Covert Court homes built in the 1800s as part of a property called Potter's Addition. Nearly 140 years later, Shawn Grate squatted in one of the two identical homes, where he committed his atrocities. *(Courtesy of Joe Lyons, Photographer/Reporter)*

Detective Sergeant Curt Dorsey, along with Lt. Tim Shreffler and Sgt. Jim Cox, located and arrested Shawn Grate after his kidnapped victim called 911. Sgt. Dorsey escorts the suspect, Shawn Grate, to his patrol car *(Courtesy of Joe Lyons, Photographer/Reporter)*

Bible found in a Mansfield City residence where Shawn Grate lived months before his arrest. Once arrested and incarcerated at the Ashland County Jail, Grate requested that Mager get him a new Bible. *(Courtesy of Joe Lyons, Photographer/Reporter)*

A shirtless Shawn Grate in the early hours of his interview with Detective Kim Mager. *(Courtesy of the City of Ashland)*

The Ashland community gathered in prayer as they awaited news regarding the search warrant results at the Covert Court crime scene. *(Courtesy of Joe Lyons, Photographer/Reporter)*

Detective Mager and Lt. Garry Alting interview citizens who approached the crime scene during execution of a search warrant. Those interviews would prove valuable during the investigation. *(Courtesy of Joe Lyons, Photographer/Reporter)*

West 2nd Street in Mansfield, Ohio, the residence where Shawn Grate lived for months before his arrest. He had rented the home for two years. Grate's landlord described him as "easygoing." *(Courtesy of Joe Lyons, Photographer/Reporter)*

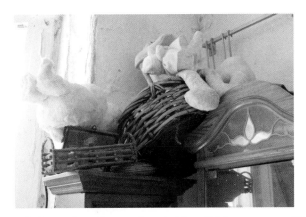

Stuffed animals located at Shawn Grate's Mansfield apartment. He was not known to have any children at that location. A large number of stuffed animals were also found in the Covert Court residence where he was arrested. He denied victimizing children but admitted that he had "thoughts" about children. *(Courtesy of Joe Lyons, Photographer/Reporter)*

Detective Mager outside the crime scene. Evidence had been collected during multiple search warrants at the Covert Court residence. *(Courtesy of Joe Lyons, Photographer/Reporter)*

Captain Craig Kiley, Officer Aaron Welch, and BCI Agent Staley at the Covert Court scene. *(Courtesy of Joe Lyons, Photographer/Reporter)*

Family and community members standing en masse near the Covert Court home. *(Courtesy of Joe Lyons, Photographer/Reporter)*

Community members created a memorial at the Covert Court scene. The collection of stuffed animals, candles, notes, and photos grew in the days and weeks after the case broke. *(Courtesy of Joe Lyons, Photographer/Reporter)*

Forensic facial reconstruction of the victim Shawn Grate called "Dana." The model was created by Ohio BCI's forensic artist, Samantha Molnar, using Grate's memory of the young woman. The woman was later identified as Dana Nicole Lowrey, 23, of Minden, Louisiana. *(Courtesy of Samantha Molnar, Criminal Intelligence Analyst and Forensic Artist)*

Still-video grab of Shawn Grate in prison garb while in the custody of Ashland County. *(Courtesy of the City of Ashland)*

Shawn Grate in a holding cell of the Ashland County jail demonstrating on Det. Brian Evans the chokehold he used to strangle one of his victims. *(Courtesy of the City of Ashland)*

Shawn Grate arriving at Ashland County Common Pleas Court for a hearing. He is escorted by Deputy Shannon Mahoney (left) and Chief Deputy Carl Richert (right) from the Ashland County Sheriff's Office. *(Courtesy of Joe Lyons, Photographer/Reporter)*

Simonson Construction Services demolished the Covert Court residence at no cost. Citizens gathered to watch, hoping to gain closure. *(Courtesy of Joe Lyons, Photographer/Reporter)*

Officers Lee Eggeman and Aaron Kline flank Ashland County Sheriff E. Wayne Risner as Simonson Construction demolishes the Covert Court property. Detective Brian Evans stands in the background as Ashland County Prosecutor Christopher Tunnell can be seen with his head lowered. *(Courtesy of Joe Lyons, Photographer/Reporter)*

As layers of the Covert Court home were removed, the rooms where the heinous crimes were committed became visible to bystanders. *(Courtesy of Joe Lyons, Photographer/Reporter)*

Detective Mager's sons, Corbin and Reed Mager. *(Kim Mager)*

Detective Kim Mager and her daughter, Macy. *(Courtesy of Dan Mager)*

15

Murdered over Magazines

On Thursday, September 15, 2016, I filed formal charges against Shawn Grate for the kidnapping and rape of Jane Doe and the murders of Elizabeth Griffith and Stacey Stanley Hicks.

There was an interest in learning more about this stranger who was squatting in our community, and reporters were hard at work digging up his past. Interviews with Grate's former high school classmates suggested his youthful good looks, piercing blue eyes, and athletic build had made him popular with the girls at River Valley High School.

"He was charming. He was always smiling, and he had those big blue eyes," one former classmate told a local news reporter. "All the girls liked Shawn."

It was a balmy seventy-five degrees, and the American flag atop the courthouse was blowing in the breeze as I climbed the cement steps to the Ashland County Clerk of Courts, a two-story limestone government building on West Second Street, just a couple of blocks from the Covert Court crime scene. Detective Brian Evans accompanied me there for the filing.

Two days had passed since Grate's arrest, and interest in the case continued to grow. There was an inordinate number of media outside the building, mirroring what we'd just seen at police headquarters. Satellite trucks were lined up along the street, with reporters standing in front of TV cameras doing live remotes about Grate's impending arraignment.

Detective Evans and I were in plain clothes—Evans was in jeans, a Harley sweatshirt, and Oakley sunglasses, and I wore slacks and a pullover. We managed to elude the reporters waiting in the hallway outside the Clerk's Office—they were out-of-towners and did not recognize us as being linked to the case. But one member of our local media spotted us and slinked into the office, trying not to alert anyone else.

When the others saw him stand up, they followed him into the office, where I was signing the charges.

Once the charges were filed, Evans and I walked over to the jail to serve Grate with the criminal complaint. We decided we wouldn't present it to him right away. We had some questions we needed to ask him; we were hoping to learn the identity of the older woman we had seen in the video on his phone.

There was also some question about how Grate had strangled one of his victims. The method of strangulation becomes important in an autopsy. We needed clarification so there would be no question when comparing Grate's statement and the autopsy report.

Detective Evans and I had worked many cases together over the years. We were among the more senior members on the force, having been hired on the same day twenty years earlier. We'd worked side by side on so many cases and could finish each other's sentences. Evans was fierce in his niche. He worked narcotics cases primarily, but our casework often intersected, so I was both familiar and comfortable with his interviewing style.

Grate's bond hearing would happen via video from the Corrections Division. This was not unusual, as Ashland County Common Pleas Court judge Ronald Forsthoefel was forward thinking when it came to technology, believing it was a way to make things run more efficiently.

Detective Evans and I would be meeting Grate in an interview room in the booking area of the Ashland County Sheriff's Office. The space is small, and the acoustics are a little bit hollow sounding. Like the interview rooms at the police station, this room had minimal furnishings with just a table and a few chairs. There was a small window about three-quarters of the way up the door, so corrections officers could monitor interactions inside the room from the hallway.

We were not permitted to carry our weapons into the booking area, so neither Evans nor I was armed. As always, I was carrying my digital recorder with me and intended to capture the interview for the official record.

As the two of us walked from the courthouse to the sheriff's office, we talked about the complaint that we'd obtained and how to handle our meeting with Grate. We decided we would not bring the charging documents into the room with us. Instead, we would wait until after he had answered our questions—and then serve him with the charges as we walked him to the designated area of the jail for his arraignment.

But our plan would soon change.

Grate seemed pleased to see me when he entered the room flanked by corrections officers. Wearing a yellow, prison-issued jumpsuit, he was clean-shaven and looked somewhat rested. As soon as he sat down, he stared at me.

I didn't say anything initially. I was trying to read his disposition.

Detective Evans broke the silence and jumped in to introduce himself.

Grate simply acknowledged him with a nod.

I opened the interview with my signature question: "Are you okay?"

To which Grate replied, "Yeah, hanging in there. How are you doing?"

I hadn't expected him to inquire about me, nor did I anticipate an apology of any sort, but he offered one.

"I'm sorry," he said. Perhaps this was his way of acknowledging that he had drawn me into a maelstrom of crime and tragedy.

Grate told us that he had seen himself on the news. "It's good to face it," he said of his situation.

I explained that we wanted to ask him to clarify some points. Because he was in jail, I had to first read him the Miranda rights.

Grate nodded in agreement, giving me a green light to proceed.

I reminded him that the Ashland Police Division had his phone. "We noticed a video where you are talking with a woman with brown hair." I told him that in the video, they were talking about phones. What I didn't say was that his penis is exposed in the footage, and he is manipulating it.

"I don't fool around with the lady," he stated. "She just likes to look at me."

He identified the woman, although we would later learn the name he provided was not her real name. She was from Ashland. Grate said he met her at the "Catholic place where you eat," an apparent reference to either the Kroc Center, where he'd met Jane, or a local church that provides meals.

He said that when the two were together, they "talked" and "even held hands."

"We thought about dating a little bit, but she just got out of a relationship, so she don't fool around," he told us. "There was never nothing, no sexual assault or anything with her."

Grate said the woman liked to look at him when he was nude.

She watched him, and he recorded it so that he could "study her more."

"She is alive and well," he added. He then admitted that she'd helped him sell the outdated cigarettes he'd stolen from the gas station in Ashland.

We would later locate the woman and confirm that she was okay.

We talked about her for a bit, then I informed Grate that, after today, I wasn't sure I would be able to talk to him anymore. Once a defendant is assigned an attorney, they are typically advised to cease all discussions with police. "Is there anything we haven't talked about yet that you might need to get off your chest?" I asked.

Grate's blue eyes widened. "Mm-hmm," he affirmed.

"What would that be?" I queried.

"Been thinking about it, but I can't get the year right, but I'm sure you can help me get the year right. It's been . . . Two thousand and six or five or four. I can't place the time . . . Two thousand and five?

"It's a cold case," he added. "They've already found her."

Two thousand and five? That was more than a decade ago. Had the killings begun then? I shot Evans a look; we had another one. But what did he mean by saying that the body had already been found?

Grate volunteered that the incident had occurred in Marion County, in the neighborhood where he had grown up. "It's kind of weird how it happened. In a way, I felt like I had to do it . . . do something. Got out of control . . . I ain't gonna lie, it did."

Grate's account came in layers. It started off in a staccato-like fashion with Grate spitting out fragments of sentences. There were some tangible details at the beginning, and it was unclear where the conversation was going. The interview soon grew into a full-fledged murder confession.

Grate claimed his mother was home sick one afternoon when

a woman selling magazines turned up at the front door. He had mentioned this magazine salesperson during our initial interview at the police station, but he'd never returned to the topic. It was still early in my interactions with him, and I didn't yet know that this was his MO—to drop hints for me to follow. Apparently, this had been one of them.

From what I could decipher, the woman had sold Grate's mother magazine subscriptions, which she paid for in advance, but she never received the order.

"That's all she complained about," Grate grumbled. "So, I ran and I found her, and she tried to sell *me* magazines as well . . . so I took her with me . . . to my grandparents' house, where I was living."

Grate explained that at the time, he was living at his paternal grandparents' house in Marion County. His grandparents had passed away, and he was remodeling their beige, one-story residence, which his father intended to sell.

"What's her name?" I asked.

"I'm thinking her name is Dana." Grate said he wasn't sure, but he believed that "Dana" was correct, although he couldn't provide a last name.

Detective Evans and I had no idea if this was the woman's real name, but we took Grate's lead for the remainder of the interview and began calling this new victim *Dana*.

"How did she die?" I asked.

"I strangled her," Grate replied matter-of-factly. "Wait, no . . . I didn't. I strangled her first, and then I dragged her down to the basement after she passed out, and I panicked, and I ran upstairs. I grabbed a knife. I stabbed her in the neck."

"This was the first time," he added, suggesting that Dana was the first person he'd killed.

The case had just broadened again, not only by miles but by over a decade of time.

Detective Evans asked Grate if he could describe Dana's physical appearance, but his recollection was scant. He estimated her age to be around twenty-six; she was a white female with a thin build and brown hair. He couldn't remember anything specific about her face or what she was wearing. "It's almost forgotten," he said.

Then, in the next breath, he admitted that he had seen a story on the news about Dana's body being found a couple of years after the murder, but as far as he knew, she had not yet been identified. He claimed that she told him she was from "somewhere else." But he suggested she could have been lying.

He said that over the years, he tried to "do some type of research to figure out her name," but he "wasn't able to keep up with the situation."

At this point, I asked Grate how much time went by between the time Dana sold his mother the magazines and the time he located her again.

"A few months," he said. He then recounted their two interactions. He said the first time he met Dana was when she showed up at his mother's place and his mother invited her inside.

"They took forever and forever," he recalled, referring to the young woman's sales pitch and eventual transaction. At one point, he went around to the side of the house to smoke a cigarette. "I don't smoke in front of my mom," he offered.

When he returned to the living room, his mother was still combing through the catalogs of magazines and books, making her selections. The *Cat in the Hat* series by Dr. Suess was among the items she chose. Grate recalled that she paid by check, but he wasn't sure about the amount.

He grew agitated recalling his mother's irritation over the months when the items failed to arrive. "All I hear is my mom complaining and griping and like, 'God is gonna condemn her' and . . . 'She's gonna meet the right person.'"

"How long was it supposed to take?" I asked.

"About a month," Grate replied. He explained that three months had already passed when he spotted Dana near the Catholic school in Marion, once again selling her books and magazines. "I wasn't out looking for her . . . it was random, like meant to be," he claimed. "I just talked to her . . . I don't know. It's weird."

Grate said he had no intention of harming the woman when the two met that day. But Dana made a fatal mistake when she tried her sales pitch on him. That took the conversation in a bad, and dangerous, direction. "I realized she was trying to do the same thing to me . . . sell me magazines. I told her I probably won't get 'em."

Grate sniggered, recalling that Dana assured him they would be delivered. So he pretended to go along with the sale, selecting several sports magazines. His tone grew sarcastic as he described Dana's follow-up sales pitch. She said she was willing to "give him a break" on the price, offering fifty dollars' worth of merchandise for twenty-five—but only if he paid her right then and there.

"It was such a deal," he scoffed, adding that she extended the offer *after* he told her he only had twenty-five dollars. "Awfully convenient," he mocked.

Grate said he had already made up his mind that she was "pulling my leg."

He then told Dana that he didn't have money on him, so he invited her to accompany him back to his grandparents' place, ostensibly so he could pay her. "I lied, but she already had irritated me and someone I supposedly care about," he said, referring to his mother. "I do try to care about my family, but it's really hard sometimes."

In his next breath, Grate once again remarked about getting a "lethal injection, eventually," for all his crimes. "Two years from now?"

He agreed to draw us a diagram of the home and describe how

the murder took place. He indicated that he and Dana entered his grandparents' house through the front door and went through the family room to the kitchen, where they sat on the barstools for a minute. He claimed he "felt her bullshit, and I felt enraged."

He said as a ruse, he invited Dana to his bedroom so he could show her his "ball cards." He explained that he had a large collection of baseball cards. "Oh, neat," Dana remarked, following him down the hallway.

"So, that's when I confronted her. 'So, you gonna rip me off like you did my mom?'" he asked her.

Grate said Dana feigned innocence. "Who's your mom?" she asked in Grate's retelling of the meeting.

He said he told her, "Oh . . . so you do it to a lot of people? . . . I was like, 'You con. You're, you know, gonna take my money and run.' She said, 'Nah.'

"I told her, '[I] could pretty much give you over to God . . . God will take care of ya.'

"I know I'm not God," he added. "I'm not meaning nothing like that."

Grate revealed that Dana "tried to get past me, and I just yanked her up . . . walked her back a little bit to the living room 'cause everything . . . all my stuff was in the bedroom. I didn't have nothing in the other rooms.

"That's when I choked her out, right there," he said, indicating a location on the hand-drawn sketch. He pointed to the area just outside the bedroom door.

"She tried to get out of the bedroom, and I kind of just grabbed her, turned her around, took steps back with her, and choked her out right there, and I believe her nose was bleeding. There was some blood. Could have been from her lip."

He then pointed to another area on the drawing, near the basement steps. "That's where she peed her pants," he stated. He said he then dragged her down the steps. "Right in the middle of the living room, there are the steps right there."

I then had Grate draw a diagram of the basement of the home; he narrated the events that had occurred there using the sketch. He referenced and labeled the washer and dryer, as well as the sump pump. "That took a lot of her blood," he stated, referring to the sump pump.

"She was right here," he continued, drawing an *X* to indicate the position of Dana's body. "And all the blood flowed down the way the floor is designed; it was just streaming right there."

I was about to ask my next question when my cell phone started to buzz. I saw that it was Captain Lay sending me a string of text messages. In one, he asked if Grate was confessing to "another one."

I responded, "Yes."

"Call me," he wrote back.

I read the text as an order from my superior—and not merely a request to call him when we were done. Still, I didn't want to break the continuity of the interview. So I pressed on, hoping my captain would understand.

I realized that time was passing and that we were going to be late or miss Grate's scheduled arraignment. But he had already confessed to one additional murder during this meeting, and I had no idea what was going to come next. I felt that I had no choice but to continue the interview and apologize to the court.

I asked Grate if he had tied Dana up after the murder, as he had done to Elizabeth Griffith. He explained that he kept her body in the house overnight, so he tied it up and then untied it when he was ready to move it from the house the next day.

He said he placed the body in the trunk of his red four-door car, wrapped in a blanket, as he had done with Candice Cunningham's. "Dana I didn't drag with care. I just threw her in the trunk, and I threw her in the woods." He then boasted about doing the "same thing" to this blanket that he had done to the one he used to transport Candice.

"I had a bonfire," he stated.

Grate disclosed that the murder occurred in the afternoon and that he already had a bunch of tree limbs in the backyard, because he had planned on having company over for a bonfire that evening. He described moving a couch in front of the basement door to prevent any of his guests from entering.

"It sounds weird, but I just finished laying her down . . . stabbed her in the neck. I heard someone knocking on the door, so I went [to answer the door] and they [his guests] were bringing wood, so I made sure I was okay, no obvious mess," he remarked, referring to his clothing. He said he told a buddy to take the truck to the back and that he would be right around. "There were only a couple of people at the bonfire, and they stayed outside," he said casually.

"Where did you take her?" I asked.

Grate claimed he stayed up all night, and at about 6:00 a.m., he transported Dana to a remote location off Highway 23, known locally as Linn Hipsher Road. He said he disposed of the body on Marion-Williamsport Road, off of Grace.

To better describe the location, he drew us a map. "It's right off the highway across these tracks past a church to the next road." He described the area as farmland and said he placed Dana on her back with "no clothes on."

Talking about her clothes, he said, "They were soaked . . . they were drenched. I stabbed her right here," he repeated, pointing to his neck. "I'm sure there's dried blood."

When asked, Grate informed us that his father had sold the house where the incident had occurred. But he raised the possibility that there could still be evidence in the home, including Dana's blood. He claimed the pressure he applied to Dana's neck made her nose bleed. She may have hit her nose as well, he added. He said the floors in the living room were hardwood, covered with carpet, and suggested the blood could have soaked through the carpet and stained the wood below.

"It's not my field," he stated. "I don't know what would be recovered through this. It's been years."

Detective Evans inquired about the vehicle Grate had used to transport the body. The question set off a reaction in him—not about Dana but about how he lost his ride.

He claimed that his vehicle was impounded by Bucyrus police after an officer stopped him for having no headlights. During the traffic stop, the officer also learned that Grate had no driver's license and that he was wanted on child support issues.

Grate was also incensed that his former girlfriend, a woman named Christina, was speaking out about him on local TV. He said he'd seen her on one of the news stations after his arrest. "I didn't want to do her any favors," he declared.

It's not clear how Grate's ex-girlfriend wound up on TV. Perhaps she approached a reporter to tell her story. But it's more likely that reporters tracked her down as they sought to piece together Shawn Grate's background and probe what could have prompted him to turn into a rapist and murderer. The story of his arrest was all over the news.

In a moment of levity, Grate said of Christina, "She's still alive." He then provided us with her last name. "Hildreth," he said, "the one on the news running her mouth constantly. She thinks she knows me. She's the one who's crazy."

Grate described their relationship as contentious and admitted to at least one incident of physical violence. "I did knock her hand a little loose once. Lost it."

He claimed the two jumped "right into a relationship" and got an apartment together in Bucyrus not long after Dana's murder, when his dad sold his grandparents' house.

As part of our investigation, police would interview Christina Hildreth. And while Grate was attempting to portray her as the "crazy" one—the same adjective he had used to describe both Candice Cunningham and Stacey Stanley Hicks—Christina's account of their relationship indicated otherwise.

Grate said that he and Christina had begun dating "like a year after" Dana's murder. The timing appeared to match the account provided by Hildreth to both the media and law enforcement.

According to Christina, she was introduced to Grate by her stepsister, who knew him from her job at a gas station in Marion.

Christina said that she began her relationship with Grate right around Christmastime. They wound up living together for five years. Hildreth described Grate as "very charming" at the start. "It was the way he looked at you, like you were so special to him," she told one reporter.

She said Shawn was fun and they really hit it off, but his charm could turn to "wickedness" in a nanosecond.

Christina claimed another side of Grate emerged once they moved in together. "He would get angry over things that most people would let slide," she said. They argued a lot, mostly over the fact that Shawn wouldn't get a job. "He was always doing things to make me late for work, trying to get me fired," she recalled. "He wanted me to quit working and said his dad would pay our bills."

Over time, Grate became jealous and possessive, and he tried to isolate her from her family and friends, she said. At some point, he turned violent. He strangled her several times, but she was too scared to leave. "He always apologized," she said. She said he'd promise it wouldn't happen again.

Predictably, it did. One evening, after she returned home from work, Grate asked her for money. He didn't have a job, but he had "straightened up the house" and thought that Christina ought to have been paying him for the work he'd done. Christina refused and told him he needed to move out, sparking an angry confrontation.

According to Hildreth, Grate pushed over the couch and gave her a black eye. He also broke her hand. When it began to swell, she begged him to let her go to the hospital for treatment. At first, he refused, but he finally relented and demanded she tell doctors that she had sustained her injuries from a fall.

In the ER, Grate was glued to her side, likely to ensure she did not disclose that he had physically attacked her. Even during the exam, he remained in the room, where a nurse asked her if she felt safe at home. "Of course, I had to say yes," she stated. "He was sitting right there."

It was only after Grate was instructed to leave the room while a technician x-rayed Christina's hand that she finally disclosed he had harmed her. Grate had been told to sit in the waiting area. Hospital staff called the police, but Grate saw the marked police car pulling up outside and took off running.

That's when the stalking began, according to Hildreth. She said the police accompanied her to her apartment so she could collect some things to take to her mother's. But she'd forgotten something important and returned by herself a half hour later. Once inside, she spotted a hammer she had never seen before on the kitchen counter and the toilet seat up in the bathroom. It was clear that someone, most likely Grate, had entered the apartment. She tried to run, but Grate grabbed her before she could reach the door and beat her savagely.

A neighbor heard the commotion and called police. But when they came to the door, Grate grabbed the hammer and held it over her head. He demanded that she keep the cops outside. Fearing for her life, she told them everything was fine.

After the police left, Hildreth endured another vicious beating that she also reported to the authorities. That second beating and police involvement sent Grate on the run.

Working with the police, Hildreth then participated in a ruse to lure Grate back to the apartment, where he was arrested on charges of domestic violence. But he was sentenced to just thirty days in jail. "He kept trying to call my work collect, and he was telling people he was in jail and what he was going to do to me when he was released."

Terrified, Hildreth began a letter-writing campaign to the municipal court judge, who extended Grate's sentence to six months, the maximum time for this offense.

In one interview with reporters, Hildreth suggested that Grate may have been the victim of some trauma when he was young. "I am not sure," she said. "It is just a feeling I had."

She indicated that his relationship with his mother might be a trigger. "He wasn't close to her," she said, adding that she'd only met her three times during their five years together.

"He [Grate] said that when he was around eleven or twelve, he told his mother there was something wrong with him and he needed to talk to somebody," Hildreth recounted. "She was very religious and told him to pray about it and go to church and he would be fine."

During the interview with Grate, Detective Evans and I asked him if he had ever told anyone or written anything down about his interactions with Dana or any of the other women he had killed. His response was noncommittal. He chuckled and said he wanted to know that, too. He then suggested we might find the answer on the eleven o'clock evening news. He said he'd seen a promotional spot, or teaser, for a TV segment that was supposed to appear that night featuring his ex-girlfriend Christina, who claimed that Grate had confessed to her about harming someone.

He then acknowledged that he had, in fact, told Christina about the encounter with Dana, but "not in so much detail." He said that during the time they were living together in Bucyrus, he broke down. He told Christina that he had done something "real wrong, something bad," he said. Adding, "It's hard for me to open up to her, or anyone, because it's killing me every day."

He indicated that he felt as though he was having a breakdown and that he tried repeatedly to get in touch with his father to talk to him about how he was feeling and to ask for help. But according to Grate, his father would not take his calls, and the messages he left for his dad on his voice mail went unanswered.

I would later have an opportunity to sit down with Christina Hildreth. I was taken by her strong sense of recall and detail, and I found her to be insightful and genuine. She described an incident during her relationship with Grate where he was found hiding in her couch. He had actually cut the framing to accommodate himself. She said she actually sat on the couch while he was inside of it, unaware that he was under her. Her account was confirmed through police reports.

Her eyes filled with tears as she recounted how he would go from charming to downright tormenting toward her. She also recalled occasions where she found IDs belonging to unknown women concealed in Grate's car. At the time, she said she found the IDs concerning. Since the case broke, her concern had elevated to suspicion.

I shared that suspicion.

16

A Dangerous Demonstration

Our interview with Shawn Grate in the booking room of the Ashland County Sheriff's Office moved into its second hour. Only Detective Evans and I really knew what was going on inside that room. The only communication either of us had had was my text to Captain Lay indicating that we had another victim.

Outside, law enforcement personnel and the public were anxiously anticipating the moment that Shawn Grate would be marched into the room at the jail that had been set aside for the arraignment. The judge had set the time, his staff was prepared to proceed, and the prosecutor was ready as well. No doubt, TV executives were ready to break into regular programming with the news from Ashland. Most importantly, the community, including families of our victims, was waiting to hear the charges in the case.

But Evans and I had only one thing in mind: drawing out further information from Grate and getting a better handle on his crimes. We knew when he started to confess that the hearing wasn't going to happen on time. At some point, corrections staff knocked at the door and said the hearing was about to begin and we needed to have Grate escorted out of the room.

Detective Evans stepped into the hall to let them know that Grate wasn't coming out, because he was talking with us.

Before diving back into the details of his interactions with Dana, we wanted to discuss some of the items we had found during the search of the Covert Court residence. I told Grate that we had discovered two Tasers in the home and asked if he had used them on any of his victims.

He said he never used a Taser on anyone, but that he thought about trying it on himself just to see if it would work.

I told him we also found makeup, and that Jane had told me that he had applied it to her face and body during her captivity. "What was the reason for putting makeup on her?" I asked.

"To cover her injuries," Grate replied. "I mean, she was bruised up pretty bad, and after I put makeup on her, I almost let her go right then and there. I mean, she looked like almost ready to go."

I then asked about the lipstick.

Grate said it was to "cover her busted lip."

Although I didn't confront him, I couldn't help but recall the photo I had seen on his phone with Jane positioned on her back with a sheet covering her breasts. Her eyes were closed, and she was in full makeup. The timing of the picture wasn't on the last day, so the suggestion that it was to cover up injuries wasn't logical.

Grate was forthcoming when I asked if he had stolen money from Jane while he held her captive. He admitted to keying in to her home and stealing some cash out of a "green thing" she kept on a stand in the living room. He said he knew the location of the money because he'd seen it during a prior visit. At the time, Jane had insisted that he stay outside. Still, Grate said that his vantage point at the threshold of the apartment door allowed him to see into her place.

In what seemed an odd transition, he asked if police were offering a reward for his capture. "If there is one, Jane should get it," he said. "She doesn't have anything."

Grate claimed that he delivered an ominous threat the night before meant to boost Jane's incentive to find a way to escape. He was convinced that this is what had empowered her to risk harm and dial 911.

I asked if he thought that Jane would tell anyone what had happened if he'd gone through with the idea of letting her go.

Grate said he thought she would. But she told him she would give him a couple of hours' grace, meaning enough time for him to get away, and he believed her. Yet he was hesitant, because "it was a bad situation."

He explained that during the ordeal, he told Jane that he loved her and that she was "going to live through it."

He then remarked that it would be cool if Jane would write to him, "but I think I ruined that." He claimed her abduction and subsequent rape was "just an incident between the two of them."

He added, "Maybe eventually she'll write me, but that ain't gonna happen."

Grate paused for a moment. He said he needed to think about how he was going to word his next remark. "Jane is safe," he began. "She was just . . . dealing with her lustful mind."

When asked if he had thought about coming forward and confessing to his crimes, Grate acknowledged that he had.

"Why didn't you follow through?" I asked.

"I keep meeting nice people . . . making hope."

Detective Evans asked Grate if there were any more "situations" like the one with Jane that he wanted to tell us about.

Grate hesitated before answering. "Nah, there's been no one. There's no Janes." He further insisted there were no other victims out there and that he'd told us everything.

Neither Evans nor I believed him.

Grate asked if he could have a cup of coffee, and I left the interview to retrieve one. While out of the room, I spoke with Captain Lay via phone and briefed him on the confession about the fourth victim, Dana.

By now, it was clear that today's scheduled arraignment would not happen. We had Grate talking, and we intended to keep going as long as our suspect would cooperate.

Captain Lay would then contact law enforcement in Marion County, advising them that Grate had just confessed to killing their victim, who had been murdered more than a decade earlier. They were advised that Grate's recorded confession would be provided to them.

While I was out of the room, Grate talked to Detective Evans about coffee and commissary. "I'm waiting for hate mail," he remarked jokingly.

Upon my return, I handed Grate his coffee, then asked him to tell us about the types of pills he had in the Covert Court residence.

He said, "A lot of them were from Candice Cunningham, because she took fifteen different psych meds." He also admitted to stealing prescription pills from Elizabeth Griffith's apartment after her murder. Apparently, he just mixed them all together in a bowl, a sort of cocktail, and offered them to guests who visited.

I told him that there was a house on Orange Street that he visited with a female and that she had mentioned the bowl of pills. I was referring to the woman I had interviewed outside the Covert Court house after my sweep of the residence that past Tuesday.

Grate shot me a look of surprise. He recalled the woman's name being Tracy. He claimed he walked up to a house on Orange Street with her but said he didn't actually go inside. He just wanted to "allow her to believe" that he lived there. He said that he and Tracy weren't alone that day; her niece and her niece's boyfriend had accompanied them on the walk and that they had all gone their separate ways once they reached the residence. Grate was adamant that Tracy never entered the house. He later admitted to bringing her to his apartment on Covert Court.

I asked why he didn't "do anything" to Tracy, why he hadn't harmed her.

He said that he massaged her shoulders while she was at his apartment and that he treated her like "a lot of others."

"I didn't flip out or anything. Things went smooth. Even though she still needs to go find God first . . . She needs to go find herself," he said. "I can't take that away from her."

I next inquired about Brittany, the young woman who'd come to the police station to tell me about her interactions with Grate while sitting outside the Orange Street apartments.

"Are you referring to the seventeen-year-old who has a child?" he asked. Grate admitted to offering his help when he saw her at the laundromat but suggested there were no other interactions between the two.

"I know it's hard to believe, especially if they've been inside, that they made it out in this situation. . . . I know a lot of people, and this has shocked them," he said, referring to news of his arrest and the crimes he confessed to have committed.

When asked what it is about a woman that angers him most, he said he didn't know. I reminded him of some of the words he'd used in our previous conversations, like *bossy* and *liar*.

"It depends on the moment," he said, adding that he can sometimes be thinking about his mother when he is with a woman. "Then it's all bad."

After another short break, I asked Grate if he had "cut" any of the women he killed. There was a nuanced indicator involving him possibly cutting someone.

"The first victim," he said, referring to Dana. Grate then indicated that he thought he knew to what I was referring and began to relate a story about one of his ex-girlfriends and an incident with a knife. Although I wasn't referring to her, I listened to his story.

He frowned as he related his displeasure at having watched her on television that morning suggesting he had once come after her with a knife. He identified her as Lisa Ball and said she was the mother of his second child, a boy, whom I will not name.

"She's still alive," he mused.

Interviews with suspects are never linear. As usual, I found myself trying to piece together a picture of Grate's background and whom he'd been involved with over the years.

From what I had ascertained thus far, Grate was still in high school when he became a father for the first time. He said he was sixteen and had just started working at the local supermarket when he met a girl who had recently lost both of her parents. I have chosen not to name her out of respect for her privacy. They were both sixteen when they started dating. Two years later, they had a daughter together, when they were both eighteen.

According to Grate, the young woman and their baby girl lived with him and his brother in their father's house in Marion for a short time. Eventually, Grate said, she met a "stand-up guy" whom she ended up marrying, and the child went to live with her and her new husband. Grate indicated he had little to do with her or the child.

He said he was twenty-three when he met Lisa Ball, the woman he said he saw on television that morning. Lisa was just seventeen when the two began dating, and she got pregnant with Shawn's second child, his son. It's unclear where they were living, but Grate claimed their relationship quickly soured, with police called to the house on two occasions.

In one instance, Grate was accused of trying to strangle Lisa. The second time, Lisa said he pulled a knife on her, so she called 911. When police arrived, the violence escalated with Grate threatening to kill her.

Grate claimed it was Lisa who was the "crazy" one, that she was the one who stabbed *him*. He then admitted that *he* gave her the knife. "That's when I knew my thinking was wrong."

He said he would come home from work to find the house dirty. He recalled one time Lisa spent the entire day watching soap operas. Her sister was at the house that day.

Grate said he went upstairs and began to pack his belongings, and he grabbed a knife. "I had had enough."

He claimed he put the knife down and walked over and "smacked 'em both," referring to Lisa and her sister. That's when Lisa supposedly went for the knife.

Grate said he took it from her and tossed it. He then tried to go down the stairs, but—according to his version of the encounter—she got the knife and ran after him. He had his baby boy in his arms, and he ducked, and Lisa gouged him twice in the back. When he turned toward her, she fell.

He claimed she cut him a few more times and her sister grabbed their son and took him outside. He said Lisa cut him eight times that day, and he lifted his shirt to show us the scars. There were various healed scars on his torso, indicating they were old. But I had no way of confirming how he had sustained the injuries.

Grate said the dispute happened in Marion and that there was a police report to corroborate his story. Because the incident did not happen in my jurisdiction, I didn't have an immediate mechanism to assess the veracity of his claims. I would later learn that his account of the altercation with Lisa was not consistent with the police report involving the incident. The police revealed that he was more of the aggressor than he had told me, and that he had grossly minimized his role in the altercation.

I told Grate that when I'd asked him about an incident involving a knife, I was referring to injuries on one of his victims' stomachs. I recalled that during our first interview, he'd lightly mentioned something about a cut on Candice's stomach. Because he had jumped over it, there was some indication there was more to the story, so I decided to revisit it here.

"Candice Cunningham," he said. "She liked to cut herself a lot."

Grate recounted that she "sliced her belly" during an argument that grew heated after she struck him with a bag of tobacco. "It's just the cost of battle with her," he said, adding that even if he hadn't killed Dana, he still would have killed Candice because of how much he had to deal with being with her.

I next brought up a second scenario Grate had skipped over in the first interview about beating up a man. He said it happened during his high school days in Marion while he was hanging out with a rough crowd. He talked about a man with a knife.

"I know I didn't kill him or anything," he said. He appeared to present the incident as if it were no big deal, but looking back, I believe this incident needed to be explored further.

I transitioned to talking about electronic devices. I asked Grate about the locations of the cell phones belonging to Elizabeth and Stacey. Neither device had turned up during the execution of search warrants at the Covert Court location or at the homes of the two women. He claimed he threw Elizabeth's phone into the creek by her apartment complex the day after her murder. He said he was on his way to walk Jane Doe to lunch at the Kroc Center that morning around 11:00 a.m. and stopped on the bridge on Holbrook Avenue to dispose of Griffith's phone. He threw it as far as he could and estimated that it landed some fifty to sixty feet off the bridge.

Officers searched for the phone, but their efforts proved fruitless.

Stacey's phone was tossed randomly when he was out driving her car one afternoon, Grate said. He then agreed to draw us maps of both locations and signed the detailed drawings he prepared.

At this point in our conversation, I asked Grate how I was supposed to know if he was telling me the truth about Dana. I challenged him to share something about the case that nobody else would know. I explained that I wasn't saying that I didn't believe him, but I told him that I wanted to make it definitive.

"I understand," he said. He then inhaled slowly, paused, and offered a detail. "I did go back after a few months, and I burned a fire."

Grate admitted that three months after the murder, he returned to the site where he had disposed of Dana's body, doused it with gasoline, and set it on fire, just as he had done with the blanket he'd used to transport her body and the knife he'd used to kill her.

"I caught her on fire to burn up a little evidence, just in case it was there," he stated. He explained that he had handled Dana's body with his bare hands and was worried he might have left fingerprints behind. He then explained that this was why he burned the blanket, to get rid of any hair that might link him to the crime.

"I've been paranoid . . . just beating myself up the whole time," he stated. "So, I took a drive back and did catch her on fire about one o'clock in the morning . . . engulfed in flames with gas and went away, you know what I mean, it calmed—"

Grate stopped midsentence.

"I could've swore someone on the highway could have seen me," he disclosed. "I was out of there, my car . . . I just wanted to run from it, and that's what I've been doing all my life."

When asked about the condition of Dana's body upon his return to the dump site, Grate said that animals were "working on it," and he saw maggots on Dana. At one point, he thought about burying her. "A lot of things went through my mind."

Detective Evans asked Grate about the make and model of the car in which he'd transported Dana. We would need to locate it; perhaps there was still evidence in the trunk?

Grate said he thought it was a 1989 Pontiac, but he wasn't certain. He told us there were holes in the back of the car, inside the trunk.

He explained that he'd punched holes through the sheet metal on the bottom of the trunk—where a spare tire is often stored—so that he could hose out the inside of the trunk and let the water drain out. Without those holes, the water and any traces of blood or bodily fluids would have remained inside the trunk.

He had obviously been keeping track of any news involving the disappearance and the discovery of Dana's body, because he knew that it had been found about two years after the murder. Grate claimed he didn't keep any of Dana's belongings as trophies and said that the murder was not premeditated. "It wasn't planned or meant to be," he said.

Next, we steered the conversation to the second point we had wanted to clarify during this interview—Grate's method of strangulation. We were trying to determine a way of testing the veracity of his earlier statements, as his verbal descriptions weren't absolutely clear. We knew he had used manual strangulation on the victims, and with Stacey, he used both manual strangulation and ligature strangulation. But we were also aware that hand/arm position during strangulation can cause hyoid fractures that are sometimes found in autopsy results.

The hyoid bone is u-shaped; it is fractured in many homicides by strangulation. Postmortem detection of a hyoid fracture is pertinent in the diagnosis of strangulation. We needed to know if what Grate had described was consistent with the findings of the autopsies.

Evans and I asked Grate about the position of his hands when he strangled all his victims.

The question seemed to get his attention. Sitting up in his chair, he replied, "Okay . . . well, with Stacey, at first it was joking around. . . . So, I just took this hand [referencing his left hand] and I put it on the back of her head, and at the same time, I put this [indicating his right arm] right in her throat.

"I'm like, 'You sure?' I kinda let go, and she looked at me and started flipping out." Then it all "went bad."

Detective Evans rose to his feet and physically demonstrated what Grate had just described.

"That's correct," Grate remarked, instructing Evans to lean forward. "And in just a few minutes . . . out," he said.

Grate told us he also used his thumb to apply pressure while pushing up on the victims' necks. "I mainly push, I don't squeeze," he clarified. "I haven't broken it down . . . I haven't dissected it, but really, I just look at their faces and see if I'm getting anywhere . . . that's what I do."

Grate's phrasing during this portion of the interview made his killings appear prolific, indicating there were more victims to uncover.

Evans asked Grate if he would be willing to demonstrate the move for us using a doll or stuffed animal.

"I was thinking of demonstrating on you," Grate replied. He stared at Evans, then looked at me, then back at Evans, who was sitting next to me and across from Grate at the table.

Because Grate appeared too eager to use Evans as his subject, I decided to test his eagerness. I asked him if he would rather demonstrate the strangulations on me. He shook his head, grinned, and said he didn't want to use me for the demonstration.

I was aware that Brian Evans is a badass. But having been around when my husband is coaching wrestling and watching my sons and my brothers-in-law compete over the years, I also knew that if a choke hold is locked in, you can lose consciousness in mere seconds.

I had worked strangulation cases in the past, and the risk was high. Evans is tough, very tough, but I thought this was a risky move under any circumstances. To make matters worse, because we were in the county jail in an interview room, neither of us was armed. Still, I believed that Brian Evans would have his hand in and that the situation would be a little more controlled.

We removed Grate's handcuffs so that he could demonstrate his method of strangulation of the various victims. Detective Evans rose from his chair and stood across the table from me. I was thinking, *Why the hell can't we use a doll?*

"Taller than all the others," Grate stated, apparently thinking of his victims. He then advised, "I have choked a man out before to slow him down."

Yet another comment referencing violence with men I hoped to explore later.

I remember looking around the room, trying to contemplate what I would do if the situation went south. I asked Grate if he was okay with us videoing him, and he gave his consent. So I began recording.

"This is Detective Mager. We have Detective Evans in the room, Shawn Grate in the room," I said. "It's September 15, 2016. The time is 1704 hours. Shawn is going to demonstrate the way he uses hands in strangulation cases that we have been discussing."

Without further prompting, Grate stated, "With Elizabeth, it's kind of shocking. We were just joking like how she wished she kind of would die, you know . . . So, I'll help ya. I'll just go like this; you know what I mean?"

He demonstrated grabbing Elizabeth's neck with his right hand from the front while using his left hand to steady her head and neck.

He said, "And she just kind of whacked my hands." He demonstrated how Elizabeth slapped his hands away from her. "She started flipping out to the point where I had to just like . . . grab her."

Grate moved behind Evans, and with his left arm, he wrapped it around the detective's neck. With his right arm, he bent it and placed his hand on the back of his neck. He pushed Evans's head forward and said, "I just leaned forward and pressed."

He literally wrapped his arm around Evans's neck. I recall seeing Evans's eyes looking at me. I was trying to determine if he was in trouble and what my next move would be if the situation got ugly. He used more pressure than the detective had anticipated. He basically had Evans in a rear choke hold, with his arm all the way around his neck, and to our surprise, the hold was locked in.

When Grate let go, Evans mouthed the words, "I will never effing do that again." I later chastised him, accusing him of letting his ego get in the way with a serial killer.

His throat was sore for the next few days.

I asked if Grate could describe what happened to Stacey Stanley Hicks. He remained standing for the demonstration. He said they were sitting side by side. "We were getting along still . . . till somewhere along the line she felt threatened . . . I'm still thinking about this, of what went wrong exactly with Stacey and I. 'Cause I didn't have no thoughts, but I do remember when she grabbed her Mace, and she missed me the first time."

Using his right hand, Grate simulated holding a canister of pepper spray. "That was a good shot, you know what I mean, but dang, I just lost it. . . . I just clinched on . . . did not let go."

Grate positioned his hands and arms as they would have been when he was strangling Stacey. He stated that it was the same hold he'd used with Elizabeth, with his arms around her neck and his other hand pushing her head forward. "And I didn't let her go," he reiterated. "I couldn't really see her 'cause my eyes were maced. I turned her around and just clinched . . . and clinched."

The visual was disturbing, but I had him talking, so I pressed on. "How about with Candice Cunningham?" I asked.

"I tried to keep her calmed down a lot, and I really didn't mean to," he said of his interaction with Candice. "I fought with her for like three days. A lot of it was mainly face-to-face. . . . We even would walk around town every night after our big fights, and then we go to bed that third night, and it's almost like she just keeps egging me on."

Grate indicated that after she smacked him in the face with a bag of tobacco, he grabbed her. "That's when I choked her, and she passed out . . . I was irritable. I'd had enough. I just finished her."

I asked Grate to tell us more about his interaction with the woman he had identified as Dana. I wanted further clarity about how he had taken her life.

Grate said that when she'd tried to exit the bedroom, he backed her out. "I turn her around . . . she comes toward me. I knocked her hands around, knocked her whole body around, and just grabbed her like she was meant to be . . . choked out."

He used both arms, moving them fluidly in demonstrating how he'd turned Dana around and gotten her into position. "I mean, it felt right in my hands," he stated.

He leaned over while still holding his arms, as if he had Dana in the strangulation hold. "I sat her back, laid her down, and then actually laid down with her; we was laid down side by side."

When I asked at what point he stabbed Dana in the neck, he declared, "She woke up." He said they were already in the basement when she suddenly revived. He admitted that he didn't know for certain if she was dead when he dragged her down the basement steps, but when she woke up, he panicked.

"I didn't know what to do. I ran upstairs, grabbed a knife . . . and the first thing I did when I went back downstairs, I stabbed her in the neck."

Grate used his right arm and made a stabbing motion. He was still standing up during his account of what transpired. At one point, he said he believed the knife was a "straight knife" like a "knife you cut onions with."

At the end of the demonstration, I memorialized it on video. "All right, the time is 1712 hours. The date is September 15. This is Detective Mager, with Detective Evans and Shawn Grate at the Ashland County Sheriff's Office."

I thanked Grate for providing the demonstrations and said that I appreciated it.

"The news is going to talk about all the missing bodies," he remarked.

At this point, I talked about his candidness with us. Being strategic, I told him that I believed he had a conscience, and I appreciated his openness.

"I try to justify things in weird ways," he replied. "I'm really warped, I think, though . . . damaged."

In a subsequent interview with Detective Evans and me, Grate admitted that after killing Dana, whenever he met someone new, he would ask himself, "Am I capable of hurting them?" He then suggested there could have been a lot more victims.

To me, this highlighted that killing was always an option for him.

Despite having confessed to four murders, Grate claimed he didn't want to "play God," insisting that wasn't his motive.

"Are you saying that you believe you are predisposed to do what you've done?" I asked.

His answer was profound. He explained that, for him, watching television was almost like reading the Bible, "when you turn to a verse and see how that verse applies to you."

He described sitting in his jail cell casually clicking the remote, explaining that three times in a row, he landed on a crime show; he saw that as a message.

"People like violence," he stated.

I asked Grate what else I was missing. I told him I recognized that without law enforcement having any knowledge that Candice

Cunningham was missing, he was honest in talking about his victimization of her. I explained that it was a choice for him to tell me about Candice, and that it was appreciated.

"They could have remained cold cases," he acknowledged. "I've been thinking about it, and it was too much all the other day. Too much all in one day." Grate would later clarify that he had only told me what he thought I could handle in one day.

There were many times during the interview where Grate appeared to be pulling back, and I'd have to redirect the exchange to reset his emotions. But at this particular moment, he was being candid, so I seized on the opportunity to explore his psyche.

I asked him what it felt like directly during and after strangling a woman.

"Oh, man. While I'm choking 'em. . . . By then, I know. Right then, I know if I should finish or not. . . . What am I supposed to do? . . . People who actually want to die and they keep . . . like, every day, just [popping] handfuls of pills," he said, suggesting that people like Candice Cunningham just popped pills to exist. "Candice Cunningham was just another nut. . . . Crazy. She should not be out in society."

Grate said that Candice was unable to work and that there "really needs to be something done about [people using the system]." He acknowledged that he viewed particular people as a burden to society. He specified that he was not referring to people who are disabled or handicapped. They weren't the problem.

At this point, I began to wind down the interview. I asked Grate if there was another case I didn't yet know about.

I wasn't surprised when he hesitated before answering. He stared at my eyes, and I stared back trying to read him, and he knew it. Something felt wrong, but he claimed there were no more bodies. I sat there recalling that just two hours earlier, he was emphatic that there were only three women he'd murdered. I also recalled during the interview on the thirteenth, he had provided nuanced hints about Dana.

"No, there's four," he claimed.

He said he wanted to be honest about that point, then he reminded me of the answer he had given back at the police station when I'd asked him this same question. "I said there were four, right?"

He justified holding back details about Dana, stating, "It's a ten-year-old case, and knowing all I've done now, I just felt like . . . I have to think about it . . . but I'd rather just get all this out right now."

Grate next expressed his concern that confessing to so many homicides might lead to accusations and charges related to open cases that he had not been involved in. "I just had this feeling I'm gonna probably be accused or charged with a lot more. But there wouldn't be no proof, 'cause I haven't done nothing else, other than Jane. I have four bodies. That's it."

I thanked him for his honesty, although I internally questioned it.

He started to get emotional, talking about how life is only temporary. Then he began to cry.

I told him that he didn't have to watch the television that was on in his jail cell.

"Watching it helps," he said.

I related that he probably assumed there were charges coming. "Are you ready for those?" I asked. I told him that I had to read the charges to him.

Detective Evans left the room to retrieve the complaint. He returned with the paperwork and a message: Marion County officials wanted to talk with me.

I left the room to make a call to Lieutenant Christy Utley of the Marion County Sheriff's Office. I told her that Shawn Grate had just confessed to a murder in her jurisdiction.

Lieutenant Utley provided me with the location where the skeletal remains of an unidentified female had been found on March

10, 2007, in a remote wooded area approximately one hundred feet east of Victory Road, north of Marion. The coroner determined that the location coincided with the site Grate had just described to us.

A local man had stumbled upon the remains while out searching for scrap metal he could sell. The area was a popular illegal dumping site—which meant that it was littered with construction and demolition debris, including pipes and electrical wire. While he was foraging around, he came across what he thought was a Halloween decoration, but upon closer inspection, he realized he had just stumbled across a human skull.

The coroner had established the remains were those of a young female and that the case was likely a homicide. A forensic anthropologist estimated the remains had been out there for at least a year. Marion authorities checked missing persons reports for Marion County and the surrounding area, but the description did not match any of the reports filed.

Information about the discovery had been entered into the National Crime Information Center's database, but there were no hits. Attempts to identify the woman through dental records and a DNA examination had also proved unsuccessful.

While out of the room, I also called Captain Lay to provide him with another update. When I rejoined the interview, Grate immediately asked if it was now time for him to hear the charges. "It's one of those things I gotta accept and find the best in it," he said.

I presented him with the court-stamped criminal complaint—Kidnapping, Felony of the First Degree; Murder, Felony of the First Degree; and an additional Murder, Felony of the First Degree.

Grate said nothing. But I could see his mind working. He asked if someone could bring him his eyeglasses from the Covert Court residence. He explained that he was worried that someone may get pissed off about one of his crimes and come to court with a gun, intent on killing him. He needed the glasses so that he could see if anyone was getting out of control.

"I would do it if someone had hurt one of my loved ones," he said.

Grate went on to say that he figured that a lot of people would be mad when they learned about his horrible acts. Still, he said that he was one of those people who believed that everything happened for a reason. He talked about how relaxed Ashland was, with people going to their jobs like it was no big deal. He said he wasn't trying to justify what he did, because he knew that his actions were "totally wrong." He said he was just trying to find a motive for his crimes.

Grate next shared his view of the city of Ashland. "Ashland is supposed to be a Christian city, too. And it's dead. All the churches are dead. People are content. There's no growth. People's faith stays stagnant." He suggested that his situation, was like "a revival . . . a wake-up" call to them. This man was literally describing our community as being complacent.

Maybe he meant that everyone thought that Ashland was a safe place to live and had no idea that people like him, evil people, walked among them. Whatever he meant, the arrest of serial killer Shawn Grate was indeed a wake-up call for our city and our state. No one could have believed that crimes like these would take place here.

Before concluding our interview, I asked Grate if he believed he did the right thing by being honest with me.

"Yes," he replied. "Someday in my life, I'm gonna be free from all this. Free from what I've done. There's a purpose for why I'm moving on to an institution."

DAY FOUR

September 16, 2016

17

"What the Hell Were You Two Thinking?"

It was late when I finally left the Ashland County Sheriff's Office that Thursday evening. Before going home, Evans and I had contacted authorities in Marion County to provide a detailed account of Grate's confession, and in the days ahead, we would coordinate with Marion County Police Lieutenant Christy Utley and Detective Nate Hildreth (no relation to Grate's ex-girlfriend Christina) to gain more insight from Grate in an effort to identify this young woman and bring closure to her family.

My mind was racing when I finally walked through the front door and was immediately confronted with angry stares from my two younger children, Macy and Reed. They had seen video of me on the evening news walking out of the courthouse with Detective Evans after filing the criminal complaint against Grate. Now, I was being confronted for not being forthcoming with them.

Being the child of police officers is difficult. I've been called out in the night and come home at 4:00 a.m. to find Reed sitting on the coffee table waiting for me. He was worried and couldn't sleep until I got home. Then he had to get up early in the morning for school and focus on his schoolwork.

My daughter, Macy, has a pulse on the family. She has incredible insight, and regardless of her age, she has always been ferociously protective of our family. I have taught her to be strong and honest. Now, my little girl felt betrayed. And so did her brother.

I told them I *wasn't* lying when I said I was helping people, and I wasn't. I just couldn't tell them the circumstances of the case and about any risk to their mom. I am well aware that hearing those sorts of things could be negatively impactful to my children. So, I shielded them. But all my kids have an uncanny ability to assess a situation, even through nuances.

That night, I explained to them that most of my job was really positive. But sometimes I had to talk to people who hurt others, people like Shawn Grate.

They asked if their dad could be in the room when I talked to Grate. I told them that wasn't really possible. Then they specifically wanted to know if Detective Brian Evans and Sergeant Aaron Kline would be in the room with me. Evans and Kline had a lot of contact with Dan and me, and the kids viewed them as protection for me. We got through the conversation and continued with our nightly routine. I silently realized my job had just affected my kids—again.

And I felt guilty.

I couldn't sleep that night, thinking about Dana's family. But I was also excited for the morning briefing. Detective Evans and I were proud of the work we'd done and anticipated big attaboys from everybody on the force about Grate's confession to a fourth murder. It had been strategic to not simply serve the complaint on Grate right away but rather talk to him before presenting the formal document. It was horrible to identify another victim, but we were optimistic that the admission would finally bring closure to the grieving relatives.

As I drove to the police station that Friday morning, I remember feeling almost like how a kid might feel after they hit a home run and their coach is about to publicly acknowledge it. Instead of accolades, however, I walked into a second confrontation—this time with my superiors.

Chief Marcelli was in the hallway about to head in to the detective bureau for the morning briefing when he spotted Evans and me striding toward him, so he stopped and waited. As we neared, I noticed his face tighten.

"What the hell were you two thinking?" he barked, shaking his head in displeasure.

Surprised by his remark, I shot him a puzzled look. "What happened?" I asked.

Somebody had shown him the video of the strangulation reenactment Evans and I had done with Grate during our interrogation, and he was not impressed that Evans's life was put at risk, even for a moment.

I explained that we had sought to clarify Grate's version of events so that we could compare it with injuries identified in the coroner's reports. But the chief didn't approve of the risk we had taken, and he let us know it.

I was willing to accept his criticism, anticipating the accolades Evans and I were about to receive from Captain Lay and the other officers in the briefing. Our interview had produced a confession of another murder, which brought the total to four. And we'd cleared a case in Marion County, about an hour from Ashland, that had gone unsolved for more than a decade.

Evans and I entered Captain Lay's office, with Chief Marcelli on our heels. The captain was at his desk, and Sergeant Alting and

BCI special agent Ed Staley occupied the two seats facing him. The chief opted to stand, so Evans and I grabbed two chairs from the table in the corner and set them on either side of the captain, facing the others in the room.

Once we were all settled in, I looked around, anticipating all the kudos. I wasn't expecting a medal or plaque, but figured we deserved a few pats on the back for a job well done.

Captain Lay looked at me, then at Evans and said, "I don't want any more surprises from you two!"

At first, I thought he was joking, and then I realized he, too, was angry.

"What are you talking about?" Evans replied.

The captain suggested that Evans and I had gone into our meeting with Grate with a secret master plan to interview him about another victim rather than serve Grate with his complaint so he could attend his hearing. In reality, everyone knew how Evans and I worked; we made a master plan in every scenario. Although we'd anticipated asking Grate some questions, we hadn't anticipated such a huge revelation.

Detective Evans took offense at the captain's insinuation, and an argument broke out. The situation went downhill from there.

"Let me give you some tips," the captain told Evans, his tone contemptuous.

Evans grew animated. Flipping open his notebook, he sarcastically retorted, "Oh, you have some tips for me. This ought to be good."

As the confrontation escalated, I noticed Sergeant Alting turn toward the window, hoping not to get drawn into the drama. Meanwhile, SA Staley sat coolly in his chair, watching the spectacle.

Hoping to defuse the situation, Chief Marcelli yelled over the escalating voices, "Fellas, come on. That's enough!"

But the dispute continued unabated. My eyes bounced from the captain to Evans as the two traded angry barbs. With each snipe, they inched closer and closer together, until they were right in front of me.

"Hey!" I yelled.

And everyone looked at me.

I explained that there had been no bad intentions and that Evans and I didn't know there was another victim when we entered the interview room the previous afternoon. I related that I had simply asked Grate if there was anything else that he wanted to get off his chest, and he'd poured out the confession about Dana in Marion.

The verbal tussle finally ended with the chief acknowledging that the Grate investigation was a lot to deal with and that everyone was doing a fine job. He commented that we all needed to take some time off and decompress.

The Friday morning blowout was never mentioned again.

And nobody took time off to decompress; there was no time for that.

It was a long day, writing search warrants, checking on Jane Doe, interviewing witnesses, and contacting law enforcement in other counties to update them on new details related to the crimes Grate had committed in multiple jurisdictions. I was also scouring Grate's statement for investigative leads. There were the trailer break-ins at Charles Mill Lake Park, the forts he'd constructed in Ashland and Richland Counties, the burglaries at the Island Trading Post and the Eagle gas station, and on and on.

Typically, each one of these offenses would have warranted a full investigation. Then there were the four murders and all the legwork that needed to be done. We were inundated with calls, and officers were taking tips over the phone, interviewing people in the community and coordinating with local, state, and federal agencies. We also assisted state and federal authorities in coming up with a matrix that would detail Grate's movement throughout his entire life.

And we had an unidentified victim—identifying her was a priority, although Marion County would take the lead on that case. *Who was Dana?*

I was eager to search the missing persons databases, hoping to put a name and face to this victim. I found many of the data banks impressive, especially the one created by the National Center for Missing & Exploited Children. But I was surprised to learn how many jurisdictions weren't utilizing that national repository.

As I moved from one database to the next, I realized that many of them had entries that were not on any of the other databases. If you didn't know which web-based tool to search, chances were high that you'd miss something that could be vital to your case. The assortment of databases was an amazing resource for law enforcement. Still, it was worrisome that the system was so fragmented. Not everyone had either the time or inclination to mount a slow, careful, and methodical search.

Broadly speaking, missing persons cases were serious matters that deserved attention from law enforcement. Certainly, some issues resolved themselves on their own. There were some folks out there who simply wanted to disappear for a period of time. But there were other missing persons cases that ended in tragedy—as I was experiencing firsthand with Grate.

The more I thought about the patchwork nature of the missing persons databases, the more concerned I became. How many cases had gone unsolved over the years simply because someone didn't check all the relevant data banks? I know from experience that caseloads for detectives can be significant. What had we missed? What had other departments across the US missed?

During my initial searches, I discovered that there were nearly

640 missing adults in Ohio alone. Some had disappeared more than sixty years earlier, never to be heard from again. Others, like Candice, who were living on the fringes of society, might vanish but never be listed as missing.

How could this be? I wondered. In the greatest and most powerful country in the world, how could we have people missing that no one had reported? Secondly, how could we have bodies that had been located that we couldn't identify? We could trace our ancestors back hundreds of years; why couldn't we ensure a proper burial for our people—men and women, children and adults?

With Grate's confession to four murders in three separate counties, the case was now interjurisdictional. We had a growing number of crime scenes, each of which needed to be thoroughly examined by a forensics team. Crime scenes had to be protected from the public, too, which required considerable manpower from different police agencies. Our law enforcement partners were conducting interviews and follow up simultaneous to me interviewing Grate.

In the weeks to come, the FBI would also be involved, with profilers from the Behavioral Analysis Unit (BAU) at Quantico, Virginia, reviewing my interview recordings and providing guidance for subsequent interview sessions.

18

"The Devil's Good-Looking, Too"

What had started out as a local case quickly grew into a full-blown, national crime story. Word that Shawn Grate had confessed to a fourth murder only served to generate more media interest. News organizations from across Ohio, across the US, and even across the pond to the United Kingdom and beyond were now reporting on the case.

The day Grate was supposed to be arraigned, the *Daily Mail*, a UK tabloid, ran an "exclusive" interview with Shawn Grate's mother, Theresa McFarland. MOM OF "SERIAL KILLER" REVEALS HER SON HAS LED COPS TO A FOURTH BODY AND SHE BELIEVES THERE COULD BE MORE VICTIMS AS SHE COMPARES HIM TO TED BUNDY AND JEFFREY DAHMER, the headline blared.

Accompanying the full-page article were paparazzi-style photos of Grate's mother dressed in a pink-and-white housecoat, peering out her front screen door. This was the only interview McFarland would grant amid reports the tabloid newspaper agreed to pay her for her story.

McFarland told the paper she was "heartbroken" over her son's admissions to killing four women but said she couldn't doubt his guilt because it was Shawn who had led police to the victims' bodies. She expressed surprise that his crimes "went so far back," referring to his latest confession to the murder of Dana, the magazine sales-person, in 2006.

"He's good-looking, but the Devil's good-looking, too," she said of her son. "He ain't [got] no red horns and all that stuff. You find out he's charming, and of course that charm can charm the pants off anybody, not to be nasty, but you just know how it works."

McFarland claimed she hadn't seen Shawn in three years. "He is estranged from the family," she said.

"I guess I can say I'm just glad he's got a conscience and now he's stopped. It's too bad it's too late for the victims. It's just so very sad, and I'm praying for them and their families. I'm praying for him, too.

"It's shocking, because I love him, and I know he loves me, too, but his love is a twisted love," she told the reporter.

McFarland described her son as headstrong and suggested he had a need for control. "You couldn't live with him," she said. "You try to help him, and the next thing, he's running your life."

I wasn't surprised to hear about Grate's deep-seated need for control based upon what he'd said to me in our lengthy interview sessions. But I didn't put much value on the impromptu interview of Grate's mother with no forensic parameters in place.

I did not interview Grate's mother or father during the inves-tigation, but I knew that detectives from Marion County were working parallel with us, conducting interviews. Our investiga-tive team, which included law enforcement from Ashland County and BCI, as well as other law enforcement partners in Marion and Richland Counties, were working hard conducting interviews and doing follow-up investigation.

I had interviewed Grate four times in the first week of the case and had gathered background about his life prior to his arrest. Much of what I gleaned was later confirmed by Grate's half sister, Barbara, during the penalty phase of Grate's capital murder trial. Barbara was the only member of Grate's family to appear in court on his behalf. She told the court that she was estranged from her mother, Theresa McFarland, and that she had not spoken to her brother Shawn for several years.

During her testimony on the witness stand, Barbara painted a picture of a turbulent upbringing. Like Grate, she placed much of the blame at her mother's feet, describing McFarland as toxic. She said her mother was just fourteen when she left home to marry fellow Kentuckian Edward Meadows, who was seven years her senior.

Theresa was placed in her maternal grandparents' care when she was two years old, Barbara said. She then related a story she said her mother had told her. She claimed that one night, Theresa's father came home after drinking all night to find his wife, Barbara's grandmother, waiting at the door with a shotgun. "She shot him," Barbara said. "He lived, but they ended up getting a divorce."

It was not clear if Barbara's grandmother was charged with a crime, but after the event, Theresa and her two sisters were taken from their parents and sent to live with relatives. Theresa, the middle child, went to her paternal grandparents in Kentucky. Her two sisters were placed with their maternal grandparents in a neighboring state.

According to Barbara, Theresa claimed she was sexually abused by her grandfather, so eloping at fourteen seemed like a good way out. The marriage was one of "convenience, not love," Barbara said. Theresa was fleeing an abusive household, and Edward was a draft dodger who wanted to get married and have a child to avoid being sent to fight in the Vietnam War.

The newlyweds drove north to Canada, where they lived for a short time before crossing back into the US and settling in Ypsilanti, Michigan, where Barbara was born in June 1969.

Barbara said her father, Edward, was an alcoholic who physically abused her mother. Through tears, she recounted an incident she said occurred when she was two years old.

"What I always thought was a dream was actually reality. I remember being in my crib and my dad coming at me, and my mom coming and hitting him over the head. And my mom grabbed me and ran. I don't know a lot of the details, but that is how we ended up in Ohio."

Theresa was seventeen at the time, so she had to wait until her eighteenth birthday, the law in Michigan, to file for divorce. Barbara said she and her mother ended up in Bucyrus, Ohio, where Theresa found a job at the family-owned powerboat maker Baja Boats. She eventually left there to become a go-go dancer at a bar in Marion. That's where she met twenty-one-year-old Terry Grate, and the two were married four months later.

In February 1974, they welcomed a son, Ronald Jason. Two years later, on August 8, 1976, Shawn Michael was born.

For the next several years, Theresa was a stay-at-home mom, and, according to Barbara, the family enjoyed a "normal, middle-class life."

"We moved to a small house in Marion," she recounted. "It was in a country setting, like somebody took a little suburb, picked it up, and put it in the middle of a cornfield."

Barbara said their new community had lots of neighbors and a lush green park that divided the area's two school districts.

"In the summertime, as soon as the sun rose, we were outside until the streetlights came on and we came home for supper," Barbara recalled. She said she and her brothers played softball and football in the backyard and socialized with the neighborhood kids.

But there was tension in the home. According to Barbara, Theresa and Terry's marriage was solid for the first two years, and then it was "on and off." There was also hostility between Shawn and his mother, she said.

Sometime around 1980, Terry lost his job, Barbara said. The company where her stepfather was employed closed its doors, and Terry found himself unemployed and without a paycheck.

To support the household, Theresa found work outside the home as a bartender, thrusting a preteen Barbara into the role of care-taker and homemaker. Two years later, in 1982, Theresa and Terry divorced, and at twelve, Barbara became "mother of the house." Her duties included making sure her two brothers, Jason and Shawn, now eight and six, were fed, did their homework, and went to bed on time.

Most nights, Barbara was already asleep when her mother came home, if she came home at all. "Mom would go out a lot," she said. "She'd get off work on Friday, and we wouldn't see her again un-til Sunday. Terry had visitation every other weekend, so when the boys weren't with their dad, it was my responsibility to take care of them."

According to Barbara, Theresa would often bring men home in the evenings, even when the children were there. She was also physically abusive and often spanked the kids.

"Mom was irresponsible when it came to her children. She was young, and she didn't give us a lot of attention. She wasn't con-nected to us."

During one of my interviews with Grate, he revealed his distress that his mother was "bringing home guys all the time." He said the men would try to talk to him. One morning, he was up early. His mother was still in her bedroom, and she told him to watch cartoons.

Grate wanted breakfast, so he was waiting for her to come out of the bedroom. He said he knocked on the bedroom door, and she told him it would be a little while. He went back and watched cartoons for a little longer, then he returned to her bedroom and knocked again. It escalated to him kicking her door, he said.

The door opened, and there was a man there, asking Grate what was wrong. He told the man to shut up, and his mom sent him to his room. According to Grate, the man came into his bedroom and sat down next to him on his bed.

"Get out of here!" Grate told him.

He tried to "handle me," Grate claimed. "I kicked him in the face." At that moment, I saw Shawn Grate as a six-year-old boy, not the killer before me.

He added, "There were a lot of strange faces growing up."

Barbara said Grate was afraid of their mother and he often described her as miserable. Aunts, cousins, and other relatives shared the sentiment, she said, portraying Theresa as mean and cold.

During one of my interviews, Grate related a story that had him falling into a creek. He described sneaking around the back of the house to hose off, hoping to avoid his mother's gaze. But she spotted him covered in mud. "That was interesting," he recalled. He didn't elaborate, but he insinuated a punishment was meted out.

There was not a lot of warmth or closeness in the home, according to Barbara. "I would not describe it as a loving house. It was a routine house. We had to get up to go to school, there was no family time, no loving, no nurturing.

"I always had a job to do, to get up to take care of my brothers, fix dinner. All three of us were different, and all three of us have a different perspective of home."

During her testimony, Barbara divulged that Grate did not talk until he was four. "He didn't have to," she said, "everybody talked for him."

He also struggled in school, she said. According to Barbara, he was found to have dyslexia, which warranted subsequent intervention.

When he was around five or six, Shawn broke his arm, Barbara said. "He didn't want anybody to see him with that cast on," she recalled. "He was embarrassed.

"My mom went to the grocery store, and she wanted him to go with her, and he didn't want to because he didn't want anyone to see him with the cast. My mother insisted, and he ended up breaking the cast off his arm. She had to have it put back on four more times, because he kept breaking it off."

Barbara claimed the battles between Grate and their mother began when he was still a toddler.

"My mom was having new carpet laid," she told the court. "And Shawn wanted a sandwich. He was hungry—and hungry *now*. She [Mom] told him to wait. She went outside to write a check for the carpet. While she was outside, Shawn went into the fridge, got the mustard, and sprayed it on the new carpet.

"It was always a battle in the household of who was going to be in control—him or her? It started with the mustard, and it just carried on from there."

Barbara said that when she was ten, she arrived home from school one afternoon to find the family's Marion home engulfed in flames. There were fire trucks parked along the curb, and "half our house was missing," she recalled. "There was extensive damage to my brothers' bedroom and my parents' bedroom. Both rooms were located in the back of the house. Firemen knocked down doors and threw them out the window. There was heavy smoke damage."

During an interview with me, Grate admitted to setting the blaze in his own home. At the time, his parents were trying to make their relationship work, he said. His mother and father "always fought." His dad would "flip out and smack a lamp." He was sure his father wanted to smack his mother, who, he claimed, "still has her ways."

Grate recalled that he was playing with a Zippo lighter during one of their fights, and he burned his finger. He then walked over to the closet and set it on fire, then ran to tell his parents the house was on fire. Grate recalled that his father moved out shortly thereafter.

As Grate got older, the battles between him and his mother continued. "When [Shawn] doesn't get what he wants, he acts out aggressively," Barbara said.

She recalled that when Grate was around six or seven, a man named Dan, whom Theresa dated for a couple of years, moved in with them while recovering from knee surgery. "Shawn didn't care for him being in the house," Barbara said. "[Dan] was trying to correct Shawn or talk to Shawn, and Shawn didn't like that. Shawn had shoes on, and he hauled off and kicked [Dan] in his knee. [Dan] moved out shortly after that."

The year Barbara turned sixteen, her mother lost her bartending job, and her stepfather, Terry Grate, moved back into the house temporarily to help with the finances. For the first time in years, Barbara was free to be a teenager.

The week after Barbara turned seventeen, she moved out of the house and in with her boyfriend. "That's when things turned to chaos," she said.

She recalled that not long after her departure, her brother Jason got off the school bus one afternoon to find "all his clothing, bedding, and possessions in a black plastic garbage bag on the front lawn next to a bag with all of Terry's belongings."

Barbara said that Theresa no longer wanted a relationship with Terry, and this was her way of letting him know. As for eleven-year-old Jason, "he had done something to aggravate her," so he had to go, too.

With Terry and Jason gone, nine-year-old Shawn was alone in the house with his mother. But two years later, he experienced a similar fate. Fighting back tears, Barbara described the day Shawn got off the school bus to find his mother had packed up the house and moved to Kentucky to be with her then boyfriend.

"He came home to nothing," she sobbed. "[Mom] took everything—his clothes, his bedding. So, Shawn went to live with his dad."

For a time, Grate was making good strides, particularly at

school, where he discovered his love of baseball and joined the River Valley baseball team as a standout pitcher.

"He had hopes and dreams of playing sports and moving forward," Barbara said.

But Grate's world came crashing down one night on the ball field when he was in the eighth grade. "He went to throw a pitch, and his arm broke from his shoulder blade to his elbow," Barbara recounted. "It turned out he had a tumor that was growing, and he had to have surgery on the arm. He was never allowed to play baseball again. He tried boxing and was sparring one day and rebroke his arm."

Not being able to play baseball marked a turning point in her brother's life, Barbara said. "Shawn fell in with a bad group of kids and started doing drugs."

On several occasions during my interviews with Grate, he alluded to his disappointment at the breakdown of his relationship with his father after he was forced to retire from the sport.

He said around this same time, his father moved out of the house and in with his girlfriend, who lived across the street, leaving his two sons, fourteen-year-old Shawn and sixteen-year-old Jason, to manage things on their own. It was during this time that Shawn met the girl who would become the mother of his first child. He told me that he got a job at the local supermarket, and his father would drive him to and from work. It was unclear if he met the young woman at the supermarket where he was employed or if she was a fellow classmate. Both were sixteen, and Grate recalled that she had lost both of her parents, but he provided no further details.

Barbara said the year Grate turned seventeen, he got into trouble at school. She couldn't remember what he had done—she was married at the time and had a family of her own. But it was serious enough to warrant a call from the principal.

However, school officials did not notify Grate's father. Instead, they contacted Grate's mother, who had been granted legal custody of her two sons after the divorce. Administrators made it clear to Theresa that as Shawn's legal parent, she would be held responsible for her son's actions.

That afternoon, when Grate got off the school bus, Theresa was waiting for him in the driveway of his father's home, Barbara recalled. "She made him go inside and pack his clothes and come live with her and her current husband. He didn't want to go; he absolutely didn't want to go."

Grate described his time living in the home with his mother and her new husband, Mike, as tumultuous. He said he never really accepted Mike because "I was torn between him and my dad." He suggested he "wasn't allowed to love Mike or respect Mike because it's just against the 'rules.'"

In one interview with me, he talked about his mother getting physical with him. He said in one instance she pushed him, and he lost his balance and pulled his mother's shirt off. Another time, his mother's husband, Mike, allegedly punched him in the mouth. The police got involved more than once, Grate claimed.

In June 1994, two months before Grate's eighteenth birthday, Theresa transferred legal custody of both of her sons to their father, Terry. That September, Grate returned to live with his elder brother in their father's house and begin his senior year at River Valley High School.

That same year, his first child, a daughter, was born. In a previous interview, he had described meeting the young woman when they were both sixteen and said she and their infant daughter lived with him and his brother for a time.

That August, Grate was arrested for strangling the mother of his child, who told police she had been trying to break up with him and that this was not the first time he had physically assaulted her. Eventually, the young woman would marry, and she and her new husband would raise Grate's daughter with no support from Grate.

On October 23, 1996, Grate was arrested again, this time for breaking into a house in Marion County with a juvenile accomplice to steal money and jewelry. He was twenty at the time and was charged with felony burglary.

In January 1997, a judge sentenced him to four years in prison. But he was granted early release in October of that same year, having served just nine months of his four-year term.

On February 16, 1999, Grate was arrested for breaking into the Marion home of his then pregnant seventeen-year-old ex-girlfriend, Lisa Ball. In one of our interviews, he'd admitted that he and Ball fought often and that during one of their confrontations, he'd contemplated killing her. He then disclosed that if he had followed through, she would have been his first victim.

That March, Ball filed for and obtained a restraining order preventing him from contacting her. But she had a change of heart about Grate after she gave birth to their son that September and asked the court to allow him to contact her. Just one month later, on October 22, 1999, she called police to her home again, this time to report the incident with the knife that Grate had described to me.

Grate was charged with a felony, and his early release for the 1999 burglary was revoked. He returned to prison in March 2000 to serve out the remainder of his four-year sentence.

His sister, Barbara, said that after his release in January 2003, he asked if he could come to live with her. He had been staying with his mother, but he wanted to get away from her.

Barbara agreed, but only if he got a job.

About a week into his stay, Grate showed up at the house just before midnight with a female friend, and the two were making a lot of noise, Barbara recalled. "I didn't see them, I just heard them. I believe at one point, I did get up and tell him, 'Hey, I have to be up at three thirty and be at work at four thirty,' and to be quiet. At that time, I was working twelve-hour shifts at the Honda supplier [in Marion], and I had to be in at four thirty in the morning."

At some point, they left, and for whatever reason, "[Shawn] left my front door propped wide open," Barbara said. "I mean, critters could walk in the house. I mean, here it is midnight, one a.m., and my door is propped wide open. I couldn't understand why he would have done that.

"It upset me, so I shut the door and locked it. He did not have a key to the house. If he didn't have that much respect, 'You can go and stay at Mom's house,' which was around the corner," Barbara continued.

"The next day, Shawn called, and he apologized and asked if he could come back. And I told him that yes, he could, but to not do that again. I told him I would leave the door unlocked for him when I left for work that morning."

Barbara recalled that sometime between 12:30 and 1:00 p.m., her mother showed up at the auto parts factory and pulled her out of work. "She wanted to catch me before I headed home. Someone had broken into my house and just totally tore my house from one end to the other."

Barbara said it was Shawn who discovered the break-in when he arrived at her house that morning. He contacted their mother, who came right over, then called the police.

"I blamed [Shawn] for doing it," Barbara said, aware that he had been arrested for burglary in the past, and, according to Barbara, the police confirmed it. But Grate insisted he was innocent.

She said responding officers took Grate to the Bowling Green police headquarters, where he consented to a polygraph. "He passed the polygraph, so, he didn't do it; somebody else did," Barbara said. "But moving forward, he stayed with my mom. 'Cause I was angry."

According to Grate, the situation with his sister is what precipitated his move to his grandparents' house in Marion. During one of our interviews, he said that Barbara accused him of the break-in and swung at him. He suggested that Barbara was committing insurance fraud and that was why she said there was a burglary. His claim was never substantiated.

It was while staying at his grandparents' house that Grate committed his first homicide, Dana. Shortly after the murder, he moved to Bucyrus, where he met Christina Hildreth, and the two were together for five years, until his arrest in June 2010, when he was charged with first-degree misdemeanor domestic violence against Hildreth and sentenced to 180 days in jail.

Upon his release, he went to live with his mother, and he even accompanied her to church. But he said he resented how he was treated at church because he didn't feel accepted.

During an interview with Grate, he bizarrely claimed that a very religious woman from the church began writing to him when he was released from jail and was encouraging him to return to the faith. He suggested that she gave him mixed messages and that their relationship actually became sexual in nature, first with phone sex and then with kissing. But he said that they were never intimate. Engaging in actual sex would have been crossing the line for her, he claimed.

Grate's purported reaction to the religious hypocrisy of secretly lustful women was palpable. He said that because this woman had played games with him, he wanted to blackmail her and play games with her, too. He told me that she had given him a Bible, and he was toying with the idea of returning it with a note demanding she give him two hundred dollars a month, until she told her husband the truth. Ultimately, he abandoned his blackmail scheme.

Grate told me about another incident when he was nineteen. He said that he found out that a guy from a Baptist church he attended had molested children and had gone to prison. He said the news came as a shock to him because he'd thought that man was a devout Christian. He said that he was so upset over the incident that he took his anger out on a Bible, tearing it apart with his bare hands.

Despite his misgivings about the church, at his mother's urging, he continued to attend.

Not long after his release, he met Amber Bowman, the woman who would become his wife. I did not interview Amber Bowman, the mother of Grate's third child, but her story was all over the news.

On an episode of *Dr. Phil*, Bowman recounted that she was the one to welcome visitors at the church, so she went up and shook Shawn's hand. "He wasn't outgoing at all; he was not one to come out of his pew," she said of Grate.

She recalled that when they first met, she'd found Grate extremely handsome. "He had a great smile and sweetness about his eyes. He was very kind and very compassionate. I fell head over heels for him, and I was smitten. I got pregnant in November, and we got married in December."

But the "normalcy of marriage set in," and Bowman noticed that "Shawn seemed very restless." In the bedroom, he was forceful with her; it was his way or no way, she said, recalling that "one time, he put his hands around my neck and pushed me down into the bed."

After their daughter was born in April 2012, Bowman said she found out that Grate was cheating on her. When she confronted him, he packed a bag and left. "I remember vividly praying over him and our marriage, but there was no other option than to divorce."

Bowman claimed that Grate began sending her threatening messages. He told her he was going to put the names of her family members in a hat and start "taking care of them one by one." He also threatened that if he couldn't see their daughter, nobody could.

Bowman claimed that during their brief marriage, Grate admitted to stabbing someone, but said he did it in self-defense. She said he didn't reveal any details about the incident, so it is unknown to whom he was referring. I would later take a call from a woman from another state claiming that she now believed the man who broke into her house and stabbed her some years earlier was Shawn Grate. She said she recognized him after seeing his eyes on the news.

When asked if the revelation alarmed her, Bowman claimed that Grate had returned to church and was trying to turn his life around. She said when she learned about the murders, she thought, *That could have been me.* She added, "For whatever reason, he did spare my life."

19

Friday Night Lights

In Ashland, there is always a ton of excitement over the Friday night football games under the lights. A lot of people go to the various high school sporting events on Friday nights—what we in Ashland call Friday Night Lights. I had been working round the clock since Grate's arrest that past Tuesday and was looking forward to a few hours with my family.

That Friday, attempting to give my children some sense of normalcy, I took them to the varsity football game my husband was coaching. His team, the Crestview Cougars, was facing off against the South Central Trojans, and it was important to get my two younger kids there.

As I sat in the bleachers next to Macy and Reed, my mind was still focused on the Grate case. My senses were heightened. I was particularly aware of the sound of the band, the crack of the helmets, the lights on the field.

I couldn't stop speculating on why Grate had repeatedly talked about—and focused attention on—one of the forts he had constructed. He kept returning to it time and again throughout our interviews, and I was beginning to suspect he was dropping bread crumbs, just as he had done with his recurring clues about Dana.

Grate had assured Evans and me that Dana was his final victim;

he'd killed four women, and he'd told us about them all. But something was gnawing at me.

After the game, I put my two little ones to bed, then sat quietly on the couch in the living room. My eldest son, Corbin, came home from a night out and walked into the living room to check on me. He immediately sensed that something was troubling me.

"I don't know why Grate keeps talking about these forts, and there's one he keeps giving me directions to," I told him.

"Where is it?" my son asked.

Coincidentally, the location as a crow flies was not far from our house, and I started to describe it. "Well, if you take 30A out of Mifflin and go up the hill, you take that first left."

Corbin interjected, "Then you take a hard right, and there's a gas well up there on the right-hand side."

I was stunned. How did he know this?

"Mom," he said, "they found a body there."

"What are you talking about?" I asked.

"They found a girl there. It was an overdose in Mansfield, and they dumped her body."

Corbin got out his computer and pulled up a map of the area, then pointed to the location where he believed Grate's fort would be located. He always had a sense for investigation. Even as a small child, he was able to figure things out by mere nuances. He told me that a body of a female had been found by the gas well by a Columbia Gas Transmission employee back in 2015, and it was allegedly related to a drug overdose and dumping.

I told my son I was unaware of a body being found in that area, so he pulled up an article about the discovery on the internet and started reading off details. "She's thirty-one . . . Her name is Rebekah Leicy. They found her body right by Grate's fort."

I told Corbin that Grate had insisted that there were no more victims out there—that he'd claimed Dana was the fourth and final.

But Corbin was not backing down. He wasn't due to enter the police academy for a little while, but he was already thinking like someone who had some training. Like a good officer, he started reeling off a variety of facts and concerns about the parallels in the murders to which Grate had confessed and the circumstances surrounding Rebekah Leicy's death—the proximity of where Grate had resided in Mansfield in relation to where Rebekah was last seen, the location of where Rebekah's body was found in relation to the address of Grate's mother's residence, as well as the location where he'd built a fort. The site was a wooded area of Ashland County that was very close to my house.

Corbin told me to grab something to write with, and we began to compile a list. He was quizzing me about the target age of Grate's victims, as well as their lifestyles, looks, and the circumstances of their deaths.

Clearly, Rebekah Leicy fit the pattern.

"Mom, he did it," Corbin said. "It's not logical otherwise. You've got to do something," he implored.

By the end of the evening, Corbin and I were convinced that Grate was responsible for Leicy's death. I told him that I would let the Ashland County Sheriff's Office know that I'd be interviewing Grate about it.

That Saturday, at 9:30 a.m. sharp, I called Lieutenant Smart of the Ashland County Sheriff's Office and informed him of the conversation I'd had with my son regarding the revelations about Rebekah Leicy.

Lieutenant Smart said he recalled the case of Rebecca Leicy's disappearance and the subsequent discovery of her body in Ashland County. Police believed that Leicy had overdosed, perhaps while partying with others, and that those unknown individuals had taken her body to this remote, wooded area, where they had dumped it. At the time, based on the coroner's finding, there was no indication that she was the subject of a homicide. But Grate's confession now indicated otherwise.

I related the parallels in the three homicide investigations connected to Grate with the circumstances of the Leicy case, just as Corbin and I had discussed the previous night. And I was told that Ashland County Sheriff's Office sergeant Jason Martin had been the officer assigned to the Leicy case. Lieutenant Smart agreed to have Sergeant Martin contact me at the police station later that day. Under Sheriff E. Wayne Risner, it was not uncommon to co-investigate cases that crossed jurisdictions between the city and county.

It would be a couple of hours before I returned to the police station; I had a family obligation that I didn't want to miss.

My younger son, Reed, had a football game that Saturday morning, and I was determined to be there. So, I attended the game and cheered my son on from the sidelines.

Coincidentally, the game was at the YMCA, which was near where Grate said he'd thrown Elizabeth's cell phone off the Holbrook Avenue Bridge. So, while Reed and his team were having their pregame warm-up, I walked over to the area around the bridge and looked for the discarded cell phone.

My feet and the bottoms of my pants were soaked from the morning dew, but my efforts were without success. Reed, on the other hand, scored a couple of touchdowns, and his team won.

After the game, Dan took the kids to Savannah, a neighboring suburb, for Macy's softball game, and I drove to the station, where I met with Sergeant Martin. He had brought his file on the Leicy case so that I could review it.

According to Leicy's family, the last time Rebekah was seen alive was January 22, 2015. Two months later, on March 16, her body was found by a Columbia Gas Transmission employee checking on gas wells in the area. Her body was positioned against a majestic oak tree on a right-of-way off County Road 1908, just south of US Route 30.

At the time, Ashland County coroner Dr. Dale Thomae ruled that Leicy's death was the result of a drug overdose and reported finding no evidence of traumatic injuries on her body. She was just thirty-one years old.

Rebekah grew up in the "Little Kentucky" area of Mansfield, the family had told a reporter from the *Mansfield News Journal* when Rebekah's body was first discovered. She gave birth to her first child at sixteen and never finished high school, her father, Robert "Bob" Leicy said. He described his daughter as a "spunky little brat."

"She acted like a little girl when she didn't get her way," he told the reporter.

He said he and his wife, Linda, had two other children besides Rebekah when they split up, and Becky, as she was known to her family, went to live with her dad.

Born on March 24, 1983, Rebekah enjoyed fishing, camping, and spending time with her three children.

Her father said that her drug use began with smoking "herb," but she was introduced to harder drugs by a boyfriend. He said he tried to help her get clean, but she repeatedly rejected his pleas. Rebekah's addiction worsened after her mother died in 2004, he said. At times, she was homeless and, like Shawn Grate, slept in tents in the woods and squatted in abandoned buildings.

If what Rebekah's father was saying was true, she was like so many other people who suffered the consequences of addiction, where there is no room for your obligations or your family, even your children, only drugs.

"She would call when she didn't have food," her father told a local journalist.

So, news of Rebekah's death came as little surprise when police showed up at Bob Leicy's doorstep the day her body was found. He told the Mansfield reporter that he believed his daughter's death was tied to her drug addiction.

Leicy was convinced that a local drug dealer had injected Rebekah with a lethal dose of drugs after she'd stolen money from him. It was a reasonable suspicion—if she had, in fact, stolen from the man.

A close friend of the Leicy family also latched onto the idea. Rebekah was telling people she feared for her life in the weeks before she disappeared, he said.

But my son Corbin and I now suspected that Shawn Grate had played a role in Rebekah's death.

I reviewed the investigative file Sergeant Martin brought to the police department. It was clear that Mansfield PD had done their due diligence investigating Rebekah Leicy's disappearance. I made copies of several of the police photographs that had been taken the day Rebekah's body was discovered so that I could use them in my interview with Grate. I then told him about my conversation with my son the previous evening, and why Corbin and I were now convinced that Grate was responsible for Rebekah's murder.

Sergeant Martin and I were reviewing the case notes when I was alerted to a call from Lieutenant Utley from the Marion County Sheriff's Office. Lieutenant Utley was eager to go over details related to the confession I'd elicited from Grate regarding the murder of the woman he called Dana. The incident had occurred in Utley's jurisdiction, and she wanted a briefing.

I told her that Sergeant Martin and I intended to interview Grate regarding a possible new victim, Rebekah Leicy, and she asked if she could be present to observe the interrogation. She told me that her agency had not yet identified the body of the female found in

Marion County whom Grate had referred to as Dana, but efforts were underway.

It was after 3:00 p.m. by the time I arrived at the Corrections Division to escort Grate to the detective bureau in the Ashland County Sheriff's Office, where our interrogation would take place. The two buildings were just across a parking lot from each other, so Sergeant Martin joined me for the short walk. I had worked with Martin on a variety of cases over the years. We were comfortable with each other's interview styles; we both knew when to talk and when to remain silent.

During the walk, I introduced Grate to Sergeant Martin, explaining that he was a detective from the Ashland County Sheriff's Office and that he would be sitting in on our conversation.

Grate seemed okay with having Sergeant Martin participate. He told us that being behind bars in jail was hard for him, in part because he was missing coffee and caffeine. He said that he had been a caffeine drinker his whole life, but his access to coffee was now limited by his incarceration.

I asked the corrections office staff if they could provide Grate with a cup of coffee, and they agreed.

Once in the interview room, I again asked Grate if he was okay. "Hanging in there . . . I am still trying to forgive myself." He stated that it would be nice to get forgiveness and said that having an interview with me helped him to face reality.

The video recorder for the interview room was not functioning properly, so I used my digital recorder to capture the audio from our meeting.

Grate asked me if I had been busy trying to "gather up everything."

I explained that I had, in fact, been busy, and that I hadn't had much sleep, to which he replied that he had been having dreams.

Now was clearly not the time to explore Grate's dreams, so I

pressed ahead, explaining that he was now represented by an attorney for the cases that had occurred in Ashland City. I reminded
him that I was referring to the alleged crimes that had taken place
in the Covert Court house—the abduction and rape of Jane Doe,
and the murders of Elizabeth Griffith and Stacey Stanley Hicks.

"Today, I want to talk to you about something completely separate than the other cases," I said. That meant I would have to Miran-
dize him first. I advised him that if he decided not to talk to me, he
would still get his coffee.

After informing him of his Miranda rights, I asked him if he
understood.

"Yes," he replied.

I told him that I had noticed that things he told me had come in
layers and that I understood his mindset of not telling me everything
at once. I reminded him of what I had told him at the beginning of
the case, that I wouldn't judge him. "And I haven't," I said. I also told
him that I appreciated his candidness and trust to this point.

Grate watched me with his icy-blue eyes as I explained why I was
there. I told him that the previous night, I had gone over the information he had given me to date, and I had made a discovery. I said
that I needed to talk to him about something, and the reason I had
Sergeant Martin there was because he had dealt with a situation
related to my finding a long time ago.

"There are some parallels in that situation and the current cases
here in Ashland," I explained. "Do you know what I'm talking
about?"

"I'm not exactly sure," he said. He looked at me, squinting in
anticipation.

I told him that there was an unsolved case in Ashland County.

"We are here to learn if you had something to do with it," I said.

Without further prompting, Grate stared at me, nodded slowly,
and stated, "Rebekah Leicy?"

"Yes, sir," I replied.

"I had a problem with her once."

Grate claimed that when he met Leicy, she got violent with him, and he was "angry and bitter" about her. "Just like Stacey," he railed.

"Elizabeth was more difficult 'cause I played around with her. She got scared and jumped the gun. . . . I thought we were more than that, but Rebekah . . ."

At this point, I removed Grate's handcuffs. As I did so, he remarked about Rebekah Leicy, "She tried to rob me."

"Rebekah tried to rob you?" I said, returning to my seat directly in front of him. "Tell me about it."

"She was number two," Grate continued. "Yeah, Rebekah was number two. She seemed like a good person and everything. . . . We've met several times as friends."

I found it strange that Grate was speaking about Rebekah in the present tense. "How did you two meet?" I asked.

"Through the street," Grate replied. "I tried to encourage her to get off crack."

I asked Grate if he was okay with Sergeant Martin asking questions during the interview, and Grate indicated that it was fine. I then encouraged him to tell us what happened with Rebekah Leicy.

"It was shortly after my best friend passed away," he said. "It was two years ago, probably, wintertime, when I took her out there," Grate stated, referring to the wooded area where he'd discarded Rebekah's body.

As I was about to pose my next question, I noticed that Grate's demeanor had changed. He now looked sullen. Lowering his eyes, he offered a half-hearted apology. "I now feel like a liar," he said, apparently feeling remorse because he hadn't told me about Rebekah Leicy in our earlier interviews.

He appeared upset that he hadn't been honest with me, as if he had betrayed me in some way. This happened several times during our thirty-three hours. He then suggested that Leicy's death "was pretty much self-defense." He claimed she robbed him, and he just "snapped."

I asked Grate where the incident with Rebekah took place.

He said it happened at his friend's shop in Mansfield. Grate identified his friend as David Kulig and said he passed away in late May of 2014.

Over the next three hours, Grate painted a picture of himself as a man without roots, moving from one temporary shelter to another, while also trying to set up some kind of wooden sign-making business for himself. He explained that his friend Dave owned a building on North Walnut Street. Dave also operated a shop out of the location, the Eclectic Tempo, where he taught poetry, music, art, magic, and billiards.

According to Grate, Dave owned both the building and the shop, and he had made Shawn a partner, although it was unclear to what business Grate was referring. "His family is not going to like this," Grate remarked.

As with all of Grate's confessions, this account would have to be verified. In the coming days, I was able to confirm the details about Dave Kulig's building and business.

According to the Richland County coroner's investigaton, Kulig died of natural causes in his apartment above the shop on May 28, 2014, and his parents, Jim and Jéan, now owned the building.

Grate claimed that back in 2014, he had a workshop in the basement of Dave's building. He said he met Dave in 2012 while he was staying at the Harmony House, an emergency supportive housing ministry for young people. He had gone there after his divorce from his wife, Amber, and was approved for a sixty-day stay. The administrators at Harmony House granted him a thirty-day extension after he was unable to secure permanent housing during the initial period.

According to Grate, Dave had a personality disorder, but over time, the two "grew a bond and became friends."

When Grate's ninety-day stay at the Harmony House ended, Dave gave him a place to live, an upstairs apartment in the building on North Walnut Street. He even offered Grate his first two months' rent for free if he agreed to clean up the shop.

Grate said he lived there for two and a half years but returned to Harmony House after Dave passed away from a heart attack in May 2014. And while Grate was no longer a tenant, he continued to maintain a small woodshop in the basement, with permission from Dave's parents. He indicated that he was good friends with Dave's whole family.

Grate said he remained at Harmony House for about five weeks, then moved to a shelter for men, where he eventually found employment in the maintenance department of the Holiday Inn on Park Avenue in Mansfield. But his failure to pay child support caught up with him, and the court garnished his wages, taking 60 percent of his paycheck each week.

When his stay at the Harmony House ended, Grate sought help from the Volunteers of America. The nonprofit organization had a branch in Mansfield, and as an ex-offender, Grate was able to get an apartment, where he stayed for about five weeks before moving into the basement room of the building on Second Street owned by landlord Jim Crisman.

A mutual friend told Crisman that Grate needed a place to stay, and Crisman agreed to let Grate work off his rent by doing odd jobs for him.

I asked Grate how he met Rebekah Leicy.

"Twenty dollars . . . that's how I met her," he replied.

"As a prostitute?" I retorted.

"Yeah." Grate claimed that after their first encounter, Rebekah started calling him, and sometimes she would come over to hang out and get away. She would bring crack over for herself, Grate said, adding that he did not partake. He admitted that he had used crack twice in his life.

Grate said he was in his woodshop in the basement of Dave's building in January of 2015 when Leicy stopped by. He had just come back from doing his laundry when she showed up unannounced. She was there about forty-five minutes when things took a turn, he said. They played a game of pool, then he walked Rebekah back to his workshop to show her some of the things he'd made.

"I went to the bathroom, right? I had some money in my wallet, and that's the first thing I did was check my wallet and it [the money] was gone.

"I confronted her. . . . She wanted to leave. I snatched her up; we fought. I ended up . . . choking her out . . . till she slept. I reached in her pocket, got my money."

Grate explained that before Rebekah lost consciousness, she'd tried to call 911. He said he grabbed the phone "after we were wrestling and stuff." Rebekah was curled up in a ball, he said, and he didn't know what she was doing, but he heard her yelling, "Help! Help!"

Grate claimed that Rebekah had two phones on her, and after he strangled her, while waiting for her to "wake up," he "grabbed the phones and . . . took the batteries out" to ensure they couldn't be used to track her location.

When she finally reawakened, Grate said he stood her up. "I was like, all right. I snapped. I treated her like a man. I squared up with her, right? I told her, 'You wanna steal from me?'

"She kept fighting me, trying to leave." He said he told her, "'Hold on there,' then I pieced her."

He made two *pow-pow*-type noises. "Boom!" he said. "Gave her a knee and put her to sleep again." While describing the episode,

Grate demonstrated the motions with his hands, indicating that he'd punched Rebekah twice. He then made a motion with his knee, as if he kneed the young woman in the face. "I didn't know what to do. . . . I panicked, so I just finished her off."

"How did you finish her off?" I asked.

"I choked her. She was on her belly . . . and I just put my arm around her, and I grabbed her other leg. . . . It was beyond trying to fix. I mean, I was . . ."

Sergeant Martin asked Grate to reiterate where the event took place. And Grate again cited his friend Dave's shop. He then suggested that if we needed any evidence, we should locate the golf club carrier he used to transport her body.

Grate explained that after killing Rebekah, he put her in an "old, plastic golf club carrier." "She barely fit," he said. He then leaned the carrier against a wall in the back of the basement, near the fire exit, until he could gain access to a vehicle.

"There's one room right when you walk downstairs," he said, sketching out a floor plan. "Over here is where I made my workshop."

Grate said the murder took place at around five in the morning, but it took him a couple of days before he could get a car to transport her away to where her body could be dumped. By then, he was living in the basement apartment of the building on Second Street in Mansfield owned by landlord Jim Crisman. Some thirty hours after the murder, he was able to use his landlord's Lincoln Mark VIII to transport her body to the dump site.

Grate said he had an extra set of Jim Crisman's car keys and that he would always ask to borrow the Lincoln. He claimed he had Jim's permission to use the vehicle that night, although Crisman apparently had no idea what Grate was up to.

He said he borrowed the car at night and parked it next to a meter so that he would have access to it in the morning. He estimated that he had Leicy's body for about thirty hours, because it was around two in the afternoon when he removed her from the building in the golf club carrier.

Grate said there was snow on the ground, making it difficult for him to maneuver the carrier. He recalled walking past an attorney's office with people watching him as he wheeled Rebekah's body to the car. Obviously, they didn't realize what they were seeing.

It was still snowing when he arrived at the location where he intended to dispose of Rebekah's body. Concerned that the Lincoln might get stuck if he tried to drive it off the paved portion of the road, he parked it on the road shoulder and dragged her body the rest of the way. He claimed that Rebekah was fully clothed in a sweatshirt and pants when he removed her body from the golf carrier.

He described propping her lifeless body up against the tree before making his way back to the car. He recalled that as he drove to the location, he noticed a police officer in a marked patrol car driving behind him. He worried that the officer had seen him with Rebekah's body, but after a few minutes, the vehicle turned in another direction, and he realized he was in the clear.

We revisited the dynamics of the crime scene, where Grate murdered Leicy.

Grate said his clothing was on the floor when he brutally strangled her to death, causing her to bleed all over his apparel. So, he bagged up the items, as well as Rebekah's shoes, and threw them in a dumpster.

Grate agreed to draw us a diagram of the location off Route 30A, where he'd placed Rebekah's body. As he sketched, he explained that it "took a while" for somebody to find her. He was in the county jail having been caught with "a few bags of marijuana" when he learned that her body had been discovered that past March. He admitted that he was also on probation for a previous offense at the time.

Grate went on to say that in recent months, he'd built a fort in the area within sight of where he placed Rebekah's body. I thought perhaps he placed his fort at that location for some morbidly twisted reason, but he claimed it was because it was close to his mother's house and he knew the area. He recalled watching the Charles Mill Fourth of July fireworks from the fort.

He talked about the view, stating, "I recommend it, because you can see the fireworks from all different areas from that spot."

I showed Grate a picture of the location, using one of the copies I had made from Lieutenant Smart's file, and he identified it as the site where he built his fort. Then I showed him a photo of the location where Rebekah's body was found, near the sprawling oak tree.

Grate intently looked over the photo. He explained that there was a cross and a memorial beside the tree, left there to honor the spot where Rebekah's body had been found.

Sergeant Martin asked Grate if he'd ever told anyone about what happened with Rebekah. "Not about Rebekah," he said.

Grate said he felt he'd "set Rebekah free" by killing her. He added, "It ain't my right. It ain't my place." Still, by murdering her, he'd "saved a lot of her family's burden of not knowing where she is anymore."

Grate drew a link back to Rebekah's drug addiction and suggested that she was "the same as Candice." The two of them would "stab you in a heartbeat," he bizarrely remarked.

Internally, I disagreed. She was a beautiful woman who was described to me as being kind and harmless. His dismissive remarks were just another layer of sadness.

To test the veracity of Grate's confession, I asked him to tell us three things that nobody else would know about the crime scene. I told him that we believed him, but other people may not. I needed to make sure that he had in fact committed the crime and wasn't just trying to take credit for all the unsolved homicides that had occurred in the area. I was relieved that he didn't bristle but rather responded in detail.

"Well, for one, you've got your memorial on the wrong side of the tree."

I asked him to elaborate.

Grate explained that he'd put Rebekah's body on the left-hand side of the tree, but whoever had placed a small white cross at the site put it to the right of the tree.

Sergeant Martin and I glanced at each other, recognizing that there was no other way that Grate would have known the precise details of where Leicy's body was found.

"Okay, what else?" I asked.

"Her pants are pulled down, but you won't find my DNA on her." Grate insisted he didn't sexually assault Leicy; he claimed that her pants partially came down when he was dragging the body from his car to the location where he left it.

He was correct again. Leicy was found with her pants down, and there was no other way he would have known that.

Lastly, he said, we would find her DNA in the golf club carrier he'd used to transport her body.

Grate claimed that after disposing of Rebekah's body, he stored the carrier "at Jim's." He described it as an "old-style" golf bag, black, with wheels. He indicated there were a couple of them in Jim's basement.

"The bent and mangled one will have Rebekah's DNA," he said.

He explained that Rebekah was bleeding from the nose and mouth when he placed her body in the carrier bag and suggested we would find dried blood on the inside of the carrier.

It was a stunning statement and one that was later verified by the Mansfield Police Department. At the end of the interview, Detective Martin and I contacted Mansfield police detectives and advised them that Grate had made a full, detailed confession of his murder of Rebekah Leicy. We further related that he had been Mirandized, the interview was recorded, and we suggested that they seal off the house where Grate indicated the golf bag would be located so they could retrieve and analyze it for DNA.

The scene of the murder was a Mansfield, Ohio, address, so MPD would handle the crime scene and investigation on their end. My involvement was the initial confession from Grate.

Forensics experts would find DNA from both Grate and Rebekah on the bag, with Rebekah's being inside, just as Grate confessed to us.

Because Rebekah's death had been ruled an overdose and subsequent dumping, nobody was looking into the circumstances of her death, and her name had not been mentioned in this investigation. I was beyond proud that my son Corbin, a fresh mind to law enforcement, had the wherewithal to recognize the parallels in Rebekah's death to Grate's modus operandi.

I asked Grate if there were any other victims he wanted to tell me about.

Based on what we knew so far, Grate killed for the first time in 2005, when he murdered the magazine salesperson Dana. There appeared to be nearly a decade between Dana, his first victim, and Rebekah Leicy, his second victim. His next murder was Candice Cunningham in June of 2016, followed by Elizabeth Griffith and Stacey Stanley Hicks, which happened in rapid succession. And Jane Doe would most likely have been number six, had she not escaped.

It was an odd spacing between the murders, and we suspected that there were others he wasn't disclosing.

"There is no one else . . . honestly," Grate replied.

"How can you go from Dana to no victims for years?" I asked.

"Regret. A lot of regret."

I asked him how long before the murder of Dana he had been having homicidal thoughts.

"Probably ten years." He then began talking about his ex-girlfriend Christina Hildreth, suggesting once again that he had wanted to murder her.

"I would have loved to have been able to do a lot [of murders]," he added. "But I knew I wouldn't be able to get away with it."

"Why couldn't you have gotten away with it?" I asked.

With regard to Hildreth, Grate said that he was pretty sure that police would have looked at him as one of the prime suspects in the case, given their relationship. "It wasn't random."

I asked about the victimization of other prostitutes.

"I've never killed no other prostitute," Grate stated.

I told him that if we ended the interview and there was still another layer that I wouldn't hold it against him.

I suggested that at the beginning of the interview, he appeared to regret not having been forthcoming with me. Now, I didn't want to walk out that door, because I was afraid that he wouldn't want to be perceived as betraying me again, as that might prevent him from disclosing information about any other victims.

"This onion is peeled all the way," he said, indicating that there were no more murders to be unearthed.

I decided it was time to move on. I told him that Sergeant Martin would be leaving the interview room and that we would now be joined by Lieutenant Christy Utley from the Marion County Sheriff's Office. She was responsible for following up on the murder of "Dana," because it had occurred in her jurisdiction. I asked Grate if he would be willing to help Marion County identify Dana.

Although he had already given me his confession about Dana, her body had not been identified. Marion County needed further information that would assist them in identifying the human remains they'd found on Victory Road.

Sergeant Martin excused himself, and Lieutenant Utley entered the room. I explained to Grate that Marion County police had looked at the sketch he drew for Evans and me of the home where he claimed the murder had occurred.

The statement elicited a sarcastic comment from Grate. He suggested the new homeowners might want to move now that they knew there was "a dead body in there."

For the next ten minutes, we reviewed details of the case that Grate had provided two days earlier—where he met Dana, how he lured her back to his grandparents' home, and more. But my focus was on identifying her so that Marion County could bring closure to her family.

I asked him if Dana had been carrying any identification the day he killed her.

He said he looked at her ID, then burned it in the bonfire. In a later interview, he told me that he felt like he might have held on to the ID for a while and thought it could be tucked in the floor joist in the basement. He recalled that an Ohio ID was among the items she was carrying. He recalled her last name being "longer," maybe eight or nine letters.

"How confident are you that her name was Dana?" I asked.

"About ninety percent," Grate said.

He described her as being about five foot eight to five foot ten but said he couldn't be certain, because of her shoes.

Lieutenant Utley spent some time clarifying when he had committed the murder and when his grandparents' house was sold.

We asked if he knew where Dana was from and by whom she was employed. I told him we didn't have much to go on, but that a composite sketch had been done when Dana's remains were first found off Highway 23 nearly a decade earlier. I then presented him with several drawings with a mix of head-on facial views and side profiles and asked if any of them resembled his victim.

He pointed at one of the head-on sketches and indicated that it didn't look like Dana.

"She was attractive, she was very pretty," he remarked.

I asked if he could describe the features of her face that made her look "pretty."

"She had an innocent look," he said. "And nice teeth. She looked like she took care of herself."

Grate asked if there were any other drawings he could look at. We told him there weren't.

To better assess his recall of the incident and the veracity of his remarks, I presented him with another sketch and asked again if he could identify the woman.

"That's Rebekah Leicy," he said. "That's a good one . . . She had a good heart, but she was torn. She had a heart like mine."

Before escorting Grate back to the jail that afternoon, I stood outside with him while he smoked a cigarette. He was congratulatory to me. "There you go," he said with a grin.

In yet another twist, this alleged serial killer was applauding me for accurately deciphering his trail of clues to determine that he had killed Rebekah Leicy.

Grate was apologetic because he'd promised me there were no more victims. "I just tell you what I think you can handle in one day," he remarked again.

"I can handle it. Don't hold back," I stated, and he responded with a smile.

Several days later, on September 22, 2016, an Ashland County grand jury returned a twenty-three-count indictment against Shawn Grate that was presented by Prosecutor Chris Tunnell. The indictment included charges of Rape, Burglary, Evidence Tampering, Gross Abuse of a Corpse, and Kidnapping with sexual motivation, as well as two counts of Murder for the strangulation deaths of Elizabeth Griffith and Stacey Stanley Hicks. These charges only related to crimes Shawn Grate had committed in Ashland County.

Marion and Richland Counties would handle the charging for the incidents that had occurred in their respective jurisdictions.

20

The Grate Deceiver

Religion had surfaced with some regularity during my interviews with Shawn Grate. During one of our exchanges, he asked me if I believed that Jesus would forgive murderers. His remark stayed with me. The truth was, I didn't know how to respond.

Now, he was asking me if I could provide him with a King James Bible that had Psalms and Proverbs. The one he had in his cell didn't include particular material that he wanted to read, and he was eager to get hold of a version that did. I remember feeling conflicted about providing this man who had done such evil things with a Bible. But I understood that he was worried about his salvation. During a prior interview at the police station, he had asked me if I believed that God would forgive him or if I thought he was going to hell. I couldn't answer him. But I could provide him with the Bible he had requested.

I approached Detective Lieutenant Joel Icenhour, the former head of the detective bureau and my first training officer. Although he had retired in 2015, Icenhour still worked part-time for the department, doing forensic analysis of electronics. He was also a Christian, so I told him that Grate was asking for a Bible, and he agreed to coordinate getting a copy of the King James Version.

Within a day or two, Detective Lieutenant Icenhour came back to me with a leather-bound Bible he'd gotten from a local pastor. I recall being taken by how beautiful it was; the leather was high-end with a distinctive, oaky smell, like a pair of fine Italian shoes. The Bible had reverence, and I don't know why, but as I held it in my hands, I suddenly felt small.

Delivering the Bible to Grate at the jail felt surreal. This was a death penalty case, and I was furnishing this special Bible to a man who had asked me about his salvation and if he was going to hell.

Grate seemed genuinely pleased by the gesture and repeatedly thanked me. I don't think he expected me to keep my word, and he then asked why I had done this for him. I told him I would never stand in the way of someone obtaining a Bible.

It was early in the morning of September 21 when ACSO Corrections Division corporal Mike Freelon advised me that Grate had repeatedly asked to talk with me. I told Corporal Freelon I would be there within the hour.

Detective Evans accompanied me to the Ashland County Jail that Wednesday morning. Grate appeared frustrated when he arrived in the booking area. Apparently, he had requested to meet with me multiple times, but he had not heard back. "I figured you'd been busy," he said.

I told him I had not received any of the messages.

He acknowledged my statement, then without any prompting, he announced, "I wanted to get some dates right."

To continue our conversation, Evans and I escorted him across the parking lot to the police department. Neither one of us had any idea what we might get him to divulge this time, but the conversation was worth having.

During the walk, Grate told us that his television had been taken away. "I've just been in my cell with my Bible." He claimed he was "trying to get back to civilized thinking" and that news reports about his crimes were making him want to "rip the TV off the wall."

He was particularly upset about statements from a "guy" being interviewed on one of the news programs who claimed that maintenance had checked the Covert Court house once a week.

"That isn't true," Grate insisted. He said he'd been at the Covert Court residence for forty days, and during that time, nobody came by to check it.

He said when he first arrived on Covert Court and tried the doors, they were locked, so he busted a window, then watched the residence for three days to make sure nobody went inside. He then broke a second window in the basement. He walked around the block and noticed two police cruisers in the area. He waited for three days in the "green building" across the street before returning to the residence.

This time, he went inside and learned that the electricity was on. He said he was able to relax, eat, and gain strength. There was even a television in the home, so he bought a VCR and DVD player to take full advantage of the small luxury. To avoid detection, he screwed the front door shut and used the side entrance to enter and exit.

He thought he had about thirty days before he was discovered. "I didn't worry about it till the incident with Elizabeth."

When we arrived at the police station, Evans and I escorted Grate to an interview room in the detective bureau, where he was provided with a cup of coffee. I then asked him what he wanted to talk to me about, and he reiterated that he wanted to "get the dates right." He was alluding to the dates he'd killed Elizabeth and Stacey.

"I don't remember the dates, but I wrote them down on this daily reader . . ." He described a white book with pink trim that he said we would find near the Christmas tree in the living room /

bedroom of the Covert Court residence that had already been searched.

Daily Bible readers had become popular in recent years, with select excerpts from the Bible for each day. Grate's featured pictures and illustrations along with the passages.

"What's in the daily reader?" I asked.

"Elizabeth's date. The date Elizabeth died . . . that would be the oldest date."

Grate indicated we would also find the date of Stacey's death. "The newest date would be Stacey's."

He explained that, at least initially, he was using the daily reader to log how many days he was at the Covert Court residence. But after Elizabeth's murder, he notated the date in the reader so that he would remember the date he killed her. He said that after each murder, he didn't sleep for about seventy-two hours. He just stayed awake to "think things through." By recording the dates of the killings, he didn't have to recall them, because he'd written them down.

"What is the reasoning in writing the dates down?" I asked.

"So I would know. I could have reference," he said.

Grate explained that he was monitoring the bodies' states of decomposition. "I was kind of paying attention with the odor, the smells. I mean, my clothes were starting to absorb the smell. Jane started recognizing the smell, my odor. 'Cause I would hang out with her every day."

I would later have to write and execute a search warrant to retrieve the daily reader, which indeed showed Grate's memorialization of the dates that he killed Elizabeth and Stacey.

In the days and weeks that followed, Grate sent me lots of kites, written requests asking to talk to me. The value of the exchanges was that he kept divulging more information, admitting to more crimes, and providing incredible insight for behavioralists to analyze. Gaining as much information as we could, while we could, was crucial.

I had two reasons for continuing to meet with him. The first was that we believed there were more victims. His pattern and the time gaps between his murders strongly suggested that there were more victims out there, and I didn't want to stop interviewing him until I had them all.

My second reason was that he was still blaming one of the victims, Stacey Stanley Hicks, for what had happened to her. He didn't want to admit that she had done nothing wrong. I was looking for the right time to confront him so that he would acknowledge that she had entered his apartment with no sexual intentions.

With each interview, I sought clarification and elaboration on the details that Grate had told us about his crimes. One point of clarification was related to whether he'd buried cans near the fort outside of Mifflin, where he had taken Jane Doe one afternoon during a hike. I was curious about the "treasure box" he had dug up and given to her to keep safe.

He said that he had buried several cans containing costume jewelry that he'd stolen from a lady in Richland County, whose home he'd burglarized. (Police would later collect the "box" from Jane Doe's apartment and mark it as evidence.) "I'm kind of an opportunist in a way . . . definitely an opportunist. I'm pretty dangerous, and I have to admit it. . . . It's not good. All my life, I've been this way."

He talked about feeling like he was never able to grow up. He suggested it was because between the ages of eight and twelve, "I didn't see my mom do nothing but cry . . . She was trying to find herself. . . . She was crying out for help."

He recalled that at the age of ten, he started gathering up trophies from his time on the baseball diamond. "That was a Dad-and-me thing," he said pridefully. He then described a time when his mother "blew up" in anger and threw the trophies at him. He described their relationship as being like "a boyfriend/girlfriend hate." "But it's a mom-and-son hate," he said.

Grate was midsentence into his next story when the building's fire alarm suddenly began to blare. I asked him if he wanted to go outside to smoke a cigarette, and he agreed. BCI agent Staley was at the station and accompanied us to the rear of the building.

While we were outside, he talked about his three children. He said he was particularly regretful of not having spent more time with his son. He recounted one Christmas he got to spend with the boy at his mother's house and remarked about seeing gifts for his son under the tree. He claimed he wanted to write his son a letter, then he began to cry.

He wanted to tell him, "It's not in his genes. That he's not a killer."

Grate then disclosed that when he was a child, his mother would tell him that she was worried that he would become a "pervert" just like her father and grandfather, who, she claimed, had both molested her. He was upset by her declaration, indicating this was something a mother should never say to a child.

I nodded in agreement and reflected on the parallels of this interview and the thousands of interviews I had conducted with children, where a recurring theme was the impact on a child when parents missed the mark. Although some children have horren-dous childhoods and move on to fulfilled adult lives, there are many who are emotionally paralyzed or arrested in development as a result of their traumatic childhoods.

Grate stated, "She [my mother] tells me so much about how warped her side of the family was and how she worried that I was gonna be like that . . . or an alcoholic . . . because it was in the genes."

At one point, Detective Evans stepped away momentarily. While we waited for his return, Grate continued to muse aloud. "I bet you deal with a lot of people who don't have a conscience," he remarked.

He told me that I had a good career, "helping people." He then admitted that sometimes he checked himself and asked, "Am I still being a deceiver?" He said he questioned himself about being honest. He tried to be polite and to say thank you to get what he wanted.

"The more polite I am, the more I get."

Before going back inside, I informed Grate that there were detectives from Holmes County who wanted to speak with him. We returned to the interview room, and I introduced Grate to the officers. They were there to question him about the body of a Toledo woman found in their county. Grate denied any involvement in the woman's death.

He was visibly frustrated when he emerged from the interview. He indicated the detectives had asked him the same question again and again after claiming they believed him when he said that he was not connected to the victim in their case.

Once back in the interview room with Grate, I had to spend time rebuilding his comfort and trust in law enforcement, and this wouldn't be the only time that occurred.

The next time I met with Grate, I was accompanied by FBI agent John Minichello. The FBI had been involved in the Grate investigation since day one. Profilers at the Behavioral Analysis Unit (BAU) at Quantico had requested audio and video recordings of my interviews to review. The bureau had also been in touch with investigators in Marion and Richland Counties, intending to put together a profile on Grate. I'd expected to get some critical feedback from them and was pleasantly surprised when they complimented my interviewing skills.

I was aware that every interview with Grate was a promising opportunity to gain information, but in partnering with Agent Minichello, I was certain we would gain more insight into Grate's psyche. Agent Minichello was also instrumental in picking up on case facets with a federal nexus and on leads from jurisdictions outside of mine and even beyond Ohio.

Our interview began with Grate telling us about all the fan mail he had received, mostly from people he didn't even know. He talked about the content of the letters; many of them addressed him as a serial killer and talked about his work in the same breath as they talked about other serial killers.

He told us that he once bought a DVD set of all the serial killers to watch. But he made clear that he was never inspired by serial killers. He said he found the Zodiac Killer interesting, because "he never got caught." He watched the recording about him three times.

He viewed Jeffrey Dahmer as "weird" and said Ted Bundy "is one of a kind."

Agent Minichello asked if he had ever identified with a particular serial killer.

"I've done things," Grate said. He talked about how Bundy had his heart broken. "Bundy was out for revenge, to let out anger."

The Zodiac Killer was a mystery because of the "codes," he said. Grate acknowledged feeling some excitement when studying serial killers. Some were "random," he said. "They don't really know their victims."

During the interview, Grate was very engaged in communication with Agent Minichello, who is particularly skilled at creating an environment where people feel comfortable being candid. Prior to the meeting, we had discussed our strategy, which included the exploration of other potential crime categories.

Having worked an enormous number of child sex offenses, I am hyperaware of the indicators of the child sexual abuse dynamic in a case. There had been a few points during my many hours of conversation with Grate that remained open-ended for me. I decided to introduce the topic of children-related crimes. I asked Grate if he had ever accessed child pornography.

"By accident," he said. When pressed, he eventually admitted to entering terms like "young girls" into a search engine. He said what he saw was really "confusing," "sick," and "messed up."

Grate then advised that when he was in his late twenties, he began having sexual thoughts about children while researching serial killers. He said he wouldn't "force" a child, but if they were "coming at" him, he didn't know how he would act. He reiterated that he had sexual thoughts about children but didn't want to hurt them.

I recognized that this revelation opened up the possibility of a broadened spectrum of potential victims—children. Grate had already told me in a previous interview that he had given a stuffed animal to a child he saw in the area, and I was aware that he had a lot of stuffed animals in the Covert Court address.

Additionally, early on in the interviews, when I'd asked him about children, his denial seemed shallow; I wasn't certain what he did, but whatever it was, he wasn't ready to talk about it. But I had him admitting to viewing child pornography.

Having dealt with offenders who targeted both children and adults, males and females, my radar was up. But despite his admission that he had accessed child pornography, he did not disclose anything further during this interview.

I asked Grate if he'd always had those thoughts about children, and he told me he felt like he had never grown up. He said that he was always trying to figure out what was wrong with him. He acknowledged that as he exposed himself to other people's attraction to children, he gained his own attraction to them, but insisted he had never acted on those impulses. He also indicated that he had an early interest in sex, but that he didn't lose his virginity until he was sixteen.

In a curious twist, Grate then began to question me, asking if I would help him come up with what his motive was in committing his crimes. He told me that a media personality had sent him an eight-by-ten photo of herself, along with a request to speak with him on camera.

"I wanted to talk with you, because you help me," Grate told me.

He said he wrote back and told the woman that the victims he murdered "were already dead" because they were accepting "government checks." He claimed he wrote that to see how she would respond.

I told him I could not advise him about what to do, but I suggested he assess the motive of those who were reaching out to him.

I would later learn that Grate accepted the interview and regurgitated a little of the information he had already confessed to. He later said he felt exploited and advised that he toyed with the reporter when he talked with her, that he had not provided her with accurate information. He said that during the interview, he was pressed for his motive.

I told him not to box himself in; that if he didn't know his motive, he shouldn't try to come up with one just to have an answer when people ask. I tried to explain that it was more important to talk about everything in his life, along with his candid emotions and thoughts, and that the information he gave could be useful for BAU in analyzing causation.

He said that after that, he didn't intend to talk to anyone, because he recognized it was pointless.

I pointed out how difficult it was to get him to talk at first and how candid he was now.

Agent Minichello and I knew Grate had many attributes of serial killers who have been assessed, including predatory behavior, manipulation, asserting power, and difficult child circumstances to mention a few. But there was so much more to learn.

We discussed Grate's dark thoughts. He said that when he was eighteen, he thought about older women. He suggested that he looked for "mom figures" when he looked for women, saying he felt that mothers provided a sense of safety, despite his bad experiences with his own mother.

Still, his victims weren't older women; instead, they ranged in age from early twenties to middle forties. I believed him to be an opportunistic killer, which are more about circumstances than a particular type of victim. Yet he was also truthful about older women, especially since I'd already viewed a video on his cell phone where he allowed an older woman to watch him masturbate, a woman with whom he held hands and considered having a relationship with.

Grate agreed but said that Elizabeth Griffith was different from the others, because she was "lost and just wanted to be loved." "She had problems her entire life," he said.

He then stated he'd been reading the newspaper and that Elizabeth's funeral was coming up; he even knew the date.

When the subject of his mother arose, his demeanor changed. He told us that she had come to see him at the jail and that during the visit, she said things to him that she should have said when he was a little boy.

"She is crazy," he stated. But he admitted that he was glad that she was coming to see him. He said she talked about his future, telling him he should become a barber, as if he weren't in jail facing at least two counts of murder and possibly the death penalty.

He said he jokingly told her that he was interested in culinary arts. He then stated, "She is stuck in herself."

We talked about the trauma his mother was experiencing at learning about his crimes.

Grate said he didn't want to talk about the past with her; he wanted to move on. "I'm not trying to blame her," he said, adding that he told her she had "raised him better than this."

He admitted that he still harbored some anger toward her and stated that he wasn't sure with which parent he had experienced "the worst love/hate relationship."

"The whole family loved and hated each other," he said.

He became tearful when telling us that his mother was planning to bring his teenage son with her when she visited that coming Monday. Theresa MacFarland and her husband, Mike, had been raising the boy for the past year. He admitted he hadn't been there for his son and said he regretted that, but he was now ready to face him. He wanted to tell him that he was not predestined to be a killer, like his father.

He pointed to his mother's suggestion that he would turn out "bad" because it was in his genes. He didn't want his son believing that.

When asked whom he had trusted in his life, Grate said that he hadn't let anyone get close to him, that he pushed people away, "the way I've been pushed away."

He felt "free" now, though, having divulged his crimes.

He suggested he didn't seek to kill people but rather, he would meet them and it would progress. He said that when he got around people, they talked about wishing they were never born or how they used drugs or had tried to kill themselves. He further described the frightening nature of his interactions. He stated that when he was making the decision of whether to kill someone, he was "not craving it but more like . . . why not? I'm doing 'em a favor."

Agent Minichello asked him if he felt bad after killing someone.

"I felt bad afterwards. I was like . . . 'Ah, man, there's another one.' . . . Especially like two or three days later, I was like, 'I wish it could be like some way to put life back into 'em and let 'em get up, go back home.'"

I asked Grate about the word he had introduced, *craving*. I told him that in an earlier interview, when he described going up the stairs with Elizabeth Griffith, his heart was beating fast.

"What was going on?" Agent Minichello asked.

"Something is about to happen," he replied. "This poor girl, there ain't nothing that she would want better than to be with God."

He compared himself to other killers who may want to take a child or a beautiful lady upstairs to "play with her body." "My heart was pounding for her [Elizabeth's] heart, not her body," he said. "Her heart has been so hurt, let down in this life. . . . The others may be different," he added, referencing the other women he had admitted to killing.

He suggested that in the case of Jane Doe, I could sense her "lust . . . her desires."

"Candice was a girlfriend for a long time," he continued. He acknowledged that he knew he was going to kill Candice days before, and he talked about her impending death. "I knew eventually it was going to happen."

I asked him about the momentum during situations when a woman angered or betrayed him.

"That's what I'm used to," he replied. "It's kind of exciting when I get betrayed."

"Because you know what the options are?" I asked, inferring that murder was now on the table.

"Possibly, yeah."

"What's the craving for?" Minichello asked.

Grate told him that he wanted people to "be real." He didn't want people to "live a lie." He said that his father, his ex-wife, his mother, and her husband "all live in a lie."

I asked him if there were times when he felt like hurting someone but there was no one there.

"Yeah, probably. I'd say so. A lot of times, I stay to myself just so I won't hurt no one."

"So, those moments are more about what you feel inside and

not somebody in particular, their particular circumstance? Am I right?" I asked.

"Yeah, I don't want to be a random killer. . . . I don't want to just hurt no one for no reason," he said.

I reminded him that in a prior interview, he had asked me to help him come up with his motive. I suggested that he talk about why he thought he killed each of his victims but that the common denominator appeared to be what *he* felt inside.

Grate remarked about how he could have had his master's degree in lying and, once again, called himself "a great deceiver." Or, as I referred to him, the Grate Deceiver.

We talked for quite some time. I had interviewed with Minichello before and was taken by how valuable the information was that we extracted that day. As the interview was ending, I asked Grate if there was anything else he wanted to tell us.

He insisted there were no more victims. "There have been five . . ." He stopped himself midsentence. He hesitated for several seconds before adding, "Women."

I didn't catch the significance of the long delay until later when I reviewed the recording of our interview. The intonation in his words, as well as the long pause before adding the word *women* to his declaration, suggested that he was either toying with me or dropping another hint. Were there male victims, too? Perhaps even children? I remain troubled by the possibility.

Grate asked if he could request me again the following week. "How about Monday?"

Why was he so eager to continue talking to me? Were there more victims he wanted to tell me about?

I would continue to respond to his requests until my superiors got wind of an alleged nefarious plan to harm me.

21

Jailhouse Informant

In mid-October, a jailhouse informant came forward claiming that Grate had confided his desire to make *me* his sixth victim. Grate was convinced that killing me—the female detective who interviewed him—would be the "ultimate" crime and admitted to his jailhouse buddy that he'd been trying to get close to me, hoping he could get hold of my gun.

The inmate wrote a kite requesting to speak with me, hinting that he could offer information on the Grate case. I arranged a covert meeting in the booking area of the jail. The man, who appeared rattled, told me that he and Grate had been talking and that Grate had divulged to him that there were more victims the police were not yet aware of, including at least one elderly person.

The man, whose identity will remain anonymous, claimed that Grate also talked about the abandoned buildings in the Fourth Street area, hinting there may be "someone" in one of them. Our officers had searched those buildings after Grate's arrest, but no other victims had turned up.

The informant next told me that Grate had bragged about "watching women" from his fort in the woods in the Charles Mill Lake Park area. In particular, Grate had spoken about watching a couple of female walkers in rural Ashland County who passed by the fort he'd built near his mother's house while he was staying there. He even described both of them being slender and blond.

His remark about the two blondes was startling. I didn't say anything, but the man was describing my sister-in-law and her exercise buddy. The two women liked to walk on that remote county road where Grate's fort was located; it was close to their homes and to mine. I recall thinking about how relieved I was that they chose to walk in a pair, rather than individually.

The informant said he suspected that Grate had harmed someone in that area and that there could even be another body there.

It was only after we chatted for a while that the informant suggested that I was in potential danger around Grate and needed to be careful going forward. According to the man, Grate had been quietly observing me—watching where I kept my gun and looking for moments when he might be able to surprise me, wrest my gun away, and shoot me with my own service weapon. He claimed that Grate wanted to set himself apart from other serial killers by harming me while he was in custody.

I began thinking back through my hours with Grate and wondering if there was any truth to this man's claim. Grate and I had spent some thirty-three hours together, a majority of it with just the two of us alone in a small room.

For most of that time, I had some colleague watching a video monitor and keeping an eye on what was happening. But that wasn't always the case. There were countless moments during those interviews when Grate was contemplating. I could see it, but I assumed he was contemplating whether or not to confess, not whether or not to hurt me.

I was not sure if I should believe the inmate. Perhaps he was telling me these things in an effort to court favor, get special privileges, or get a shorter sentence. But I will never know, unless someday I have the opportunity to interview Shawn Grate again.

When Captain Lay learned of the threat, he called me into his office. "I don't want you talking to Grate anymore," he instructed. "I think he's trying to get in your head."

I don't buck the system too much, but hearing this, I felt enraged. The captain probably had my safety top of mind. But I was intensely focused on the case and willing to put the threat aside under the circumstances.

"I'll tell you what Grate needs to worry about—he needs to worry about *me* getting into *his* head!" I barked, turning and walking out of his office and back to mine.

I slowly sat down in my chair, then peeked out to see if the captain was coming down the hall after me. "I got him to confess to killing five women!" I fumed under my breath.

Despite the captain's admonition, I continued to meet with Shawn Grate, but for security reasons, our sessions now took place at the jail, where no weapons were permitted, rather than bringing him to the police department.

Two days after my meeting with the jailhouse informant, I received an urgent message from Corporal Freelon telling me that Grate had been asking for me repeatedly. I told Freelon that I would meet with Grate that afternoon.

Prior to our meeting, I was given paperwork describing a variety of jailhouse infractions that had been perpetrated by Grate. He sure was making an impression there, and it wasn't a positive one.

When I arrived at the jail, I learned that Grate had just trashed his cell. He had broken the sprinkler head and flooded his cell, and he was threatening to continue with the destruction until I arrived. Apparently, he had been sending kites requesting to talk to me for more than a week, but I had not been alerted to any of them. I was also told that he had been moved to a cell away from other inmates due to his bad behavior.

Sometime later, I learned that Grate had carefully wrapped up the leather-bound Bible I had given him, swaddling it like a baby before he broke the sprinkler head and urinated all over his cell that day.

Soon after his outburst, I met with Grate in a private room in the back of the jail, where he was secured. I greeted him and told him to relax. Yet again, I presented him with his Miranda rights and asked if he understood before I opened our discussion.

He said yes, and I asked him what was going on.

"I want to hurt 'em," he said.

"Who do you want to hurt?"

"I don't know. It don't matter."

Grate claimed that "jail staff" was playing games with him and that it was "hard to handle." He said he was put in a cell with two other people, and he was accused of trying to teach one of them ways to strangle someone.

But Grate insisted that the claim was false. He casually said that if the other guy in the cell were "more my size," he'd "try to strangle him," but not to kill him. He seemed to believe that his cellmate was just testing him. "I don't have nothing to lose," he added.

I told him that it wasn't an option for him to hurt someone in jail.

"I'm not trying to," he retorted. "I just want to be left alone."

I asked him why he had flipped out and destroyed his cell—especially after being reasonable every time I sat down to talk to him.

Grate agreed that the way he had acted was unacceptable but that he was "giving them what they want."

"Don't do that," I said. My demeanor with Grate during this

interview was different from prior meetings; I was admonishing Grate with genuine concern.

"It's too late," Grate remarked. "I'm going to have to sit in the hole"—solitary confinement.

It had been two days since I'd learned of his supposed plans to harm me, and I deliberately opted not to raise the issue with him. I was accustomed to not making my cases about me with both victims and perpetrators, but this time around, I had to be especially careful not to come right out and ask him what the hell he'd said about me to his cellmate. But it was not far from my mind.

I listened as Grate complained that he had no coffee, that all he had now were his dreams.

I advised that tearing up the place wasn't working and that when I came over to meet with him that day, I hadn't known about his episode. I then explained that I had a new protocol regarding when I could talk to him, but I didn't reveal why the new measures had been put into place.

At this point, we were advised that we had to move to another interview room in the booking area.

While walking in the hallway, Grate acknowledged that his behavior was a choice. He said that trashing his cell would give him thirty days in solitary confinement. It was a weird thing to be worried about, given that he was facing life in prison, and potentially even the death penalty. He then complained that a corrections officer had lied to him.

"That's what started it all," he said.

Once we settled into the room in the booking area, I talked to him about perspective. We discussed the fact that destroying his cell only made matters worse.

Grate suggested it couldn't get any worse, that he was attempting to fix his toothbrush holder and it cracked. He said he wrapped it, and at that point, the staff thought he was making a weapon.

I reminded him why he was in jail and asked if he thought it was unreasonable for corrections officers to suspect that he was making a weapon.

He jumped past my reasoning, complaining that the inmates took turns staring at him and waved to him when he walked by. He found it pathetic that they looked up to him. He thought they were giving him props for doing things that "they couldn't do or wanted to do."

"It sucks," he said, and he started to cry.

He insisted he didn't want to be around anyone and threatened that it was going to get worse unless jail staff "reset" the situation. That morning, he started writing on the walls of his cell. He then told me about his plan to harm one of the corrections officers. He said he was going to cover the camera in his cell so that the officers would "rush in."

"'Cause I want to focus on that one dude," he explained. "I'm gonna get him."

"Meaning what?" I asked. "Meaning you want to hurt him or you want to kill him?"

"Whatever I can. I'll do whatever I can."

Sitting across from Grate listening to him sketch out plans to hurt or kill jail personnel was beyond belief. I asked if he still had "thoughts," if he still had a desire to kill.

"I'm afraid the desire probably grew," he replied.

He suggested that with Stacey, there was a desire. He then pointed to the time period between his murders; he claimed that during those time periods, he was alone with women and had plenty of opportunities.

He said he didn't know if he felt a "hunger to kill" the first four victims, but it was different with Stacey. He admitted to having that feeling with her.

"And I'm feeling more of it now," he stated in regard to the hunger.

I wasn't sure if he meant he was feeling the hunger in general or if he was feeling the hunger at that exact moment, while I was in the room with him. But I remained composed.

He then announced that he had thought about killing his cellmate, but he hadn't followed through because he didn't want to do the guy "any favors." "He's a little snitch who needs to stay behind bars," he grumbled.

He talked about plotting to murder his prior cellmate but said it would take "too long" to kill him the way he killed his other victims. He then admitted that he contemplated "stepping on his throat."

"I was going to get him to look in the bathroom . . . like a bug was in there, in the sink," he said. The plan was to have his cellmate lean down to look, then he would knock him out and step on his throat.

He also thought about putting the man's head on the toilet seat and "killing him like a bug." He said he suspected his cellmate was trying to talk to him when they were together in the cell so that he could get information to pass along for better treatment. "I know not to talk to him. . . . 'I'm just here to play cards and watch TV,' I told him."

Grate recounted that when he and his cellmate were in view of the camera in their cell, his cellmate reached out to shake his hand. "I jokingly asked if he wanted me to strangle him on camera."

He said he then put his hands on his roommate's neck, simulating strangulation, and they both laughed. His cellmate told him it was a win-win situation for them to be housed together, because if his cellmate killed him, he would be viewed as a hero; if Grate killed his cellmate, he would be out of the way.

Grate stated that the following day, he found his cellmate on his bunk crying, yelling, "Get me out of here!" Grate appeared amused.

He went on to express his annoyance at corrections officers for confiscating a news article he had in his cell with pictures of Elizabeth Griffith and Stacey Stanley Hicks.

I told Grate that we had received a tip about another possible crime he had committed in the City of Ashland.

He claimed that his cellmate had suggested that he "make up a story." "Oh, man, if he wants to be set free, then I'm going to set him free . . . the wrong way!"

"Meaning kill him?" I asked.

"Yeah." He said by the time the ambulance arrived, it would be too late, because he would have already crushed the guy's throat.

I realized when he was describing wanting to murder his cellmates and the corrections officer that his hunger was not just about killing women but rather he had an insatiable hunger for killing, period.

Grate claimed he hadn't lied to me yet, and he would lose his word if he made up a story like his cellmate wanted him to. "Maybe I haven't answered everything totally, but . . ." He stopped midsentence, as if to suggest he was holding something back.

It felt open-ended and still does.

Grate said he felt doomed. He now wished he had not been so forthcoming so that he would have leverage, another crime to dangle in front of me.

"Do you regret telling me about the five victims?" I asked.

Grate shook his head. He stated that he didn't regret confessing. He then returned to his plot against the corrections officers. He reiterated that he could get them to come to his cell if he obscured the camera or the window. "They are going to come in, and the momentum is going to cause me to target someone," he said.

At one point, he suggested that the five women he killed had been brought into his life by God "for a reason." But he now believed he may have been deceived. That it was not God but the devil speaking to him, telling him to commit murder. "I've done the devil's work in a way," he said. "My penalty for this is death."

I again raised the concept about his actions being a choice.

"I was seeing red earlier. I appreciate you coming to talk to me," he said, and once again, he started to cry.

He told me he had a dream that he was free, and everywhere he went, the news was on, and he was apologizing to everyone for having to see the stories about him. In his dream, he had a second chance. Then he woke up. "I deserve to be in a cell," he remarked.

This would be one of my last interviews with Shawn Grate. He would continue to send kite after kite requesting to speak with me. Due to a log-in issue, I did not receive those kites for several weeks. Eventually, I was not permitted to talk to him any further, although I felt like there was still more to learn. In every one of our interviews, he'd provided disclosures, even if they were to lesser crimes or simply information about the dynamics of his life. He even wrote out his thoughts and provided them to me.

During my last two or three contacts with Grate, Chief Marcelli pulled me aside and said, "I don't want you talking to him. I think he only has prurient interests, and I am afraid he is trying to make you a victim."

If I have a serial killer who is willing to talk to me, who is still relatively fresh and not yet "poisoned" by having undergone multiple interviews with other police agencies and the media, I am going to continue to try to gain any information that BAU can potentially use in their analysis, so history won't repeat itself. For me, it was that important. And for BAU, gaining data early on is valuable for the study of serial killers. But the higher-ups in my department did not agree. I would continue to receive inquiries from jurisdictions where Grate may have been regarding unsolved cases.

Not long after my jailhouse interview with Grate that October,

I was contacted by a detective from the Delaware County Sheriff's Office who was revisiting several unsolved homicides from the 1990s. He told me it was his understanding that Grate had worked at a hotel in the area during that time, although the hotel had since been demolished.

He informed me that the woman who was running the hotel had been stabbed to death and her body was dumped near the border of Delaware and Marion Counties. He also related details of a second unsolved case involving a girl who went missing in 1996 and whose remains were found in 2004. But authorities could not link Grate to either murder.

A few months after Shawn Grate's arrest, I would continue to pick away at the follow up on this investigation. I would also try to find ways to reconnect with my family. In late December 2016, my husband, Dan, and I took our two younger kids, Macy and Reed, and my nephew Brock for an afternoon of skiing at Snow Trails, a family-owned resort in Richland County. Usually, the kids like to ski, but on this day, they opted to go tubing, so Dan and I got to relax outside the lodge by the big, open fire.

It was late in the evening, and we were getting ready to leave when I noticed a bus from one of the local churches unloading in the parking lot. Dan and I watched as a group of teens came tumbling out of the bus.

It was unusually cold that day, below freezing, and I noticed that one of the boys in the group was not wearing a coat. He was the only one. As they neared the lodge, I recognized the child. It was Shawn Grate's teenage son.

I saw him standing there in the cold with his arms crossed for warmth. The elements made him look especially vulnerable, so I struggled to get a read on whether he was okay. I wanted to approach him and tell him that he was his own man and he could create his own future, but it wasn't the time.

I pointed him out to Dan. That handsome, innocent teenage boy with the weight of the world on him. I wanted to make it all okay.

Dan, the most steadfast and compassionate man I've ever met, took his winter coat off, called a youth leader over, and handed him his coat, telling him to give it to the boy. We watched from our truck as the young man put it on and scanned the crowd, having no clue who had given him the coat.

I couldn't make it all okay, but I could have reassured him that there were kind people out there.

22

The Trial

On Monday, April 9, 2018, jury selection began in Shawn Grate's capital murder trial. Grate's court-appointed attorneys were Robert and Rolf Whitney, a father-and-son team from Richland County. The two lawyers were well known and well respected in the area. The duo had filed a plea of NGRI, not guilty by reason of insanity, on Grate's behalf, which mandated their client be assessed by a doctor from the Mansfield Forensic Center. But the doctor who did the assessment found him "sane" at the time of the alleged offenses, so the insanity plea was withdrawn.

The defense had hired its own expert to assess Grate's legal culpability. Dr. John Fabian was a forensic and clinical psychologist as well as a fellowship-trained clinical neuropsychologist who specialized in criminal and civil forensic psychological and neurophysiological evaluations. According to his website, he was formerly director of a state court psychiatric clinic and had worked in an adult and juvenile court psychiatric clinic, a state forensic hospital, and a Federal Bureau of Prisons forensic center in the state of New Mexico.

Dr. Fabian had performed an evaluation of Grate the previous year and determined he had "a number of complicated mental health issues." But since Grate had been deemed competent to stand trial, Dr. Fabian would only testify during the penalty phase of the proceeding.

A section of the street adjacent to the courthouse had been closed to traffic in anticipation of Grate's arrival that first day. Security had been increased, given the high-profile nature of the case and the intense media interest. Satellite television trucks were lined up along the curb when sheriff's deputies pulled up and led a handcuffed Shawn Grate out of the vehicle.

Grate was dressed for court in a starched white shirt, navy slacks, and a purple tie; his brown wavy hair was neatly combed and, at the temples, streaked with gray, as was his closely trimmed beard. His piercing blue eyes were visible through metal-rimmed glasses.

Television cameras captured Grate's entrance into the courthouse; he seemed to revel in the media attention and looked directly at reporters as he strode past them.

Ashland County prosecutor Chris Tunnell was already in the courtroom when Grate was escorted in. He had spent the better part of the last two years preparing to argue the case on behalf of Ashland County. Grate was being tried on twenty-three felony counts, including aggravated murder in connection to the deaths of Elizabeth Griffith and Stacey Stanley Hicks. That meant in addition to his already full caseload, Prosecutor Tunnell had to sort through every piece of evidence, read every report and witness statement, and familiarize himself with every hour of the interviews with Grate. It was a bear of a job and had him working tons of late nights and weekends. Assisting him were his chief investigator, Doug Smetzer, and investigator Tony Shambaugh.

Chris Tunnell has a particular skill at trial work. He relates to people, and I've watched him adapt to situations with ease. He's "that guy," the kind of leader you need when faced with the most difficult circumstances. The one who is observant, relentless, and unshakable. His leadership, in the opinion of so many, is a huge reason why justice was brought to our victims.

Because this was a death penalty case, Tunnell had two special prosecutors, Michael McNamara and Mark Weaver, to assist with various aspects of the prosecution.

Ashland County Common Pleas judge Ronald Forsthoefel would be presiding over the trial. There was concern that jury selection could take weeks due to the enormous media attention the case had garnered. But Judge Forsthoefel was confident that a jury would be impaneled. He intended to break the pool up into eight large groups, bringing in two a day, with a goal of reviewing all the possible jurors within a four-day period.

The process got off to a good start, with nearly half of the first group of fifty possible jurors asked to remain at the end of the morning session. But the second day, Grate offended some in the group when he waved to them after his defense attorney Robert Whitney introduced him to the group. The simple gesture took some of the prospective jurors by surprise—and prompted fifteen of them to ask to be excused. They told the judge they did not think they could be fair and impartial when deliberating the case.

"I do not hate this person, because I am Christian," one of the released jurors told a reporter for the *Mansfield News Journal*. "But I hate and despise what I feel happened."

Another admitted he had already settled on Grate's guilt. "You've got the evidence. I don't even know why you have him on trial," the man stated.

Still others were too forthcoming with their views on Grate when questioned by the attorneys, prompting Judge Forsthoefel to issue a warning, instructing them to explain *why* they couldn't be impartial "without stating opinion."

On the third day, other potential jurors said they couldn't be impartial either—because they personally knew others attached to the case—whether it was one of the defense attorneys, a witness in the case, one of the victims, or the defendant himself. Others in the jury pool said they knew one another. This was not unexpected; Ashland is a small community where everyone knows everyone. Still, a handful of the conflicts came as a surprise to everyone in the room.

One woman related that Shawn Grate had asked her for a date, telling the court, "I was at [Miller's] Hawkins grocery store. He was sitting on a bench. He walked up to me and said, 'You're such a beautiful lady. Would you consider going out with me?' If I'd accepted that, I would have probably been a victim."

Judge Forsthoefel opted to excuse her from consideration. "It's a little too close to home for you," he told her.

Another potential juror explained that her son played football with Grate's son. "It's a small school," she said, adding that her participation in the trial could "affect my son."

She had already indicated on the juror questionnaire that she had discussed the case with her family and thought that Grate was probably guilty.

In light of the potential conflicts, Robert Whitney requested that she be "excused for cause."

But Special Prosecutor McNamara wanted to keep her in the jury pool. "She's not using information that she might have previously received," he told Judge Forsthoefel. "I think she's been very clear in that."

The judge agreed, finding that the woman's conflicts were not of "grave concern."

On Friday, April 20, ten days into the selection process, a seven-man, five-woman jury was impaneled, and Judge Forsthoefel scheduled opening statements for the following Monday.

Ashland County prosecutor Chris Tunnell kicked off the proceeding that Monday morning, April 23, with a ninety-five-minute opening statement. Dressed in a dark-colored suit, his long, full beard partially obscuring his tie, his deep voice boomed from the podium at the center of the courtroom. "This isn't a 'whodunit' case," he began. "This is a 'he did it' case."

Family and friends of Grate's victims, members of the media, and local citizens listened from the gallery as Prosecutor Tunnell described the brutal deaths of Grate's multiple victims.

Grate had some supporters in the courtroom, but no one knew if any of them were members of his family.

In an unexplained development, Grate's defense attorneys waived their right to an opening statement.

After a short lunch break, Prosecutor Tunnell called his first witness, Ashland County dispatcher Sarah Miller. Once Miller was on the stand, Tunnell played Jane Doe's terrifying 911 call for the jurors. A dead hush fell over the courtroom as the panel listened to Grate's only living victim, Jane Doe, plead for officers to hurry up.

Miller's testimony was followed by that of Ashland Police sergeant Jim Cox, who was one of the three officers to respond to Doe's early-morning call for help. Cox spoke to the men's valiant efforts to locate Doe, recalling that she was naked with a restraint hanging from one arm when they rescued her that morning.

Another chilling moment came later in the day when BCI special agent Ed Staley took the stand and related grisly details of his team's methodical search of the Covert Court residence, where they found Elizabeth Griffith's body in an upstairs closet and the body of Stacey Stanley Hicks under a pile of trash and debris in the home's basement. Crime scene photos accompanied Staley's testimony, including images of the bed where Jane Doe was held captive with the restraints still attached, and the Tasers Grate had stolen during one of his burglaries.

Agent Staley kicked off day two of the trial with a continuation of his testimony, followed by Elizabeth Griffith's therapist Tina Swartz, who first alerted us to her disappearance. Officer Kody Hying, who took Swartz's call, and who played a role in the search for Griffith, was next up.

Stacey's son Kory also took the stand, delivering emotional testimony about his final conversations with his mother from the gas station where she had gone for help after discovering her car had a flat tire.

Family friend Wayne Bright, a farmer in Ashland who had agreed to go to the BP station to help Stacey that night, also testified that Tuesday. But his misidentification of Grate in the courtroom raised eyebrows. When asked by Prosecutor Tunnell to identify the man he'd encountered that night at the gas station, Bright pointed to Special Prosecutor Michael McNamara, who was seated at the State's table, which was clearly marked "plaintiff." The blunder caused a momentary silence in the courtroom, surprising even Shawn Grate, who was between his attorneys at the table marked "defendant."

For the most part, Wednesday's testimony focused on Stacey Stanley Hicks. The prosecution called fifteen witnesses, including Sonny Phan, the owner of Nails 2, where Stacey had gone for her late-afternoon manicure, and BP gas station employee Nathaniel Keck, who recalled Stacey buying a cup of coffee that evening accompanied by Shawn Grate, the man who had helped her with her flat tire.

My brother-in-law Cody Mager, a deputy at the Ashland County Sheriff's Office, also testified that day. Cody, a combat veteran of the U.S. Marine Corps who was awarded a Purple Heart related to his service in Iraq, had received some of the kites from Grate requesting to speak with me. He testified to his role in passing along those messages.

On Thursday, April 26, Jane Doe bravely entered the courtroom to testify against her attacker. Victim coordinator Ruth Rafeld was there to provide support. Throughout her testimony, Jane never looked in Grate's direction. But he was transfixed on her, listening intently as she recounted her ordeal.

In response to Prosecutor Tunnell's questions, Jane told jurors she'd met Grate at the Kroc Center in the summer of 2016. At times, she became emotional. Through tears, she described her three-day ordeal at the hands of Shawn Grate, who repeatedly raped her and kept her tied up in the Covert Court residence. But midway through her testimony, Jane regained her composure and forged on. She told jurors she was in Grate's living room / bedroom reading him passages from the Bible when he suddenly got up and walked to the kitchen. When he returned, she said, his demeanor had changed.

"He started pulling the Bible out of my hands. I looked at him, and that's when he said, 'You're not going anywhere.'"

Sexual Assault Forensic Examiner (SAFE) nurse Lisa Riley, who had treated Jane Doe at the hospital after her victimization, also testified that day.

Other witnesses included Ashland County Sheriff's corporal Mike Freelon, Elizabeth Griffith's friend Tamara Whelan, and Ashland Police Division officer Curt Dorsey. Detective Brian Evans and Detective Lieutenant Joel Icenhour were also called to testify during the trial.

Captain Lay was the last to be called that afternoon. He testified about his involvement in the case, as well as his interview with

Grate when he was first brought to the police station on September 13. The captain continued his testimony the following morning.

Then it was my turn to take the stand. Entering the court that day, I kept my focus on the front of the room. Once on the witness stand, I looked over at the defense table, where Grate was flanked by his two attorneys. He slowly blinked, then nodded.

Eighteen months had passed since I'd last seen him. I wasn't sure if he knew why I had stopped responding to his kites. In one of his last messages, he had threatened to never speak to me again if I did not meet with him. He also claimed he had information to share with me about another victim. But my superiors had made it clear that I was not to speak with him; our role in the investigation was over, and I was to focus on my caseload, which was plentiful as always. I was directed to pass the information to the FBI.

I could see family members of the victims, citizens from my community, and jurors looking at me. Prosecutor Tunnell was also surveying me, trying to get a read on how I was doing.

At that moment, the courtroom got super quiet. I was sworn in, and Prosecutor Tunnell asked his first question. As I started to answer, I noticed Grate lean back in his seat, put his hands on his forehead, and start to cry. It was the first time during the trial that Grate showed emotion, according to media who were in the courtroom.

My testimony picked up the following Monday, with Prosecutor Tunnell playing portions of my interviews with Grate. I had to hear my voice and Grate's voice as we interacted; it was surreal.

The whole scene was particularly awkward because the audio had been captured on the small backup digital recorder that I had been carrying on my person. That September 13 morning in 2016, I'd dropped the digital recorder down my blouse.

I knew to expect that the quality of the recording wouldn't be as crisp as if it were captured on our professional equipment; what I hadn't anticipated was to hear my stomach growling as the morning wore on and, more importantly, the sound of my heart beating faster at various pivotal moments during the interview. I didn't know until that moment that my heart rate changed depending on the progression of the interview. Now, the audio was being played over the courtroom speakers for all to hear.

When Grate heard himself talking to me about his interactions with Elizabeth, he reached for a tissue, wiped his tears, then bowed his head.

At one point, jurors heard Grate tell me that he should "probably get the death penalty."

I provided testimony over the course of two days. Leaving the courtroom, I felt like I didn't get to say everything. We were only prosecuting the cases that happened in Ashland County, so the recordings of the confessions Grate gave me on the cases had to be forwarded to the jurisdictions where the crimes occurred. It was not an option to talk about the other women whose lives he had taken. And while Chris Tunnell drew out all the information we were permitted to provide, it felt incomplete.

The trial continued on Tuesday, May 1, with testimony from Ashland Police Division officers Garry Alting, Lee Eggeman, and Tim Shreffler. Dr. Todd Barr, the forensic pathologist who had performed the autopsies on Elizabeth Griffith and Stacey Stanley Hicks at the Cuyahoga County Medical Examiner's office, also took the stand.

Dr. Barr told jurors that Griffith's body was in an advanced state of decomposition when he examined her, so he used dental records to make the identification. He ruled Elizabeth's cause of death as "asphyxia by compression of the neck," suggesting the likely manner of death was a "sleeper hold."

The forensic pathologist pointed to similar findings in Stacey's autopsy, although he indicated that she had a scarf wrapped several times around her neck. He testified that a ligature likely caused her death also by "asphyxia by compression of the neck."

Dr. Barr said he was able to identify Stacey through fingerprints.

On May 2, eight days into the trial, Grate surprised everyone and pleaded guilty to fifteen of the felony charges against him, including one count of Rape related to Stacey Stanley Hicks, Kidnapping with sexual motivation with relation to Jane Doe, as well as Burglary, Tampering with Evidence, and Gross Abuse of a Corpse. There was no explanation for his sudden about-face. The fifteen charges carried a sentence of fifty years in prison.

When jurors returned to the courtroom that afternoon, Prosecutor Tunnell advised them that some of the charges in the original twenty-three-count indictment had been resolved. He then resumed the presentation of his case. Judge Forsthoefel said he would schedule a sentencing date after the remaining charges—four counts of Aggravated Murder related to the deaths of Elizabeth Griffith and Stacey Stanley Hicks, three counts of Kidnapping, and an Aggravated Robbery charge—were adjudicated.

Tunnell told the jurors that the murders of Stacey Stanley Hicks and Elizabeth Griffith were premeditated. To illustrate his declaration, he played jurors more clips of the interviews that Captain Lay and I had conducted with Grate.

Five days later, on May 7, a jury found Shawn Grate guilty of all the remaining charges. Prosecutor Tunnell had been successful in bringing this man to justice.

The guilty verdict meant Grate now faced the death penalty.

On Friday, May 18, jurors returned to the courthouse for the sentencing phase of the trial. The prosecution rested its case without presenting any witnesses.

Grate's defense attorneys put up two witnesses to offer mitigating circumstances that could help sway the panel to sentence Grate to life in prison instead of death.

Grate's half sister, Barbara, was one of them. Barbara was professionally dressed and appeared poised as she told jurors she had basically raised Shawn beginning when she was twelve and continuing for four years until she turned sixteen. She portrayed a homelife absent of love and nurturing. And she described her brother's early challenges—his diagnosis of a learning disability and other emotional challenges, and their mother's failure to address it.

She told jurors that she was estranged from their mother, Theresa McFarland, whom she described as "toxic."

Grate listened intently to his sister's recollections about their childhood and his challenges both at school and at home. For much of her testimony, he remained expressionless, even as she disclosed how her repeated calls to family members—aunts, uncles, cousins, even Shawn's father and brother—to implore them to come to court to testify had gone unanswered.

Barbara's testimony was followed by that of neuropsychologist John Fabian. Dr. Fabian had evaluated Grate the previous year and wrote a mitigation report for the defense. He told jurors that he had spent about twenty-five hours with Grate, during which time he'd administered about twenty-five tests.

In response to questions from the defense attorneys, he testified that Grate's brain was "hardwired differently" and that when he was born, he was compromised in "neurological development." Based on his findings, he diagnosed Grate with a litany of disorders—persistent depressive disorder, unspecified bipolar and related disorders, a specified trauma and stressor-related disorder resulting from a complex childhood trauma, a language learning disorder, borderline intellectual functioning, mild neurocognitive disorder due to traumatic brain injury, attention deficit hyperactivity disorder, cannabis use disorder, and personality disorder with antisocial, schizotypal, schizoid borderline and narcissistic traits.

He said he determined that Grate's IQ was eighty-three, putting him in the thirteenth percentile.

"In my opinion, his brain's not working right," Dr. Fabian told jurors. "As an analogy, if a car has four wheels, we've got about three."

Dr. Fabian stated that during the assessment, Grate expressed disdain for his mother and disclosed early fantasies of wanting to kill her, claiming he wanted to take her out of her misery. He also indicated that Grate admitted to "being pretty dangerous."

"The bottom line is, he's very impaired," Dr. Fabian testified. He then suggested that these impairments could be considered as mitigating factors in deciding Grate's sentence.

On cross-examination, Special Prosecutor Mark Weaver was unleashed on Dr. Fabian. Special Prosecutor Weaver questioned the validity of some of Dr. Fabian's diagnoses, citing definitions from the *Diagnostic and Statistical Manual of Mental Disorders*, or *DSM*, to make his point.

The cross-examination was one of the best I had ever seen in my career.

While the defense had declined to offer opening remarks, at the end of Dr. Fabian's testimony, Grate's attorney Robert Whitney stood to present closing arguments. He told jurors that putting Grate to death would "add a third corpse to the case" and suggested that life in prison without the possibility of parole "would be an adequate sentence."

"A death sentence will solve nothing," he implored. "This [Grate's death] would just be another murder."

In the end, the twelve men and women were not swayed. After deliberating just two hours, jurors returned two death penalty verdicts, one for the Aggravated Murder of Elizabeth Griffith and a second for the Aggravated Murder of Stacey Stanley Hicks.

I was in the courtroom that day seated in the front row. When the death penalty verdict was announced, I glanced over at Grate to see his reaction.

He looked up, and we made eye contact. "It's okay," he mouthed.

The verdicts were met with tears and quiet cheers from family, friends, and local community members seated in the gallery. Relatives of both of Grate's victims were among those in the courtroom to hear the jury's unanimous decision.

And while emotions ran high, Shawn Grate remained stone-faced when the verdicts were read, although he smiled at onlookers as Ashland County Sheriff's Deputy Shannon Mahoney led him out of court in handcuffs.

On Friday, June 1, 2018, Shawn Grate was sentenced to death, with Judge Forsthoefel setting an execution date of September 13, 2018, exactly two years to the day of his arrest. But Grate would be granted a stay of execution pending an appeal to the Ohio Supreme Court.

In light of the death penalty verdicts, Prosecutor Chris Tunnell offered remarks. He reminded the public that Ashland County was typically a safe place to live and work. "We're mostly law-abiding, peaceful folks here in Ashland County," he said. "Shawn Grate is the rare exception of a blackhearted person who wandered into our community from elsewhere and took advantage of the kindness and goodwill of people who tried to help him. He's now learned that Ashland County takes serious crime seriously."

On March 1, 2019, Grate pleaded guilty to the murders of Rebekah Leicy and Candice Cunningham in Richland County. I had testified before the Grand Jury in the Richland County cases, which had resulted in the indictments. I attended the hearing with Richland County prosecutor Gary Bishop. Grate was sentenced to life in prison without parole for the murder of Rebekah Leicy and seventeen years to life for the other related charges, with the sentences to run consecutively.

This sentence was in addition to his death penalty sentence in Ashland County.

Meanwhile, the quest of Marion County to identify the woman known to us only as Dana did not cease. In December 2016, a clay model of Dana was created by Criminal Intelligence and Missing Persons Analyst Samantha Molnar of the Ohio Bureau of Criminal Investigation in an effort to help Marion County authorities identify Grate's first victim. Ohio attorney general Mike DeWine and Marion County sheriff Tim Bailey subsequently released the facial reconstruction in the hopes of generating leads about her identity. DeWine would later become governor of Ohio, and Dave Yost became the attorney general and made identifying Dana a priority for law enforcement.

"It's frustrating, very, very frustrating," Sheriff Bailey told *People* magazine. "Particularly for my people who want to identify her and get her back to her family."

In January 2018, isotope analysis indicated she was likely from the southern United States. In June 2019, Marion County investigators were finally able to identify her through the DNA Doe Project, which uses genealogy to identify Jane and John Does. Grate's unidentified victim now had a name—Dana Nicole Lowrey of Minden, Louisiana.

Twenty-three-year-old Lowrey had two daughters, ages one and four, and was separated from her husband at the time of her death. It was the DNA from one of Lowrey's daughters that helped to positively identify her remains, which were returned to her family in Minden.

Fourteen years after twenty-three-year-old Dana Lowrey suddenly stopped calling home to speak to her two children, the family finally had closure. Upon learning the news, local media descended on the home of David Cobb, the father of Lowrey's two children.

"We had a falling-out and we separated—never got married," Cobb told KTBS 3 in an exclusive interview. "She called one day and said she was in Ohio selling magazines. The girls were ages four and one then. She just stopped calling one day. She used to call three or four times a week to talk to the girls. May of '06 was the last time I heard from her." Cobb told the reporter he assumed that Dana had simply "moved on" with her life.

In reality, her life was taken by Shawn Grate.

Four months later, on September 11, Grate pleaded guilty in Marion County to the kidnapping and murder of twenty-three-year-old Dana Nicole Lowrey. Marion County prosecutor Ray Grogan led the case against Shawn Grate. Grate was sentenced to life without parole, plus another sixteen years for the counts. But as with the verdict in Ashland County, an appeal was imminent.

On July 21, 2022, Judge Ronald Forsthoefel rejected Grate's post-conviction petition to set aside the jury's verdicts and order a new trial. The petition had been filed by the Ohio Public Defender's Office, which represented Grate during those proceedings. The filing alleged there were errors committed by Grate's defense team in the presentation of psychological evidence, among other issues.

Grate's prior appeals to the Ohio Supreme Court and the United States Supreme Court were also unsuccessful.

As of this writing, Shawn Grate is scheduled to be put to death in 2025.

Epilogue

Demolition Day

The court verdicts against Grate and the judge's subsequent decision on June 1, 2018, to sentence him to death provided some degree of closure to the city of Ashland, but not for the families of the victims.

The pair of boarded-up and faded houses on Covert Court stood as a painful reminder of our lost victims and Grate's brutalization and rape of Jane Doe over a three-day period. So, people here were quietly relieved when Ashland mayor Matt Miller announced that a local firm, Simonson Construction Services, had offered to demolish the abandoned places at no cost to the city.

Simonson Construction had stepped up to help the community many times before, so no one was all that surprised at this latest sign of the company's generosity.

On June 12, twelve days after Grate was sentenced to die, I stood among the area residents, public officials, other members of the law enforcement community, and the families of Grate's victims who were gathered on Covert Court to watch a heavy-duty payloader knock the places down and rid our beloved city of this symbol of evil.

I was standing with Prosecutor Chris Tunnell, Detective Brian Evans, and Officers Aaron Kline and Lee Eggeman when the tract excavator began its work. I noticed that a member of Stacey's family was among the crowd, who said she was there hoping to find closure.

"Knock that SOB down!" Prosecutor Tunnell shouted.

I thought that the slow and methodical removal of those houses would finally bring me closure, but that was not the case. Instead, it was almost like a wound being reopened. I had been inside the house where Shawn Grate held Jane Doe for three days and knew the interior by memory. Now, I stood and watched as the construction machinery knocked down one wall after another, exposing rooms where Grate had murdered women and tossed their bodies aside. The noise from the machinery tearing apart the old structure made the scene even more surreal for me.

Months earlier, I had researched the pair of Covert Court homes and learned that they were designed and built in the 1880s. Drawings showed the structure at 363 as part of a larger complex that was planned in the late 1870s called Potter's Addition. The first owner of the home where Grate had committed his crimes was a woman—which was unusual in those days.

As the yellow excavator continued its work, I imagined how grand the whole downtown area must have looked when those houses were new. I also knew that tearing them down would help the city and its residents move beyond the tragedy at some level. But their demolition didn't make the pain go away; Grate's arrest and my subsequent interrogations of him have remained with me.

There were dozens of people around me that June afternoon. The media was there, too, capturing still images and video of the work being done a couple of hundred feet away. I was trying to maintain my composure. But the reality was that it hurt like hell.

I could only imagine what the pain was like for Jane Doe and the families and friends of Grate's victims. They, too, would have to live forever with their incredibly heart-wrenching memories.

The following day, the *Mansfield News Journal* ran a picture of me wiping away tears as the homes were demolished. I remember being asked by a local reporter named Dylan Sams how I felt watching the structures be erased from our town.

"It's difficult to find the words," I told him. "The house is so tangible. We are all feeling the same thing, yet from every different perspective."

I left the scene that day knowing that the house where Grate had committed some of his atrocities was gone. But I still felt unsettled, unresolved, as if I'd missed something during those eight interviews. I reflected on how Grate had indicated that this happened because we were complacent. And I recognize that although we want to forget these atrocities, we have to analyze every facet of Shawn Grate and the heinous dynamics of the crimes he perpetrated. I also realized that those involved in this situation or any like situation must scrutinize the systems, processes, and the case as a whole.

If we don't learn anything, then what is our purpose? Why are we here? How can we stop future Shawn Grates from committing the same horrific crimes?

Acknowledgments

This book would not have happened without the guidance and support of Ben and Kim Ferguson. Dan and I thank and appreciate you.

To Dana, Rebekah, Candace, Stacey, and Elizabeth, whose lives were not lost in vain; your memories will always be cherished. May your families find peace and comfort in knowing their killer has been brought to justice. To Jane Doe, whose courage and sound faith continues to be an inspiration to me.

To our editorial team, Charles Spicer and Hannah Pierdolla, and all the members of the production team, Ken Silver, Lizz Blaise, Catherine Turiano, and copy editors Sara C. Robb and Chris Ensey at St. Martin's Press, thank you for your patience, kindness, and attention to detail.

Literary agents Rick Richter of Aevitas Creative and Madeleine Morel of 2M Communications, we salute you.

To my fellow law enforcement officers throughout Ohio, it has been an honor investigating alongside you.

To Lisa Pulitzer, my collaborator and friend. I saw your passion for authenticity when you came to my community to immerse yourself in small-town America. You listen intently, investigate like a detective, and have the gift of articulation. You've been incredible to work with.

And to Lisa's husband, Douglas Love, for his editorial and technical input. I appreciate your support through the countless hours Lisa has devoted to working with me. I recognize the sacrifice.

To Ohio BCI special agent Joe Dietz, an exemplary mentor and friend. Thank you for taking me under your wing during my early career.

On a personal note, I thank my intelligent, capable, and beautiful daughter, Macy, who brings me immense joy every single day. Don't step off your path. You are going to have a tremendously positive impact on children and families.

To my strong and steadfast son Corbin, who gave us daughter-in-law Kaylee and precious, little Mylah, your ongoing ability to see what others don't brought justice for one of the victims. I'm beyond proud.

To my son Reed, who has grown up during the writing of this book to become so protective, strong, and incredibly wise, you are a man of your word and I'm proud to be your mom.

To my sister, Tamra Bower, you keep me grounded every single day. I am thankful for you, Dana, and Brock.

And, to my husband, Dan, the most principled and amazing man I have ever met, by the grace of God, I have you. I've been blessed with having you and your huge family, all of whom I acknowledge here, to surround me with love.

About the Authors

Kim Mager

Detective **KIM MAGER** is a thirty-year law-enforcement officer who retired from Ashland City Police Division in 2022. Mager is employed by a prosecutor's office and still holds a law enforcement commission. Mager specializes in sex offenses, violent crime, and child abuse and has investigated over two thousand cases. She has a BA from Ashland University and graduated Top Gun of her Police Academy. Mager is married to husband, Dan, and they have three children, Corbin, Macy, and Reed.

Douglas Love

LISA PULITZER is a former correspondent for *The New York Times*. She is the author of more than a dozen nonfiction titles, including *New York Times* bestseller *Stolen Innocence* (with Elissa Wall) and *Portrait of a Monster: Joran van der Sloot, A Murder in Peru, and The Natalee Holloway Mystery* (with Cole Thompson).